The
Seventymile Kid

Harry Karstens in 1906

The
Seventymile Kid

The Lost Legacy of Harry Karstens and the First Ascent of Mount McKinley

Tom Walker

THE MOUNTAINEERS BOOKS

THE MOUNTAINEERS BOOKS
is the nonprofit publishing arm of The Mountaineers,
an organization founded in 1906 and dedicated to the exploration,
preservation, and enjoyment of outdoor and wilderness areas.

1001 SW Klickitat Way, Suite 201, Seattle, WA 98134

First edition, 2013
10 9 8 7 6 5 4 3 2 1

Distributed in the United Kingdom by Cordee, www.cordee.co.uk
Manufactured in the United States of America

Copy editor: Joan Gregory
Cover, book design, layout, and maps: John Barnett/4 Eyes Design
Cover photograph: Karstens Library

Library of Congress Cataloging-in-Publication Data
Walker, Tom, 1945-
The Seventymile Kid : The Lost Legacy of Harry Karstens and the first ascent of
Mount McKinley / by Tom Walker.
    p. cm.
Includes index.
ISBN 978-1-59485-729-4 (pbk) — ISBN 978-1-59485-730-0 (ebook)
1. Karstens, Harry, 1878-1955. 2. Mountaineers—United
States—Biography. 3. Mountaineering—Alaska—McKinley, Mount. 4.
McKinley, Mount (Alaska)—Description and travel. I. Title.
GV199.92.K363W35 2013
796.522092—dc23
[B]

2012034594

To Mary Anne

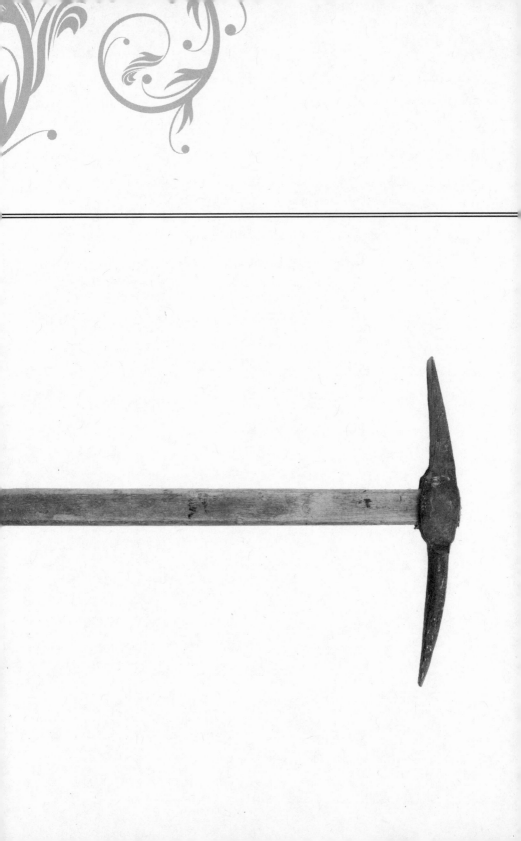

Contents

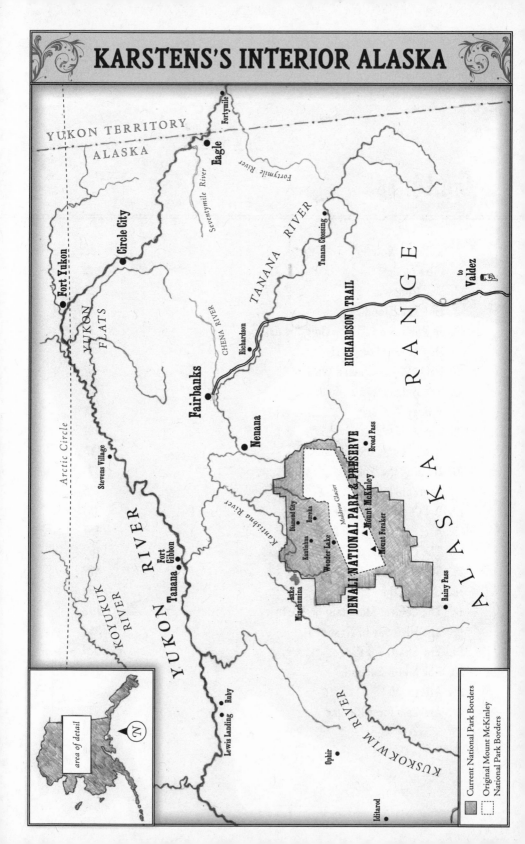

1913 SUMMIT ROUTE

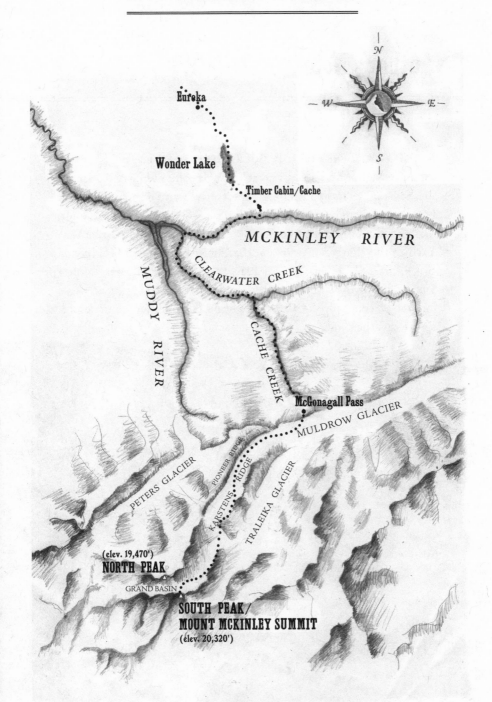

Eureka

Wonder Lake

Timber Cabin/Cache

MCKINLEY RIVER

CLEARWATER CREEK

MUDDY RIVER

CACHE CREEK

McGonagall Pass

MULDROW GLACIER

PETERS GLACIER

PIONEER RIDGE

KARSTENS RIDGE

TRALEIKA GLACIER

(elev. 19,470')
NORTH PEAK

GRAND BASIN

SOUTH PEAK/
MOUNT McKINLEY SUMMIT
(elev. 20,320')

Author's Note

AN IMPORTANT PART OF THIS BIOGRAPHY concerns itself with the first ascent of Mount McKinley, arguably a high point of Harry Karstens's life. Several writers and climbing experts have written about the climb, but most of them have based their stories on Hudson Stuck's account, *The Ascent of Denali*. This book differs in a critical and important way. Each of the climbers who made that first ascent in 1913—Hudson Stuck, Harry Karstens, Walter Harper, and Robert Tatum—kept a journal during the climb. The story told here is based largely on those journals, secondarily on *The Ascent of Denali*, offering a unique perspective on the climb.

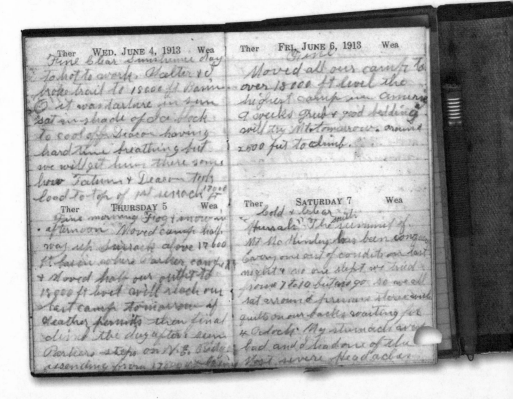

The journals of Harry Karstens and Walter Harper have been published as parts of other books. Both journals are spare and, when read alone, offer little to Hudson Stuck's account in *The Ascent of Denali*. Karstens said he didn't write much because Stuck was tasked with keeping the climb record. A few years ago, the American Geographical Society made Stuck's journal available on disk. The journal is very detailed and gives new insight into the expedition's dynamics. Missing from the disk, however, is a critical piece: the section detailing the week of the actual attack on the summit. To cut down on weight during the ascent, Stuck had switched from a full-size journal to a small pocket diary.

My frustrating search for the elusive pocket diary finally lead me back to Susan Peschel at the University of Wisconsin–Milwaukee, the new home of the American Geographical Society Library. Susan put me in contact with Peter Lewis, then acting director of the AGS, who then located the pocket diary in New York. He and his staff carefully photographed the fragile book and sent me images of the crucial pages that completed the record.

The journal of Robert Tatum was the "missing link." I knew that Tatum had kept a journal, but I had never been able to find it. My occasional enquiries turned up nothing. In late 2011, Ken Karstens, Harry Karstens's great-grandson, located Tatum's journal in the archives of the University of Tennessee, Knoxville. Tatum's journal, the most personal of the four journals, added key information for piecing together the complete picture of the first ascent of Mount McKinley.

All quotations in this book come from letters, diaries, memoirs, or other historical documents, and in places, from published books, news accounts, and magazine articles. My intent is simply to tell a true story and give credit where credit is due. The problem of nonfiction is to put aside what we "know" and filter it through what we "know now." And what we "know now" about the first ascent of Mount McKinley is a story quite different from that told by Hudson Stuck.

Harry Karstens kept spare notes on the climb in this small pocket journal.

Introduction

THE FIRST TWO DECADES OF THE TWENTIETH CENTURY are storied as a golden age of geographic discovery. Indomitable adventurers sought the Northwest Passage, the South Pole, the North Pole, and viewed Mount Everest as "the third pole." It was an era when explorers became international celebrities.

By the late 1890s, the lower forty-eight states and territories had been explored and mapped, the only remaining blank spots on US soil being in the Territory of Alaska. As one geographic prize after another was bagged, American and British adventurers began to focus their ambitions on unclimbed mountains. Inevitably, the mountain the Athabascans called *Denali*, "The High One," drew their attention. Mount McKinley, at 20,320 feet North America's highest peak, was romanticized as the last remaining geographic prize on the continent.

Early explorers and climbers had no understanding of the elemental forces that had shaped the mountain. We now know that the thrust of the Pacific Plate diving beneath the North American Plate pushed up Mount McKinley, a granitic pluton formed some fifty-six million years ago. McKinley's granite has resisted the erosion that has shaped the surrounding peaks of the Alaska Range.

The English explorer George Vancouver sighted Mount McKinley in 1794 from an ocean inlet 140 miles away. He described it as "stupendous." Russian explorers called it *Bulshaia gora*, the "Grand Mountain," and sketched the first maps. In the late 1870s and early 1880s, intrepid gold prospectors sighted the peak and marveled at its size. Prospectors Arthur Harper and Frank Densmore spoke repeatedly of their "ice mountain." A few miners called it "Densmore's Mountain," in much the same manner that Yellowstone was once called "Colter's Hell," after the mountain man who first explored the region.

In 1896, prospector W. A. Dickey named the Alaskan peak for the future president William McKinley, then Ohio's governor and champion of the gold standard. Following a long prospecting trip, Dickey sent the

New York Sun an account of his trek on the south side of the Alaska Range. "We had many glorious views of Mount McKinley and an unnamed companion southwest," Dickey wrote. "Mount McKinley is in this valley as ubiquitous as the Washington monument in the city of Washington." On his return home, he learned that he'd been hailed as the "discoverer" of the mountain. A couple years later, Robert Muldrow, of the US Geological Survey, was the first to measure the peak. He estimated its height at 20,600 feet, a little over its actual elevation of 20,320 feet.

Frederick Cook, who attempted to climb McKinley in 1903, wrote that his trek around the mountain ranked among other American epics such as Lewis and Clark's journey to the Pacific Ocean. He conveniently failed to mention that Alaska was not terra incognita. For at least three decades prior to Cook's expedition, fur traders and gold seekers had forged across the territory, exploring land already well known to aboriginal Alaskans and pioneer prospectors. Government expeditions that followed were astounded to find traces of their passing. "Who were these lonely travelers of the wild region?" asked geologist Alfred Hulse Brooks. "These pioneers make journeys that would put to shame . . . many a well-equipped government expedition."

The discovery of gold in the Klondike, in 1896, ignited a worldwide frenzy. The era known as the Gilded Age was golden only for the privileged classes that controlled the wealth. The masses went hungry, with little prospect for advancement. The huge Klondike strike was an irresistible lure, especially for the disadvantaged. And Henry Peter Karstens was definitely at a disadvantage.

Karstens was just seventeen when he ran away from his Chicago home. In 1897, in Billings, Montana, he heard of the gold strike and immediately joined the stampede to the Yukon. Few of the tens of thousands of stampeders struck it rich. Many turned around and went home, their dreams turned to ashes. Others, like Karstens, fanned out across the Yukon and Alaska, intent on making their own way. Karstens failed to strike it rich, but in Alaska found a life of high adventure.

As one historian put it, "The Alaskan wilderness setting was mythologized as the nation's 'last frontier,' and the Alaskan prospector, or 'sourdough,' fittingly took his place at the center of this myth—just as the cowboy had captured the role of mythic hero in the Far West."

In 1913, Harry Karstens led the first successful ascent of Mount McKinley. His role as climb leader has been largely overlooked. Here, for the first time, is the complete story of the Alaska pioneer who conquered Mount McKinley.

Henry P. "Harry" Karstens, age twelve

1. The Runaway

ON MAY 2, 1913, FIVE CLIMBERS HUDDLED in their makeshift camp near the Great Icefall on the Muldrow Glacier of Mount McKinley. Sheer ice walls towered thousands of feet above them. Burdened by tons of fresh snow, the slopes on either side of them thundered with avalanches. Under the huddled climbers, the glacier groaned and boomed as if a living, breathing thing. Through brief rents in the clouds, the climbers glimpsed their goal: the 20,320-foot summit of Mount McKinley. Until forced to camp by deteriorating weather, their movement up the glacier had been fluid, the use of dog teams to freight supplies a total success. But two days of heavy snow, wind, and temperatures well below freezing had halted their progress, forcing them to camp halfway between their 8,000-foot camp and their planned high camp at 10,800 feet. Breaking trail through the heavy snow had exhausted the men, further necessitating the unplanned and unwelcome stop. Although well supplied with a tent and food to last several days, they were anxious to keep moving, to establish a high camp at the base of the ridge, from which they could begin their final ascent.

Earlier, on April 30, just before the storm had hit, all five men had broken trail to the 10,800-foot level and established a new cache. Their route, marked as they progressed with willow sticks, snaked around crevasses and house-size blocks of ice. During their enforced layover, they decided to relay the remaining gear, food, and firewood from their temporary camp to the cache at the base of the ridge. It would take two trips; the first would be the hardest and most dangerous. After two days of snow, many of the trail markers had been blown away or buried, parts of the route completely obliterated. Without markers, a trailbreaker risked a lethal fall into a hidden crevasse. Already, the climbing leader, Harry Karstens, had broken through but had been saved by his rope. A lead dog had also punched through, but had landed safely on a snowy ledge above the yawning abyss.

Robert Tatum tended camp while the others went ahead with the two small dog teams, using dogsleds to haul the gear up to the advance cache. Karstens and John Fredson paired with one dog team, while Walter Harper and Hudson Stuck took the second team. One man led the dogs, with the other man just behind the dogs at a position in front of the sled. The sled man steered with the gee pole and hauled on the tug line, often working harder than the dogs. Steep ascents required the combined strength of men and dogs, the thin air quickly exhausting them all.

The two-man teams trudged upward, breaking trail though deep, heavy snow and re-marking the route as they went. Without serious mishap, they reached their cache at 10,800 feet by midday. They separated their loads into two piles—supplies in one, firewood in another. At a break before heading down, they passed around thermoses of hot chocolate and dried snacks. Karstens and Stuck lit up their pipes and relaxed atop the mounded supplies.

Their return over the broken trail was swift and uneventful. After a hot lunch prepared by Tatum, the four took off with the second load. As they moved up glacier, the temperature plummeted, a sharp wind cutting like a knife.

When almost within sight of their cache, Hudson Stuck spotted tendrils of smoke twisting in the wind. Astonished, the men shared wild speculations. Had someone come over from the south side of the mountain? Were other climbers on their way down from the summit? Could this be a sign of some starving party that stumbled upon their cache and built a rescue fire? As far-fetched as it seemed, there was only one possible answer: *their cache was on fire!*

Leaving the dogs and the loaded sleds, the climbers rushed forward as fast as the rising trail and altitude allowed. Topping an intervening shoulder of ice, they discovered their cache almost completely reduced to ashes, nearly everything destroyed but their firewood.

Gone were three high-altitude silk tents, a sack of new socks, Karstens's fur parka, underclothes, coveralls, gloves, mittens, tobacco, and ax. Up in smoke were Karstens's camera and film, as well as most of the film for Stuck's camera. Irreplaceable foodstuffs—sugar, baking powder, flour, powdered milk, dried fruit, pilot bread—all destroyed.

The only possible explanation for the fire could be traced back to their break at the end of the first relay. Either Stuck or Karstens had dropped a match or an ember on one of the silk tents and it had smoldered unnoticed as the cache was covered with the canvas tarp. The afternoon wind lifting the tarp fanned the fire to life and it had quickly spread to the wooden boxes.

Hudson Stuck, according to Karstens's written account, came undone, shouting, "We're ruined! We're ruined!" Karstens lashed back and told him "to keep still [until] we find out how badly we've been set back."

Clearly, the disaster, borne of carelessness, imperiled the expedition's continuation. Further progress would require all of their combined ingenuity, resourcefulness, and tenacity. The wilderness of the Far North had tested and honed them all, none more so than Harry Karstens. Now, more than ever, the success of the entire expedition would rest on his shoulders.

Henry Peter "Harry" Karstens was born on September 2, 1878, to John Jacob Karstens and Emma Terveen Karstens, the fifth of seven children, four boys and three girls. His father was born in Holstein, a duchy fought over for centuries by Denmark and Germany. Although Harry Karstens's ancestry was German, he always claimed to be a Dane.

The opening of America's Great Plains for settlement in the 1840s attracted thousands of land-hungry German immigrants. Chicago grew rapidly, emerging almost overnight as an industrial and commercial center. By mid-century, Germans constituted one-sixth of Chicago's population, the largest ethnic group in the city.

The extended Karstens family immigrated over a period of years, some settling in Chicago, others in Iowa and South Dakota, where they nurtured large farms and families. Rapid construction and expansion of the nation's railroads promoted shipment of grains and the growth of their businesses. Using crops grown by their relatives, the Chicago Karstens family owned feed stores, bakeries, and a variety of labor-intensive small businesses.

German immigrants tended to settle in close proximity to one another, reinforcing an ethnic identity based on work, family, and religion. They conversed in German, less so in English. The Karstens family was a typical German household, extremely hierarchical and formal, the father stern and distant. Discipline of a very physical sort could be severe, displays of affection rare, especially for boys. Even the youngest children worked in the family enterprises with well-defined chores and responsibilities. In the German tradition, the eldest son inherited everything, with younger male siblings left to make their own way.

As an adolescent, Harry Karstens attended school full-time and worked in his father's feed store and livery, unloading shipments of hay, grain, and flour; and feeding and cleaning up after the horses and mules. Under the rules of primogeniture, his future in the family was limited. The J. J. Karstens Flour, Feed, and Grain at 177 West Harrison Street, located near the shipping canal, would pass to his oldest brother, John Henry, or if something happened to him, to the next eldest, George.

Harry's father, John Jacob, is remembered as a "thoroughly disagreeable man," a lifelong womanizer who would one day run off with his mistress, abandoning his wife and children to fend for themselves. John Henry, four years older than Harry, was as mercurial and difficult as his father. The physical punishment and domination endured by John Henry was passed on, with apparent gusto, to his younger brothers.

After Mrs. O'Leary's diabolical cow sparked the Great Fire of October 1871, which claimed 18,000 buildings and left 100,000 homeless, the "Chicago spirit" rebuilt the city as a tangible force that not only exceeded what was destroyed but made it the nation's leader

John Henry Karstens in 1898 after his return to Chicago from Alaska
and a failed attempt to reach the Klondike

in manufacturing, commerce, and architecture. When Chicago surpassed Philadelphia as the nation's second-largest city, the gentry loudly celebrated.

In 1890, wealthy Chicagoans viewed their world as increasingly modern, offering the promise of unbridled success. Indeed their city expanded rapidly, growing ever bigger, taller, and richer. The city's architects built the first high-rise, reporters coining the term "skyscraper."

The city's leading lights included Clarence Darrow, Philip Armour, Marshall Field, George Pullman, Aaron Montgomery Ward, and a young Frank Lloyd Wright. On the seamy side, the infamous Mickey

Finn ran his Lone Star Saloon. The Pinkerton National Detective Agency prospered in a city plagued with crime.

Worldwide, the last decade of the nineteenth century saw rapid modernization and development. Wilhelm Röntgen discovered X-rays, Nikola Tesla invented the wireless radio, Pierre and Marie Curie discovered radium, Ferdinand von Zeppelin invented a rigid lighter-than-air ship, Thomas Edison patented a motion picture camera with the first moving picture being shown on a public screen, and Henry Ford built his first gasoline-powered automobile, the "Quadricycle."

For Chicago's working classes, the "Gay Nineties" were anything but lighthearted and prosperous. A thousand trains a day chugged through the city, while horse-drawn trolleys, carriages, cabs, and freight wagons jostled for space on streets choked with pedestrians. Typhus, cholera, diphtheria, and influenza stalked the crowded tenements. The Union Stock Yards slaughtered sixteen million animals a year, emitting a tremendous stench of death, rot, and burning hair. Uncollected manure and garbage added to the stink. The slaughter yards employed twenty-nine thousand people, with one-fifth of Chicago depending on the yards for economic survival. Wages were low and rents in the "company towns" exorbitant.

The decade that opened with such promise soon experienced a financial depression that trended from bad to worse to disastrous. The world's financial system began to collapse. Banks and businesses failed and money dried up. Labor unrest spread. Chicago, far from immune, had already experienced death and mayhem during the Haymarket Square Riot.

Despite the looming panic, and for the sake of city honor, Chicago in 1893 took on an impossible task and won the right to host the World's Columbian–Exposition. This mega-construction project, employing thousands of workers and spreading cash across the city, delayed the economic crisis quickly seizing the world by the throat. At a cost of $22 million, about three-quarters of a billion dollars today, the fair proved sensational, the greatest world's fair ever staged, attracting an estimated 27.5 million visitors, including presidents, poets, and princesses.

One event galvanized the city's children: Buffalo Bill's Wild West Show. City kids, honed on dime novels of frontier adventure, clamored to see Buffalo Bill, Annie Oakley, Sioux and Cheyenne warriors, cavalrymen, and a herd of live buffalo. The restaging of "Custer's Last Stand," featuring Indian veterans of the deadly fight at Little Bighorn, topped the spectacle. As he watched wide-eyed, the fifteen-year-old Harry Karstens did not know that within months he would be riding the Montana range not far from the fabled battlefield.

The close of the exposition ushered in the full force of the Panic of 1893. Chicago banks failed, and wages spiraled downward while prices remained high. Not surprisingly, the Pullman Strike of 1894 turned violent. The German-dominated areas of commerce and trade suffered along with everyone else. As prices soared and unemployment expanded, crime, filth, and vermin proliferated in the alleys of Harrison, Halsted, and Levee Streets. Although horses and draft animals remained vital to life and commerce, even the feed business faltered.

John Henry, the combustible and unpredictable eldest son, suffered multiple stresses. In 1894, when nineteen, he married sixteen-year-old Lillie Wishart, and within a year had fathered two girls, the first of seven children. The strain of marriage, fatherhood, and a looming partnership with his father, combined with the economic crises, served to inflame his already volatile nature.

Early in 1895, in the barn behind the store, John Henry got into a shouting match with his little brother. What came next is family lore. Perhaps Harry had failed to do his chores, or hadn't done them fast enough to suit. More likely, the ill-tempered John Henry needed little excuse for his violent outburst. Harry's own temper flared. The two began fighting. Hard punches were thrown, likely a lip cut or an eye blackened. But this fight was different from past scuffles. A barn knife flashed in the dust-speckled light. The struggle turned desperate and in the melee, John fell, blood spurting across his chest and left upper arm. Out of fear, horror, or shame, or perhaps because he was just sick of the whole damn scene, Harry Karstens fled into the filthy streets, and out of the family.

Two years would pass before Harry Karstens, then somewhere in the wilderness of the upper Yukon, got word that his brother was still alive.

The *Al-ki* steamship, on which Karstens loaded freight
in exchange for passage to Dyea

2. Ho! The Klondike

FOR TWO YEARS HARRY KARSTENS WANDERED the Northern Plains working on frontier cattle ranches, often just for room and board. In June 1897, he and Tom Cavanaugh, another young drifter, stopped for coffee in Vaughn's Restaurant in Billings, Montana. There they met "Windy Bill," a mail carrier just down from Alaska, who enthralled them with tales of the "excitement" up in the Klondike. He painted vivid, exaggerated stories of the rich claims and gold just for the taking. *Nuggets big as hens' eggs!*

Windy Bill's tall tales stirred the whole town and infected Karstens and Cavanaugh with gold fever. According to him, this was no time to ponder or hesitate. With hundreds already headed toward Seattle, every day's delay lessened the chance for a strike. With nothing to lose, the young partners gathered their gear and hastily left town.

Two days after contracting the fever, Karstens and Cavanaugh milled in the throng gathered at the Helena, Montana, railroad depot. Cheers greeted the arrival of a train loaded with 11,400 ounces of Klondike gold. The next day, the American National Bank displayed a 125-pound ingot in its front window. Local newspapers proclaimed the gold shipment as merely a taste of the golden harvest. The two young partners caught the next train to Seattle.

The main route to the Klondike began at tidewater in Alaska, nine hundred miles north of Puget Sound. The Chilkoot Trail followed an ancient Tlingit trade route through the jagged, glaciated Coastal Mountains to the headwaters of the Yukon River. Over time, alternate routes, some impossible and lethal, would be pioneered through Canada and Alaska. Now, the way north led through two boomtowns in Taiya Inlet at the head of Lynn Canal, Dyea and Skagway, already billed as "Gateway to the Yukon."

"The train was full of parties going to the Klondike and all terribly excited," Karstens recalled. "At Seattle, the crowd was tremendous. . . . We tried everywhere to get passage but it seemed hopeless. We heard of the old [steamship] *Al-ki* being taken out of the Bebe [ship] yard where she was condemned. We looked up the operators and made a deal to pay passage and help handle freight."

By the time they reached Seattle, Karstens and Cavanaugh had less than $200 between them. From this grubstake, they bought a simple cooking kit, two buckets, two mackinaw jackets, four blankets, two suits of long underwear, a small tent, two blue shirts, moccasins, socks, and two hunting knives. They purchased three sacks of flour, fifty pounds of sugar, fifty pounds of bacon, baking powder, a bag of salt, a case of canned milk, and a few pounds of tea and coffee. In addition, Karstens carried his .45-70 rifle and a supply of 405-grain bullets, a favorite combination of old-time Plains buffalo hunters. Other stampeders laughed at Karstens's and Cavanaugh's skimpy provisions. Most Klondike "outfits," as a party's collection of supplies, food, and tools were called, cost five to ten times as much and were far more robust.

The port city of Seattle was both outfitting point and bottleneck. Even with every old tub placed into service, there simply weren't enough boats to handle the throng demanding passage. By badgering the purser and offering to handle cargo for a dollar an hour, Karstens and Cavanaugh got two tickets on the *Al-ki* for their last $40. By fall, the cost of a steamship ticket had skyrocketed—one sold for $1,500, ten times its face value. On August 2, the *Al-ki* set off, loaded with livestock, 350 tons of supplies, and 110 people—leaving behind a thousand more who had demanded passage.

In the first five weeks of the stampede, twenty steamships packed with humanity forged north from Seattle to Skagway. The first shipments of Klondike gold had electrified the country. The United States was still reeling from the Panic of 1893 that had left millions jobless and hungry. Because the nation's monetary system was tied to gold reserves, people hoarded the scarce metal, only worsening the financial depression. To a growing immigrant population and the disaffected poor, the gold strike promised a way out of poverty. At the time of sailing, Karstens was just eighteen years old and, at 170 pounds, in "work shape." Cavanaugh, at twenty-two years, was equally fit, "with good staying qualities and [not afraid to] tackle most anything." The partners relied on their determination, strength, and youth to win through to the Klondike. "There was nothing like quit on our calendar," Karstens said in a remembrance written years later.

Two weeks out of Seattle, the rattle of chain and anchor, accompanied by the ship's whistle, signaled the *Al-ki's* arrival at Skagway. Without a wharf, and at low tide, teamsters lightered the livestock and supplies to the mudflats, where the passengers scrambled to get everything to high ground. "The fighting and cursing was terrible," Karstens recalled. "Freight was dumped ashore any old way without system, and a swarm of men and women clawing over it to see if they could find any with their mark on it." Freight and baggage were stolen, lost, and destroyed. "It was terrible to see that crowd working like mad men, young and old, some of them who never had done a day's work in their lives . . . struggling with impossible packs."

Karstens and Cavanaugh found the streets of Skagway jammed with hordes of gold seekers. The new town, built around steamboat captain William Moore's cabin at the mouth of the Skagway River, was a hodgepodge of tents and shacks in use as boardinghouses, restaurants, stores, saloons, and "sporting houses." Thieves and con men of all kinds, the most notorious being Jefferson Randolph "Soapy" Smith, preyed on the stampeders. The town of Skagway, goes an oft-repeated phrase, "was conceived in lawlessness and nurtured in anarchy."

From town, the White Pass Trail—a route that brought out the worst in the stampeders—also led forty-five miles through the mountains to the Yukon headwaters. Karstens learned that the trail was swampy, muddy, and longer than the nearby Chilkoot Trail. In fact, Skagway had grown in size because hundreds had turned back due to the White Pass's deep snow and harsh trail conditions. Five thousand stampeders attempted White Pass that fall, but few made it to Dawson before freeze-up. Of three thousand horses used on the trail that first year, likely none survived the route that became known as the Deadhorse Trail. The situation repelled Karstens. "We heard there were over 1,700 dead horses and mules on the trail at that time," he recalled.

And things were only going to get worse. The great stampede was just beginning. More than a hundred thousand people set out for the Yukon in 1897, with an estimated one million more planning to do so as soon as they could book passage. How many would have turned back had they known that Yukon pioneers had already staked the Klondike's best grounds?

A little daunted by lawless Skagway, Karstens and Cavanaugh reboarded the *Al-ki* for the short run west to Dyea, a boomtown rising at the head of the Chilkoot Trail. The trail paralleled the Taiya River, cutting through lush stands of Sitka spruce and cottonwood, home to black bear, brown bear, and nesting bald eagles. Just a few weeks earlier, Dyea had consisted solely of John J. Healy's trading post and a small Tlingit Indian village. Karstens found Dyea as rambunctious as Skagway, although smaller and without the same type of bottleneck. The Chilkoot Trail, though steeper and six hundred feet higher than the White Pass route, was ten miles shorter where it ended at Lake Lindeman on the headwaters of the Yukon River. Already a series of camps had sprung up along the trail, offering meals and services to the heavily laden stampeders.

The trail, still in use today, rises gradually over its first twelve and a half miles. From Sheep Camp, located just below the pass, the trail veers sharply upward, with the last few hundred feet approaching vertical. Even in summer, snow covers the final approach to the 3,525-foot summit. Weather and terrain compounded the hardships of moving heavy freight over the rugged trail. Most stampeders were city dwellers unused to physical labor of any kind. During the peak of the stampede, three to four men died daily from exhaustion, illness, and accidents. Grifters and thieves preyed on the hapless stampeders.

The Chilkoot sorely tested everyone's mettle, brutally sorting out the unfit, foolish, and ill prepared.

As in Skagway, freight was lightered to shore at Dyea, and Karstens and Cavanaugh quickly recovered their simple outfit. By late afternoon, they had set up camp and relayed their first load up the trail. "That was really the beginning of the worst hardships I have seen or endured," Karstens recalled. Their tent and clothing proved inadequate for the high winds, freezing rain, and plunging temperatures. Ahead of them stretched days of brutal labor, often without food other than unadorned cornmeal or rice. Nearly broke, with only twenty dollars between them, they lacked the money to add to their outfit. Wildlife was scarce to nonexistent, so living off the land was not an option. Somehow they had to earn money to buy more food or their enterprise would fail before it began.

All along the trail, people were constantly on the move. Dozens of men, a few women, and pack animals toted heavy loads toward the pass. Most parties had mountains of supplies, their outfits dwarfing in size that of the two young partners. Consequently, packers were in high demand. Tlingit packers had formed a block, and set prices that ranged from five to fifteen dollars per hundred pounds, the standard load size. At a location called "the Scales," just below the pass, packers reweighed everything with the price going up, a few desperate men paying a dollar a pound to have their gear toted over the summit. Karstens and Cavanaugh hired out as packers, trading labor for food. Sometimes they worked all day for a can of vegetables or a pound of butter.

Neither Karstens nor Cavanaugh could cook, so they struck a bargain with a man and his wife, who was hailed as a chef. The couple had forty-five hundred pounds of gear with only one horse and a burro to move it all. Getting right to work, Karstens and Cavanaugh loaded the animals with 200 to 250 pounds of freight each, and loaded themselves with packs weighing 75 to 100 pounds. Over the next two weeks, and powered by the woman's hearty meals, the two young men relayed most of the enormous load to the base of the pass. There, with their strength restored and the season growing late, they decided to quit and focus on their own quest. They collected $150, just half of what they had been promised for their backbreaking work, and spent it all on extra supplies, purchased at exorbitant prices.

On September 2, Harry Karstens turned nineteen, a birthday celebration he likely missed, every day blending into the next in a stupor of labor, blisters, and fatigue. Three inches of snow fell at the summit on September 12, six inches at Lake Lindeman.

Time after time, Karstens and Cavanaugh trudged up the steep face of the pass. Sometime in late September, with winter close at hand, the partners finally relayed the last of their outfit over the Chilkoot summit. "From the time we left the Scales [below the pass] and started down the river [from Lake Lindeman] it was a pleasure of sleet, rain, blistered feet, calloused shoulder and back," Karstens remembered.

After freeze-up that fall, and as reports of famine trickled in from Dawson City, the North West Mounted Police instituted rules that required each person entering the Yukon to possess a year's supply of food, about 1,150 pounds. In total, each man needed a ton of food and equipment to enter Canada. Some stampeders took three months or more to relay their required supplies up and over the Chilkoot, slogging more than thirty times up the steps, the so-called Golden Stairs, carved in the almost perpendicular ice and snow. Summer or winter, a single climb could take six hours. Karstens and Cavanaugh beat the new law by mere days.

From the pass, the trail tapered downhill, gradually losing altitude. Even in late autumn, snow covered the ground, enabling the two men to sled some of their supplies while backpacking the rest. Beneath snow line, the trail traversed lovely alpine meadows and open spruce forest. Constant fog and drizzle chilled and soaked them as they toiled under their outsize loads. Six inches of wet snow fell on September 30.

Drenched by ceaseless rains, Karstens and Cavanaugh spent several long days relaying their outfit to Lake Lindeman. A tent city had sprung up on the shore of Lindeman's turquoise waters. Nearly 150 tents crowded the clearing by the inlet stream with half as many boats being built by frantic stampeders. Shouts and curses in English, French, Russian, and a gamut of languages accompanied the din of axes, hammers, and saws.

Here just inside the Yukon Territory, and almost six hundred miles from Dawson City, Karstens and Cavanaugh met two elderly Germans who had the tools for boatbuilding but knew nothing of boats or boating. Karstens struck a deal: equal shares in the entire outfit in return for helping them get to Dawson. In addition, the Germans pledged to pay their new partners' customs duty at the police post on Tagish Lake.

Karstens and Cavanaugh had struggled for nearly eight weeks to reach Lake Lindeman, but now a sense of urgency set in. Winter was near and the wind carried a sharp bite. On each clear morning, frost tinted the ground, and shore ice crept farther into the lake. The water temperature, barely above freezing in midsummer, began to fall. Ahead of them danger lurked on the chain of lakes that birthed the muddy Yukon, flowing in a two-thousand-mile arc to the Bering Sea. Sudden squalls could swamp even the best boats; river rapids could splinter heavy scows. Already men had drowned in the short, frothing run between Lakes Lindeman and Bennett. A dunking could be fatal, the loss of supplies catastrophic. The two men would need luck to reach Dawson City before freeze-up.

The two Germans had cut some spruce logs for saw boards and now with added help, the timbering and hauling went quickly. While Karstens and Cavanaugh set to work hewing out boat ribs, Karstens put the Germans to work whipsawing lumber. "It took some time to get the hang of it," he wrote, "but we eventually turned out lumber at a satisfactory rate." Inevitably, the younger men took over the saw. Over a pit, they built a tall frame onto which the spruce logs were rolled and braced. One man stood atop the rack and another below. In tandem they worked the two-handled saw back and forth the length of the log. It was dirty, backbreaking labor. Getting boards of equal thickness took experience, teamwork, and intense labor.

While sawing boards, the partners faced the stampeders' classic dilemma: Build fast to gain a lead over their rivals? Or take the time to craft a good boat likely to see them safely through to Dawson? Some of the cruder boats under construction looked ominously like coffins. Whether it was from Karstens's experiences on Lake Michigan, or from mutual prudence, the four partners opted to build right, losing a few days of precious sailing time in favor of quality construction.

With sufficient boards finally cut and stacked, Karstens selected a bent spruce to hew into a keel. Once the ribs were attached to the keel, the construction progressed swiftly with each lapped board sealed with melted spruce resin. The men erected a mast and hewed a spar, oars, and a wide sweep for steering. When finished, their square-stern boat measured twenty-six feet long, six feet abeam, and three feet deep.

The men launched their boat on October 11. After patching a few small leaks, the partners stowed their combined outfits on board. In an evening lull, they tested their boat's handling and rebalanced the load accordingly. Now the sense of urgency that gripped every stampeder—the *Hurry! Hurry!*—burned red-hot.

At first light the next morning, the four men shoved off. In the early calm, each man took a turn at the tiller, but as the wind picked up, Karstens was the only one who seemed able to keep the boat headed into the wind and down the lake. "She was the hardest proposition to keep up in the wind," Karstens said. "If I relaxed on the steering oar, she would skid to one side and try to swamp us." By default, Karstens would be the helmsman for the entire run to Dawson. It would be his job to steer, choose routes, and command the rowers.

In early afternoon, the men beached their boat above the lake's outlet and the rock-strewn rapids that separated Lake Lindeman from Lake Bennett. Here they faced their first major decision. Should they run the whitewater or portage around? The frothing main channel was lined with immense boulders. A head-on collision would end the journey before it began. The men scouted a bad stretch of rapids and saw a huge boulder midstream with the wreckage of two boats on top. Portaging the boat and gear would take two days. With a narrowing window of time, the partners chose to line their boat through the rapids. Despite every precaution, "we very nearly lost our outfit," remembered Karstens.

Below the mile-long rapids, the stream debouched into mountain-rimmed Lake Bennett. Here, where the White Pass and Chilkoot Trails converged, was another stampeder encampment with yet more

Claim filing receipt, showing that on December 8, 1897,
Harry Karstens paid fifteen dollars for the rights to mine
on the left fork of the Yukon's Henderson Creek

boats under construction. The Mounties assigned a number to each boat and carefully recorded, in case of accident, each person's name.

Less than a quarter of the stampeders who left their homes for the Klondike in 1897 reached these headwaters lakes. Hundreds arrived after freeze-up and were joined by thousands more coming over the winter trail. A mass of humanity wintered on the lakes, building their boats in anticipation of spring breakup.

Karstens and his partners did not linger at Lake Bennett. With cries of "Hurrah for the Klondike!" they hoisted their twelve-foot sail and set out in a building wind. Halfway down the lake, and in a sudden lull, they saw a man waving wildly from shore. Pulling in, they heard a chilling story. The man was the only survivor of a party of three Frenchmen whose boat had overturned in the frigid waters. He offered half his remaining outfit if they would take him along but, already overloaded, they refused. Strangely calm, "he seemed to take the drowning of his friends as all in a day's work," Karstens recalled.

The wind soon picked up again, pounding the boat with whitecaps. Beyond where Lake Bennett hooks east and narrows, a dangerous crosswind whistled out of Windy Arm. Drenched with spray and shipping water, Karstens's boat washed ashore on the rocks of the so-called Bay of Broken Dreams and threatened to turn turtle. All four men jumped into the icy water to prevent a battering and pushed the boat out through the surf. Somehow the men powered their boat into the blistering wind and eventually reached Tagish Post without further mishap.

At the North West Mounted Police post, the partners paid their mandatory duties. After logging in the boat number, the Mounties warned the four "cheechakos" (a term for newcomers or greenhorns) of the lethal rapids and river ice forming downstream. Ahead lay five hundred miles of river, with the unrelenting grip of winter tightening.

As the days grew shorter and colder, ice formed on the boat, oars, and sweep, adding weight and hindering maneuverability. The partners floated past boats that had swamped. The survivors "offered us all kinds of inducements to help them through but we could not handle more than we had," Karstens wrote.

Under a tarp in the middle of the boat, the partners kept a stove and hot coffee going at all times. Karstens sat at the stern exposed to the elements. Working the sweep warmed him a little but "my feet were very cold with shooting pains up my legs."

Late in the second day after leaving Tagish Post, the roar of thundering rapids warned the partners to shore. At Miles Canyon, the Yukon narrows to one-third its size and plunges through a basalt gorge with what pioneers described as "an unholy whirlpool at its center." Here were two perilous rapids: Squaw Rapids, where the river pours over a succession of jutting rocks, and the White Horse Rapids, so named because the whitewater resembled bolting horses.

Karstens was sobered by what he saw. From atop the sheer canyon walls, he looked down at thick sheets of ice encrusting the basalt cliffs and a river running with brash ice. The roar of the plunging river drowned out all conversation. His partners pointed to boulder-strewn rapids and ice-encrusted sandbars. They noted jumbles of timber choking the eddies. Where the whirlpool spurted into Squaw Rapids, the Yukon narrowed to thirty feet. Only Providence could spare anyone tossed overboard into the icy tumult. Boat debris offered mute testimony to the lethal danger facing them

After careful scouting, Karstens decided to run Squaw Rapids. With pulsing dread, the men pushed off, trusting to their teenage captain. Immediately the current seized the boat and tried to spin it. Karstens screamed orders and with all his strength lunged into the sweep. Quickly righted, the boat narrowly shot past a jutting rock and into the four-foot waves. In the maelstrom the boat lurched right and left, only constant and frantic effort keeping it headed downriver. Once fully in the river's grasp, maneuvering was impossible. The only thing to do was keep the bow pointed downstream—and *pray*.

Now the extra effort to build well paid off. More than once the boat glanced off rocks and once scraped against the ice-encrusted walls. With luck and effort, Karstens dodged lethal boulders and swept past the deadly whirlpool. Freezing spray drenched the stampeders, the boat shipping water. Much more and the extra weight of water and ice would spell catastrophe. Just as the boat began to wallow, it bobbed out of the foam and floated placidly into a calm eddy.

In the eddy below Squaw Rapids, the men rowed to shore. Quickly they built a roaring fire and bailed the boat. The nearby wreckage of several stampeder boats mocked them. Spooked by their run, they shivered from the cold, fear, and dread of the whitewater ahead— White Horse Rapids. Once back on the river, they soon saw a small tent encampment with dozens of boats tied up. They pulled ashore, where a Mountie met them and explained the situation.

Earlier that summer, White Horse Rapids had claimed 150 boats and taken the lives of ten men. To stop the carnage, the Mounties had placed restrictions on travel through the rapids. The lawman inspected Karstens's boat and ticked off some basic but vital rules.

Freeboard was measured and Karstens quizzed as to his competence as helmsman. Perhaps sobered by the river's power, or by order of the Mounties, the partners hired a pilot to take their boat through the five miles of whitewater.

Wrecked and damaged boats lined both riverbanks below White Horse Rapids. Piles of goods, tents, and crude shelters disappeared under the softly falling snow. Several stampeders, who had lost their outfits in the rapids, called it quits here, planning to return home as soon as the river froze.

Safely through the rapids, the partners continued on, with Karstens again at the helm. Each day the running ice thickened, complicating navigation. No one could stay warm. Karstens wrapped two blankets over his mackinaw but was still chilled to the bone. Wet cotton or leather gloves offered no protection. The damp cold bit deep; chilblains tortured bare hands.

On Lake Leberge they checked in with the Mounties before hoisting their sail for the thirty-mile run down the lake. Beyond the outlet, they floated the Thirtymile, a lovely but treacherous stretch of the Yukon that claimed many boats. Farther downstream, Karstens easily navigated Five Finger Rapids, squirting through without trouble.

On October 23, with a hundred miles still to go, the temperature fell to −5°F. The boat wallowed with layers of ice. The men's mittens, clothing, dunnage, and tarps were caked. No one rowed now—instead the men used their oars and sweep to fend off the floes and force a way into open water.

In the last days of October, the Yukon above its confluence with the Klondike River ran heavy with ice. Now, though, if the river froze, Karstens and his partners could go ashore and walk to Dawson in two days. The personal tensions that had developed during the trip likely surfaced here. No doubt, Karstens, as helmsman and the youngest partner, had become the target for the ire of the two Germans. The long desperate journey down the Yukon had allowed plenty of opportunity for second-guessing and criticism. Close to their goal, each man no doubt began to ponder his personal dream of fortune and start scheming a way to shed his partners. A reckoning was not far off.

Five miles upstream from Dawson City, Karstens began edging the boat through running ice to the east side of the river. On November 1, nearly four months after leaving Montana, he steered safely to shore at Lousetown, on the south side of the Klondike River opposite Dawson. The following day the river froze completely, making Karstens's boat one of the last down the Yukon that fall.

The village and trading post that Karstens operated
at Tanana Crossing on the Eagle Trail

3. In Yukon and Alaska Gold Fields

HARRY KARSTENS AND TOM CAVANAUGH could not believe their eyes. At first they thought they'd been robbed, their outfit stolen. Slowly the truth sank in. Their German partners on the river trip had dumped them, taking most of the food and supplies. All that was left was a little grub, a small tent, and four blankets. So much for splitting the outfit in four equal shares.

Shock turned quickly to puzzlement, then anger. If it hadn't been for Karstens's boat-handling skills, the two Germans likely would have been stranded on the shore of Lake Lindeman, or worse, frozen in somewhere far upriver. Apparently they had resented Karstens's abrupt style and orders more than they had let on. Sneaking off like this, after all that the four had endured together, seemed a particularly treacherous act.

In growing darkness, Karstens and Cavanaugh pitched their tent in a stump field on the edge of Lousetown. Cavanaugh gave his friend plenty of space; he'd seen Karstens's anger before. Perfidy was something Karstens did not tolerate. During the long, frigid, restless night ahead, the two friends pondered their desperate situation—not only their lost gear, but all the sobering and discouraging news they had learned during their first afternoon in Dawson.

Earlier that day, after landing the boat, Karstens, Cavanaugh, and their two German partners had toted their outfit up the twenty-foot-high bank and stacked everything safely above the grinding floes. Unable to pull the ice-encrusted boat out of the water, they had unloaded it as a precaution should the ice suddenly move. They had come too far and worked too hard to lose their boat and precious gear now. Trusting to luck, or maybe the vigilant eye of the North West Mounted Police, the four men had covered their outfit with a tarp before trudging into town.

A hodgepodge of tents, a few shacks, and some log cabins covered both banks of the river, extending up the hillsides to the north. Dawson City sprawled across the mile-and-a-half-wide muskeg flat on the north side of the Klondike River, with Lousetown, or Klondike City as it was officially named, spreading across the smaller clearing on the south bank. The latter, built on the site of an old Indian fishing camp, supported shops, services, and two saloons, but it was Dawson that lured newcomers. The four men had crossed the frozen Klondike, a palpable air of excitement propelling them. Here, finally, they'd reached the golden mecca of their dreams.

A thin fog from the freezing Yukon drifted over the town, mixing with the acrid smoke of woodstoves and open fires. The shouts and curses of teamsters driving their teams along the churned, hard-frozen streets provoked the barking of dozens of sled dogs. The din of the saw-mill, the clanging of steam-powered machines, and the rasp of countless hammers and saws signaled a frantic race into winter readiness.

Ankle-deep snow covered the ground and every building. Workers rushed to finish the town's first substantial buildings—warehouses, saloons, the mining exchange, and the North West Mounted Police barracks and jail. The four partners had split up, planning to rendezvous at their gear cache before dark.

Karstens and Cavanaugh had wandered the crowded boardwalk of Main Street, passing log hotels: the Klondike, Dawson City, and The Brewery. Toward the end of the street, they had seen the big warehouses of the Alaska Commercial Company and the North American Transportation and Trading Company, and noted the armed guards standing conspicuously outside. Tents of every size, many marked with hand-lettered business signs, filled the spaces between the big log buildings. Vacant restaurants and mess tents whispered of shortage and hasty escape.

The two young men had ducked into all the public houses, the M.&M., Pioneer, Moosehorn, Dominion, and Palace. Each was filled with idle men warming by the stoves. In "Big Bill" McPhee's jam-packed Pioneer saloon, Karstens and Cavanaugh marveled at the giant moose heads leering from the walls, the gamblers, the painted dance-hall girls, and the free flow of liquor. They listened to all the gossip, but with their inexperience, were unable to separate fact from fiction. Grizzled prospectors told them about Big Bill. They said that McPhee first came north in 1888 and wherever there was a strike, and miners to mine, he soon opened a bar. To some men, McPhee was a saint, grubstaking dozens of prospectors, notably Clarence Berry, who owned some of the richest claims in the Klondike. While miners like Berry were beholden to McPhee, others loathed him for encouraging their friends to drink themselves into insolvency. However, the two young men also heard that late at night, when the revelry died down, McPhee allowed people to sleep on benches and tables for want of any other shelter.

McPhee was part of the usual boomtown mix—scheming businessmen, devout clergy, prim schoolteachers, hard-eyed lawmen, grifters, brazen prostitutes, dance-hall girls, and miners and laborers who slaved long hours on the creeks. Even in late afternoon the Pioneer did a roaring trade.

During that first day in Dawson, Karstens and Cavanaugh repeatedly heard stories of the wild stampede *out* of town that had occurred just before freeze-up. When the news broke that unseasonably low water had stranded five stern-wheelers near Fort Yukon 350 miles downstream, halting shipments of much-needed food, four or five hundred people had bolted out of town in a panic. Fear of starvation drove off cheechako stampeders and old-timers alike. (Alaskans and Yukoners commonly used the term "old-timer" to identify a person who had come north prior to or during the Klondike stampede.) A typhoid scare had sent others fleeing. Despite the looming famine, thirty-five hundred people, including just a hundred and fifty women, stayed in Dawson.

Many of the men crowding the saloons blamed the trading companies, who apparently had stocked up on liquor and hardware instead of winter foodstuffs. With their shipments stranded far downstream, the trading company warehouses contained hardware and little else. Scarcity sent food prices soaring. Flour cost $125 a sack; milk, $2.50 a can; a glass of milk, $5; and butter, $5 to $10 a pound. Worse yet for Karstens and Cavanaugh, who were nearly flat broke, paper money was nearly worthless. Coins were accepted, but "dust"—gold dust—was the currency, worth $17 an ounce.

On Karstens's first afternoon in Dawson, the irony of his whole journey became obvious to him. Even before he had left Montana five months before, the rich ground had already been claimed. The whole mad, brutal dash had been a cruel joke, on him as well as the thousands who were yet to follow. As with every previous strike, the real wealth had gone to the first arrivals.

When Karstens arrived in Dawson in late 1897, the upper Yukon Basin was not entirely unexplored wilderness. Scientists, explorers, fur traders, missionaries, and prospectors had probed the Yukon River and its tributaries. Gold strikes on both sides of the Alaska–Canada border in the mid-1880s had sparked small stampedes that spread gold fever far and wide, attracting prospectors from around the world.

Then, on August 17, 1896, came the strike that precipitated the huge Klondike Gold Rush. Prospector George W. Carmack and his Indian partners, Skookum Jim and Tagish Charley, struck gold on Rabbit Creek, a tributary of the Klondike River. They panned gold in a quantity beyond imagining. At the moment of discovery, they were standing on the richest gold-bearing ground in the world. Although they didn't know it, they had found El Dorado. After staking their claims, Carmack rushed to Fortymile City to record them. (Rivers here derived their names from their distance below old Fort Reliance, located six miles downstream from Dawson City.) In Bill McPhee's saloon there, he trumpeted the electric news that emptied the town overnight, sending hundreds of "Fortymilers" (akin to California's "forty-niners") plunging into the frontier to stake their claims. Less than a week later, Bonanza Creek (the new name for Rabbit Creek) was the scene of frantic convulsion as men staked and fought for claims. By the end of August 1896, the entire stream was staked.

A horde of gold seekers descended on the Klondike River, and by summer's end, nearly every south-flowing tributary was staked from source to mouth. Boats arrived at the mouth of the Klondike until freeze-up, disgorging dozens of prospectors and entrepreneurs of all stripes.

When the news finally broke across the world in July 1897, reaching men like Karstans and Cavanaugh, Dawson City was already a booming tent city, with riverboats bringing supplies up the Yukon from the coast and delivering ever more gold seekers. Some Dawson pioneers saw the early stampeders as interlopers and fools; others viewed them with cunning and avaricious eyes; and still others, the claim owners, welcomed the influx of new labor. Until early in 1898, the townspeople were blissfully ignorant of the horde of humanity then streaming northward.

In joint after joint, Karstens and Cavanaugh, who had envisioned themselves as "Klondike Kings," absorbed the same disheartening news. Any chance to stake their own rich claims was long gone. Talk of the impending famine sobered them even more. Menial labor seemed their only chance to survive. Laborers were in high demand, but the steady jobs went to experienced Yukoners, who worked the rich claims of their contemporaries. After their perilous journey and all of their hard work, Karstens and Cavanaugh must have found the barroom chatter crushing.

"We visited all the saloons and dance halls," Karstens remembered, "and did not return to camp until late in the evening . . . we found our own little tent and personal things but the Germans were gone with their outfits." That night, restless in their cold tent, Karstens and Cavanaugh must have wondered what they had gotten themselves into: they had no money, no work, no gold, not enough food, and were far from home in a northern wilderness boomtown with the savage winter setting in.

Early the next morning the roar of grinding ice rousted the partners from their frost-covered tent. They could only watch as the moving ice reduced their boat, and dozens of others, to kindling.

The destruction of their boat galvanized Karstens and Cavanaugh. Their priority was securing winter shelter. To survive they needed a cabin and firewood, but they lacked a stove and basic tools, like an ax and saw. From the piles of equipment abandoned during the autumn exodus, they scrounged what they could use. After a meager breakfast they packed their gear a short distance up the Klondike and began building a "beartrap" cabin, a small, crude, flat-roofed shelter.

Once they had shelter and a quantity of firewood, they sought work, anything they could find. Their search taught them a hard lesson. Young men, especially cheechako stampeders without contacts, family, or mining experience, had no power, no leverage. Good jobs were scarce and were snapped up by insiders. In late November, the thermometer bottomed out at −67°F, forcing the two young men to "hole up" in their crude cabin. As food supplies dwindled in town, the last restaurant closed its doors. The two partners, like dozens of others, went hungry, a constant reminder of their folly.

Even the rich claim owners lived a surreal existence, accumulating gold in fantastic quantities but unable to buy much more than bacon and beans. No other place in the world had a larger number of potential millionaires, yet everyone in Dawson that winter lived in a squalor exceeding the worst city slums. Even the saloonkeepers, growing rich from the sale of watered-down whiskey and a vile rotgut called hoochinoo, experienced gnawing hunger.

Unlike towns such as Skagway and Circle City on the American side of the border, Dawson was relatively free of serious crime. The North West Mounted Police zealously enforced the law. During the stampede years, the Mounties hanged eleven convicts, burying them in hidden, unmarked graves, which have only recently been discovered.

In early December, when clouds brought snow and moderate temperatures, Karstens explored Bonanza and Eldorado Creeks. He staked two bench claims on gold-rich Skookum Hill above Bonanza, but his claims were disallowed. "I was not allowed to record either of them. I guess I looked pretty young to be taken seriously," he explained. More likely, he'd run afoul of the whole staking mess then embroiling the strike.

The frantic stampede to Bonanza and Eldorado Creeks produced utter chaos. Prospectors jumped claims, crossed boundaries, ran crooked lines, and staked more, or less, ground than allowed. Anarchy reigned, with only the Mounties preventing open conflict. It would take months to straighten out the mess.

In mid-December, news of a reportedly rich strike seventy-five miles up the frozen Yukon on Henderson Creek, near the Stewart River, sparked a small stampede. Despite their dire circumstances, Karstens and Cavanaugh joined the rush.

It took real courage to stampede in midwinter. The "strong cold," as old-timers called it, seemed relentless and the chiaroscuro landscape somehow menacing, offering not even a hint of warmth or comfort. Neither partner had proper clothing or provisions. By then they'd suffered minor frostbite and knew the risks of winter travel. A mishap on thin ice or with an overflow could maim, even kill. (Even in midwinter, water can be forced up and over the ice, running under an insulating blanket of snow. The hidden slush, or "overflow," forms a lethal trap for unwary travelers.) They joined the rush anyway.

Three days after leaving Dawson on foot, Karstens staked claim #31 on Henderson Creek and Cavanaugh claim #32. A claim farther upstream belonged to Jack London and another to Elam Harnish, whom London immortalized in his book *Burning Daylight*.

Almost nothing is known of the association of Karstens and London, but they had much in common. Jack London's childhood, like Karstens's, was chaotic and difficult. At seventeen, he went to sea on a sealing schooner bound for the coast of Japan. On his return, he tramped about the States and did jail time for vagrancy. A devastating exchange with his estranged father propelled him north. When he was twenty-one, he set sail for the Klondike, just two weeks ahead of Harry Karstens.

London was starving and suffering from scurvy (not uncommon in Dawson and the Yukon Territory, with the lack of fresh produce) when he stumbled into St. Mary's Hospital in Dawson. Run by Father William Judge, the Jesuit "Saint of Dawson," the hospital provided shelter, food, and medicine for those in need; independent sorts avoided it. London eventually lost four teeth from scurvy, but he credited Judge for saving his life.

Karstens and London likely first crossed paths at Henderson Creek, and their probable association, however brief, is the source of one enduring legend—that London modeled his main character in *Burning Daylight* at least partially on Karstens. It is true that few men knew Elam Harnish by any other name than "Burning Daylight," a nickname earned each morning when he roused his sleeping companions with the complaint "Get up, we're burning daylight." However, some old-time

Alaskans claimed that "Burning Daylight" was also Harry Karstens's nickname. One man, who knew both Harnish and Karstens, swore that London had written about Karstens, not Harnish. Elam Harnish's grandson reportedly said that London's portrayal of Elam Harnish was fairly accurate, but with one exception: Harnish looked nothing like London's character. Karstens, on the other hand, though in the winter of 1897–98 still a pink-cheeked nineteen-year-old cheechako with absolutely no northern experience, bore more than a passing resemblance to the man described in the book. Perhaps London, like all novelists, took traits from many people to build his portraits and characters, and Karstens was one.

Returning to Dawson, Karstens saw less and less of Cavanaugh, who soon took a job working in the mines. "Tom was too speedy for me and I saw little of him," Karstens recalled. Karstens took any work he could find, no matter how menial. Mine labor paid $1.50 an hour, ten hours a day. Menial work paid sixty cents an hour. "Some of the rustling to get by was amusing and others tragic," he said.

By late December dog teams and horse-drawn sledges opened a trail on the Yukon River and began delivering food supplies from downriver. A lunch counter opened in a saloon where "a meal cost $3.50 and one had to call for a second helping to be fairly well fed." In contrast, a similar meal in the States cost twenty-five cents at that time. It took Karstens six hours to earn enough money to buy lunch.

Growing disillusioned with the Klondike, Karstens teamed up with a young Swede, Soren Sorensen, to explore the reputedly rich strike on Mission Creek in Alaska. In late February of 1898, they set out down the frozen Yukon River, pulling their own sleds by hand. The majority of northern trails followed frozen waterways, these natural highways abandoned only to cross mountain passes to access adjoining drainages.

Old-timers considered February and March the best months for cross-country travel. Snow covers the brush and muskeg and usually safe, solid ice sheaths the rivers and lakes. The days grow longer but the sun lacks the strength to soften and melt the trails. Exploring new country away from the watercourses becomes a matter of breaking trail, the swamps solid underfoot and the tussocks flattened with snow. Even in "spring," however, the thermometer can bottom out at −70°F.

Downstream of Dawson the river meanders through rolling hills and high bluffs. Jumbles of ice line the river's edge and pile up on the snow-covered sandbars. Cottonwood and willow hem the banks, with scattered black spruce on the open, tundra slopes. The tops, or "domes," of the hills are rocky, bleak, and wind-swept. Along the river, the stabbing wind is a constant implacable foe, creating a windchill far below the ambient temperature, with frostbite a constant menace. When Karstens and Sorensen set out, the ice on the Yukon River measured fifty-five inches deep.

At Eagle Bluffs, near the abandoned trading post of Belle Isle, about 110 trail miles downstream from Dawson and just 8 miles inside the Alaska border, Karstens and Sorensen met another group from Dawson. Discontent had swept through town that spring, spawning an exodus to earlier diggings downriver. The winter brush with starvation, the high prices, the lack of unstaked Klondike ground, and anger at repressive Canadian mining laws propelled many old-timers back to Alaska, to the pioneer camps and claims, and the lax laws on the US side of the border. Mission Creek, first mined in 1895, was the first stop for those leaving the Klondike. Still a cheechako prospector, Karstens staked claims on Mission Creek and on American Creek, its tributary.

Karstens and his new companions explored several drainages, following an old trail overland to the swift-flowing Seventymile River. Upstream of the "The Falls," an ice-armored cataract, Karstens staked a "bar" claim—a claim on the alluvial deposit of sand and gravel well above the river's low-water mark. Most claims on the Seventymile were bar claims, with limited but easily recovered placer gold. Ten years earlier, a prospector there, using just a pan and simple rocker, had taken out fifty dollars per day, a sum considered good pay. New finds on the Seventymile suggested the possibility of similar returns.

After staking their claims on the Seventymile, Karstens and Sorensen hauled their sled back up the Yukon River toward Dawson, stopping at a new boom camp at the mouth of Mission Creek. Karstens attended a miner's meeting that elected a district mining recorder. He helped lay out a town site that, after considerable debate, was named Eagle City. The new town seemed to grow overnight. Log cabins replaced tents and the first saloon opened its doors. In the spring, when the riverboats began running, the trading companies built warehouses and stores. A municipal government formed and a newspaper cranked out its first edition. By summer, the population swelled with miners and newcomers quitting Dawson to 1,700. Only two years later, in 1900, the number had dropped to 286, including 22 women.

During one miners' meeting, Karstens loudly proclaimed the wonderful riches of the Seventymile River. The gathering listened to the youthful Karstens with ever-growing amusement and when he finished, Lyman Burrell, a veteran of the Seventymile prospects, nicknamed him the "Seventymile Kid." In that era, almost everyone had a nickname; Karstens's would last a lifetime. Even into his seventies, old-timers called him "Kid" or "Seventy."

During that forty-five-day, three-hundred-mile round-trip from Dawson to the Seventymile and back, through the coldest part of Alaska, Karstens learned about overflows, thin ice, and how to survive without shelter. He learned the critical importance of a good ax—how to use it to build a shelter, cut firewood, and chop ice to melt for water. If he did not already know how, he learned how to build a fire quickly.

He also learned about game. He saw that caribou wandered constantly, one day here, the next day gone. He heard from old-timers that snowshoe hares were cyclic, sometimes darting through the brush in incredible numbers, only to disappear for years at a time. He traveled terrain that ptarmigan favored and the forests where spruce grouse lived. An old-timer likely told him never to kill a porcupine unless he needed meat, as this was the one animal a starving man could easily run down and kill with a stick. Old-timers reinforced the obvious—a winter traveler could not rely on wild meat for survival.

After long days on the trail, Karstens returned to Dawson penniless and without supplies. Significantly, he and Sorensen had suffered no serious injury despite the fierce cold they had endured. No doubt he'd learned a truth that would last a lifetime: the northern wilderness, especially in winter, presented uncompromising challenges; to survive, a traveler must always be on guard.

By April, Karstens had had all he could take of Canada and the Klondike. His best claims had been disallowed and he had no money to pay Crown fees. As soon as the ice went out, he planned to leave the Yukon for good. He sold an option on his Henderson Creek claim and used $200 to buy grub and a year's outfit.

The spring of '98 in Dawson was unusually warm and pleasant. Snow went quickly and the first wildflowers sprouted on the south-facing slopes above town. On May 8, the river began to break up. An ice jam diverted the flood into town, inundating most every street and building. Finally, on June 5, the jam broke and the river drained away as though a plug had been pulled on a bathtub. Three days later, the vanguard of a ragtag fleet of seven thousand boats, built on the headwaters lakes and carrying thirty thousand stampeders, flooded into Dawson.

Many of the stampeders wandered the streets in a daze, their dreams clearly dashed by what they found and heard, and the lunacy of the whole Klondike stampede obvious. "There are many men in Dawson . . . who feel keenly disappointed. They have come thousands of miles on a perilous trip, risked life, health, and property, spent months of the most arduous labor a man can perform, and with expectations raised to the highest pitch, have reached the coveted goal only to discover there is nothing here for them," read an editorial in the *Klondike Nugget*.

Karstens needed no such epistle to remind him. As soon as the ice went out, with the stampeders pouring in, he bought a scow, loaded his outfit, and set off down the Yukon bound for the Seventymile River. When he left town, the waterfront was four to five rows deep with sunken scows extending a mile up and down the river. He said that the men he had bought his scow from had "expected to shovel the gold up like gravel."

That spring Karstens helped build a cabin on Great Bear Bar, one-quarter mile above The Falls of the Seventymile. He and several others panned gold from the exposed bars and did "fairly well" until the color played out. In early autumn, Karstens's companions quit work. Four of them hired him to do the required assessment work on ten claims for $650, which equaled $6.50 per day.

With another winter closing in, Karstens continued to "run a cut" in the main bar and "got pretty fair results." The gold Karstens recovered from his five claims paled in comparison with the riches of the Klondike, but at least they were his, recorded in his name and protected by American mining law.

After freeze-up, he set out for Eagle, which had grown considerably since his last visit. The Alaska Commercial Company had built a large store, five saloons did a roaring business, and everything sold at the usual inflated prices. The US Army, responding to reports of lawlessness and starvation along the upper Yukon River, had begun building Fort Egbert. The post's picturesque setting near Eagle Bluffs was wasted on the troopers, as the location was one of the coldest and windiest points along the Yukon.

Harry Karstens was not the only member of his family infected with gold fever. Late in the winter of '98, his older brothers, John Henry and George, joined the rush to the Klondike over the "All-American" route out of the port of Valdez, Alaska. This route, according to boosters, led stampeders to the heart of the gold fields without the financial drain levied by Canadian customs. No mention, however, was made of the sprawling glaciers and chain of peaks shouldering into the sky, nor the power of the giant, muddy Copper River draining the highlands, all of which had to be traversed. The rumors of "an old Russian trail" were completely false.

Within hours of landing at Valdez, George and John were in trouble. No one in their party knew where they were going, least of all the leaders. The Karstens brothers soon found themselves trudging up the steep, icy incline of the Valdez Glacier. The slope to the top was twenty miles long, with a nine-mile descent to the inland basin that drained into the Copper River. In all, thirty-five hundred stampeders tried to cross the glacier in 1897–98, most between March and June. Few made it over the summit. Hidden crevasses and massive avalanches menaced the stampeders. Spring temperatures brought snow, then thaw. Rain, sleet, and wet snow stranded anyone caught in the open. Food spoiled, and without wood, warming fires were impossible. On April 30, 1898, eight feet of snow fell, triggering an avalanche that killed at least five people. The Karstens brothers helped pull the twisted bodies from the snow.

The vast majority of those who attempted the glacier suffered injury, hunger, or scurvy. By one estimate, only ten people out of the frenzied hundreds made it to the Klondike. George Karstens was one of them. John Henry left Valdez on September 24. After his return to Chicago, he never left home again, rarely even left the house. Family members thought the ordeal of the trail, especially the recovery of the dead, had unhinged him.

George Karstens forged on and reached the upper Yukon River in the early winter of 1899. It appears that by happenstance, George and Harry Karstens met up somewhere on the Yukon River. In August of that year, George recorded an interest in his first claim on the Seventymile River. Through the following winter, and into the summer of 1900, George and his brother Harry collaborated on several mining ventures, developing a shared claim on Great Bear Bar.

A gold strike at a small creek near Nome, Alaska, on the Bering Sea, sparked a winter stampede, with seven thousand people draining out of Dawson and emptying smaller camps along the Yukon River. The Karstens brothers listened to the wild tales of "golden beaches" and egg-size nuggets, but ignored those all-too-familiar stories. Perhaps chastened by the hardships endured in the Klondike rush, they continued to develop their claims. In retrospect, the decision to avoid the Nome stampede was a pivotal moment in Harry Karstens's life.

In the autumn of 1899, George Karstens abruptly quit the country, leaving his younger brother to face the coming winter alone. For over three years, Harry had faced challenge after challenge and persevered, his grit and determination obvious. When George left, he picked up his shovel and pan and went back to work.

Karstens, right, poses with newspaperman and store owner
Frank Cotter in Valdez, 1901.

4. Dog Team Mail Carrier

ALASKA'S LONG, BRUTAL WINTERS scoured some men's souls. The stabbing cold threatened everyone; no one held immunity from the possibility of gruesome frost injury. Most people prepared for the weather and took their chances according to their skills and conceits. Many more, however, were unprepared and unable to deal with the subtler challenges of the northern extreme: darkness and silence.

The gold stampedes lured north rural people and city dwellers, farmers and factory workers. Few of them had ever experienced a land locked so tight that even *sound* seemed frozen. The stillness created an air of expectancy, a breath-holding, and a warning of the danger lurking in a land of ice and snow. In the heart of winter, with its mix of unrelieved silence and darkness, the solitude exacted a terrible toll. Violence, depression, suicide, and insanity were hallmarks of the sub-arctic winters.

Those who could afford it wintered "Outside" (the Alaskan term for the Lower 48), with return tickets for the following spring when runoff again provided water for the sluices and gold pans. Some of the men who stayed behind were often those least able to cope with the isolation and the killing frost. Many sought relief in the saloons' glare and the flow of watered-down liquor.

A few old-timers, and fewer cheechakos, spent much of the winter in tiny crude cabins on their claims. The isolation sorely tested even the most resolute, with most miners moving into town at freeze-up in search of companionship and diversion. On the Seventymile River, not far from Harry Karstens's claims, George Curtis, a stampeder new to the North, slaved through summer's clouds of mosquitoes in a fruitless search for gold. After freeze-up, he turned up in Eagle desperately seeking work but finding only a town full of miners in similar straights and jobs scarce. Curtis lacked the gold dust to buy even a trapping outfit, a winter pursuit that could turn a small profit. The town had grown considerably, with sundry businesses, a new judge, a court, and a jail. Saloons did a roaring business. With little else open to him, Curtis snapped up an offer to carry the mail south through the hills to the Tanana River, where he would hand off the mail to another carrier heading downriver for transfer to a carrier bound for Valdez.

Jim Fish, owner of the Valdez Hotel, held the government contract to haul the mail from Valdez to Eagle. He divided his route into sections and hired carriers for each segment. He supplied Curtis with a dog team and the necessary start-up money to carry the mail from Eagle to Tanana Crossing on the Tanana River. Curtis was expected to keep on schedule regardless of weather.

Old-timers in Eagle, some veterans of the 1886 Fortymile strike, knew what winter could do and undoubtedly saw the danger signs in Curtis. A man could come in from the creeks but carry the solitude and fear with him. As the days shortened and the cold intensified, Curtis spent increasing time in the saloons, soon losing all his expense money to liquor and gamblers. Broke, desperate, and despondent, he tried to kill himself.

"For a week a number of us took turns staying with him as he tried to hang himself several times," Karstens said. "At the end of the week he seemed to be rational, wrote a few letters, so we let him alone." That very night, less than a week after solstice, Curtis hung himself from a cabin ridgepole.

In the wake of the tragedy, and without Jim Fish's knowledge, Eagle's postmaster cast about for a new mail carrier. At first she found no takers. Without start-up money, the venture seemed financially, as well as physically, risky. With a long winter still ahead and with few appealing work prospects, the Seventymile Kid volunteered for the job.

Although Karstens had no money, he did have a small dog team. "I knew some supplies were left at the Tanana Crossing," he recalled, "so I borrowed in debt but got enough to pull out with the mail on time. Me, just 20 or 21, out of a big city, my only experience one dog and a sled on the Seventymile and four days with a nine-dog team on the Yukon."

Karstens had no idea what he was really getting into. It was a "thing that I believe changed my whole life in the north and filled me with the wanderlust," he remembered. Government contracts detailed load sizes and schedules. Carriers were required to keep a journal detailing each day's travel, pace, mileage, weather, and trail conditions. A typical contract paid seventy-five dollars a month to make thirteen trips a winter on a schedule of six days on, one day off. The mail carrier provided his own dogs and sled. Rigid delivery schedules had to be met. Any delay was penalized. Consequently, carriers were forced to travel in any weather and temperature. By contrast, the Yukon government prohibited commencement of travel—except in life-or-death emergencies—when the temperature was −45°F or lower. No such regulation curtailed travel on the Alaska side of the border. Just to keep their schedules, and jobs, reluctant mail carriers were forced out even at −65°F or colder. Old-timers had a saying: "travelling at 50 below is all right as long as it's all right." One small mishap, one broken item, one missing glove or mitten, one ill dog, could quickly turn lethal.

With the flood of people entering the Yukon and Alaska, mail took on enormous importance. The tidal wave of letters and packages overwhelmed both the Canadian and American systems. Postmasters in hubs such as Skagway, Valdez, and Dawson City were desperate to move the mail. People badgered mail clerks for letters from home and also demanded the timely shipment of their outbound correspondence. "To see the excitement that the mail from outside makes, to see the eagerness with which the men press up to the postmaster's desk for their letters, and the trembling hands as they are opened, and the filling eyes as they read, touches the heart," recalled one observer.

It often took a hundred days or more for a letter to reach Dawson City from any place in the central or eastern United States. Bulky packages and heavy items took much longer, languishing in the far corners of the post offices, awaiting shipment by summer steamboats.

With dog teams, weight was a critical issue, with room only for first-class mail.

On every trail, mail teams had the right of way. In fact, many trails were open only due to the passage of mail carriers. At roadhouses and shelter camps, carriers got the choice seats at the table, the best food, and the cushiest bunks. They hung their mitts and parkas in reserved spots near the stove and brought their lead dogs inside to sleep under their bunks. Karstens's route from Tanana Crossing to Eagle was almost totally undeveloped. With few exceptions, he was on his own, the only shelter a hastily pitched canvas tent or spruce lean-to that he built himself. Night bivouacs were possible only with a roaring fire and plentiful firewood.

Dog driving, or "mushing" as it was called, was grueling and dangerous. Only the stouthearted and resolute succeeded as mail carriers. All of them had their tales of stabbing cold, raging storms, thin ice, overflows, and close calls. They told their stories with missing fingers and toes, and faces blackened by the implacable frost. The price of frostbite was often disfigurement for life.

Even experienced carriers fell victim to the strong cold. James Wickersham, the newly appointed federal district judge, told the story of a whole team—driver, dogs, and sled—that fell through thin ice, the musher's hat lying on the ice the only clue to the disaster. While scouting out a route for a military telegraph line between Valdez and Eagle, 1st Lt. "Billy" (William L.) Mitchell found a sled with a frozen body slumped over the mail sacks, a match between the man's teeth and a matchbox between his knees. "No hardier, braver, or more capable men ever drove a stage across the American plains . . . than these pioneer mail carriers of the Yukon," Judge Wickersham wrote. Episcopal Archdeacon Hudson Stuck, an experienced winter traveler, agreed. "So far as there is anything heroic about the Alaskan trail, the mail carriers are the real heroes," he declared.

When Karstens left on his inaugural trip to Tanana Crossing, there was little snow, so he went on foot. He toted a backpack and perhaps had each of his three dogs carry a bundle of mail. He forged his way across the 5,000-foot-high hills south of the Yukon River, waded creeks running with ice, and staggered across vast tussock flats.

Without a trail to follow, he bushwhacked, enduring dropping temperatures and bitter winds. Alone he pioneered a ninety-mile route over the hills to the Tanana River.

At the mission at Tanana Crossing, he claimed the mail carrier's supplies and outfitted for the return trip. When the carrier from the south pulled in, Karstens swapped loads and left for Eagle. By then, winter had seized the land in its rending teeth. Over the ensuing short, frigid days, the country sorely tested Karstens's strength and will.

The wilderness of the upper Yukon River, near the Canadian boundary, is one of the coldest spots in Alaska, a land where in winter even prime caribou struggle to survive. Karstens experienced a cold snap so severe that parts of Steele Creek, which drains from the hills south of Eagle, froze solid overnight.

Back in Eagle, Karstens dropped the incoming mail from Valdez at the post office in the Northern Commercial Company store, hitched his three dogs to a sled loaded with the remainder of the Valdez mail pouches, and set out down the Yukon for Circle City, 150 miles away.

Compared to the rugged trail from Tanana Crossing, the Yukon River trail was a superhighway that saw travelers of all stripes—stampeders, trappers and traders, woodcutters, market hunters, and mail carriers. Roadhouses were spaced about twenty-five miles apart, a distance equal to a day's travel by dog team. Ben Downing held the mail contract from Dawson City downstream to Fort Gibbon, at the confluence of the Yukon and Tanana Rivers. Between roadhouses, he maintained cabins and shelter tents for the safety of his mail carriers, other travelers in need, and their dogs. Each was stocked with provisions, stoves, and wood, with the strict proviso that all supplies be immediately replaced. An inviolate law of the trail required that dry kindling, firewood, and matches be placed next to the stove, ready for immediate use by a desperate musher.

Despite the roadhouses and shelters, the Yukon River's howling winds, ruptured ice, and killing cold tested everyone. Shelters saved lives and limbs, with the inexperienced Karstens no exception. Yet Judge Wickersham, in his memoirs, *Old Yukon: Tales, Trails, and Trials*, painted a rather romantic description of trail life: "For a dog, any journey is preferable to confinement on a chain in the dog lot. On the trail there is change and exercise, long and exciting races with other teams along the icy surfaces of the river trail, bells jingling sweet music in the clear and frosty air . . . there are the friendly meetings with strange teams and sometimes jolly good fighting at the overnight roadhouses, and more often with passing teams crowding in narrow snow trails."

Regular winter travelers could recognize one another at a distance by their dog teams. Heavy clothing, often with face masks, hid identities, but the few people who regularly ran the trails knew one another on sight. Despite the wilderness and solitude, mushers often avoided each other on the trail, passing at distance or on opposite sides of the river to prevent dog tangles and fights. Karstens frequently encountered Episcopal Bishop Peter Trimble Rowe, with his two-dog team, and Judge Wickersham, with his own team or with a guide. Given that a mail carrier might cover four thousand miles a winter, the three would cross paths numerous times in the years to come.

With only minimal experience, Karstens had a lot to learn about dogs and dog driving. He made up for his inexperience with guts and a remarkable capacity for work. Over the next dozen years, he would gain a reputation as one of the best dog drivers in the North, but at first he relied on his remarkable endurance to see him through. Many times he hauled the mail on foot, pulling a small sled tied to his waist, wryly remarking later that "the man is often the biggest dog of all."

On a hard, fast trail, Karstens's three-dog team made excellent time, but his small team struggled with heavy weights, often unable to break an uphill trail with any size load. Clearly, he needed to develop a better team and learn the best methods of mushing and caring for dogs. His life depended on it.

Probably because they were cheaper than prized huskies, Karstens's first team was comprised of dogs imported from Outside. With limited capital, he likely started on his mail route using an Indian sled or some handmade contraption. On one trip over the Eagle Trail, Karstens transported the mail on a dried cowhide fashioned into a crude toboggan. What happened to his sled and dogs is unknown, but all alone, in slicing winds, raking cold, and darkness, he broke trail for forty miles while pulling the makeshift sled by hand.

Dogsleds ranged from toboggans to top-of-the-line hardwood sleds, two feet wide and eight to fourteen feet long. Many mushers used Indian-made, spruce-basket sleds with handles and long runners at the rear where the driver sometimes stood. A "gee-pole" for steering extended forward from the right side of the front end of the sled. While guiding the sled with the gee-pole, the driver ran next to or astride the low-hanging towline and guided the team with his whip and voice. Most sleds had moose-hide lashings, iron runners, a snow brake, and cotton rope for securing loads. These sleds took a terrible beating from pounding over uneven surfaces or battering against trees and ice-covered rocks and hummocks; many did not last long without major repairs.

Mail loads by contract were not to exceed four hundred pounds, but the weight varied greatly. Besides the mail, a typical load included dog food, provisions, blankets, robes, clothing, ax, extra dog harness, rope, waterproof tarpaulin, and snowshoes. The best dog drivers aimed for fifty pounds per dog, but the loads often topped out at twice that weight per dog. Dog drivers walked, ran, or broke trail ahead of their teams, rarely riding the runners except on sections of level, hard-packed trails.

Karstens carried the mail over his five-hundred-mile round-trip route for about a year and a half. He said he got enough experience, and caution, to last a lifetime. He survived howling storms, bitter cold, treacherous overflows, deep snow, and reluctant or recalcitrant dogs. Toward the end of his first stint as a mail carrier, he began to master the essentials of dog care and sled travel. By taking the carrier job, which bound him for its duration, Karstens lost all his mining claims for lack of the required assessment work. "I thought I would make a trip or two and get out of it and go up to my claims," Karstens recalled. "What a lovely dream."

After spring breakup, Karstens ran the trading post at Tanana Crossing, swapping goods for furs trapped by local Athabascans. In early winter he went back to Eagle and hunted caribou for the army troops at Fort Egbert. The riverboat bringing the beef ration had frozen in while coming up the Yukon, and the soldiers were desperate for fresh meat. The Fortymile caribou herd, numbering in the tens of thousands, wintered or wandered through the high hills southwest of town. From a camp on the divide between Mission Creek and the Fortymile River, Karstens and other contract hunters killed dozens of animals to feed the troops. He used his dogs to sled heavy loads of meat back to Fort Egbert.

Two years earlier, in July 1900, the US Army began construction of a military and commercial telegraph line across Alaska. When finished, the Washington–Alaska Military Cable and Telegraph Service (WAMCATS) linked Alaska's far-flung military posts to Valdez, the terminus of an undersea cable connecting Alaska to Seattle. In 1901, 1st Lt. Billy Mitchell, twenty-two years old, arrived in Eagle to take charge of the construction of the line from Valdez to Eagle, with orders to speed up the process. Bucking heated opposition from both his troops and local muleskinners, Mitchell ordered his men to continue work throughout the winter. Despite his youth, this son of a US senator and Civil War veteran proved tough and resolute. He never ordered his men to do something that he himself would not do. He proved adept at winter travel and learned to mush dogs with some skill.

Mitchell bypassed the indolent and contentious muleskinners then employed and contracted with others to haul the 150-pound coils of wire, insulators, tools, and food needed to sustain winter operations. Ignoring the mutterings and hard stares of the fired muleskinners, the Seventymile Kid signed on as guide and teamster for the troops working in the murderous conditions.

That winter the cold exacted a grisly toll in horses and mules: lips froze where their bits touched them; sweat resulted in frostbite; overflows caused frozen hooves and legs; animals collapsed from improper food. Dozens were shot, but the work progressed.

The troops suffered as well. Frostbite claimed fingers and toes, and some men nearly perished from the biting frost; others deserted. Despite the best efforts of the packers and teamsters, food, medicine, and supplies were often inadequate. Soldiers and officers alike toiled in the seasonal extremes of heat and mosquitoes, and bitter cold and darkness. Little over a year after they started, Mitchell's solders completed the 420-mile Eagle-to-Valdez segment of the line. Within two years, WAMCATS stretched 1,396 miles, connecting fifty-four

Alaska locations. Karstens remembered the work as "exciting times" but suffered like everyone else. He returned to Eagle in "pretty bad shape with pains across the shoulders."

After recuperating, Karstens decided to return to Chicago for the first time since running away. From Eagle, he walked up the frozen Yukon River to Dawson. There, he took the stage to Whitehorse and then caught the train to Skagway, where he boarded the steamship to Seattle. In the Windy City he avidly read the newspaper stories of Alaska, which highlighted a new gold strike in the Tanana Hills and another rush to Nome. His return visit to his childhood home lasted six or eight months and was difficult. "I had been away five or six years," he recalled. "Everything was strange, and I didn't fit in. I held out as long as I could, then went north."

In late August 1903, Karstens stepped off the steamship SS *Bertha* in Valdez and looked up his former employer Jim Fish, who then held the contract to transport mail from Valdez to Fort Gibbon on the Yukon River via the new boomtown of Fairbanks. Fish hired Karstens and Charles "Mac" McGonagall to haul mail over the northern portion of

Karstens on Birch Lake near Fairbanks, in a 1903 photo taken by miner Leon Kellum, who had been mushing with him on the Richardson Trail at thirty below

the route. On the day Karstens arrived in Valdez, a climbing expedition led by Dr. Frederick Cook began its assault on Mount McKinley.

In Mac, Karstens found a partner and friend to rely on. McGonagall was an experienced mail carrier and musher. He had come north from Chicago in 1896 and, with two partners, floated the Yukon to the Fortymile strike. On the journey, McGonagall and his partners had camped on an island near the mouth of the Klondike River, just a short distance from the as-then-undiscovered bonanza.

The next winter, McGonagall hauled the mail down the Yukon River from the town of Fortymile to Fort Yukon. In 1898, while carrying the mail, McGonagall spent thirty-four straight days outdoors when the temperature never rose above −50°F. For over two years, he freighted between Dawson and the downriver camps.

When he heard of the Nome strike in 1900, McGonagall charged off with a two-dog team. Less than fifty miles from Nome's "golden beaches," he and his partner were quarantined through the entire summer because of a smallpox epidemic. Once released, his dream of gold evaporated, McGonagall returned to Dawson City.

Karstens and McGonagall spent their first summer together driving Fish's horse-drawn freight wagons over Thompson Pass. Valdez residents referred to Karstens, then just twenty-five, as an "old sourdough" or "old-timer."

After freeze-up, Karstens and McGonagall led a string of packhorses to Gakona Junction, on the Copper River, a way station on the Eagle–Valdez Trail. There they exchanged the horses for a single dog team and headed into the mountains. Their maps were inaccurate, with the route from the Copper River to Fairbanks unestablished. Three rugged trails led from the river to the main pass (Isabel Pass) through the jagged and glaciated Alaska Range. Fish had given them directions to a mine on the Chistochina River, but from there they were on their own.

Overall, the route from Valdez to Fairbanks was called the Richardson Trail, and the segment through the Alaska Range was considered the most difficult portion. The mountains did not get the deep snows of Thompson Pass just outside of Valdez, but the deep cold, wind, and alpine terrain combined for unique challenges.

Before leaving the established mine trail, Karstens and McGonagall cut willow wands to mark the thirty miles of open trail to the head of the north-flowing Delta River. Fresh, deep snow in the mountains slowed them, and they broke trail on snowshoes, the dog team wallowing in their wake. The first day they made fifteen miles and camped in heavy willows at the head of the Gakona River. The next day they broke trail to the upper Delta, pioneering the route they would use throughout the winter.

By the time they reached the confluence of the Delta and Tanana Rivers, they were low on food, with only cornmeal and tea for supper. When the ravenous dogs scented a camp, they bolted. "Before we could get to them, they were in a tent, tearing things to pieces," Karstens recalled.

When the tent's owners returned, they fed Karstens and McGonagall and told them of a cache of meat four or five miles downstream on the opposite bank of the Tanana River. "The river was exceedingly dangerous, as it had jammed [with ice] in the last forty-eight hours with lots of open stretches," Karstens said. "We made a ticklish crossing, but we found no meat cache and had fifty miles to go to Salchakat . . . where old-timer Billie Munson was building a roadhouse. We stopped a couple of

Miners and dance-hall girls at a roadhouse on the Richardson Trail
en route to Valdez from Fairbanks, 1904

days with him." The two partners helped with construction in exchange for food.

From the confluence of the Delta and Tanana Rivers, the Richardson Trail snaked along a series of low forested hills and bluffs on the north, with the broad Tanana Valley sprawling to the south. The forty-thousand-square-mile valley was largely uninhabited away from the rivers that cut through it. Except for a few small camps of Alaska Natives, and trapping and mining cabins, the dense spruce/birch forests were without trails or development of any kind. The pioneer trail paralleled or followed the Tanana downstream to Fairbanks, and from there to Fort Gibbon at the confluence of the Tanana with the Yukon River.

The men made the nearly forty-mile run from Munson's Roadhouse to Fairbanks in one day. The situation in Fairbanks looked bad to Karstens. Food was scarce and the diggings unproductive. He thought that the whole stampede to the Chena River was built on rumors. Later that spring, when the creeks proved rich, he lamented that "mail carriers were not allowed to take time out and stake their own claims."

In Fairbanks, Karstens bought another sled and seven dogs, at seventy-five to a hundred dollars per dog. Fully outfitted, the partners pushed off on the 125-mile trail down the Tanana to Fort Gibbon. There they flipped a coin to see who would carry the first mail east and south back over their new trail to Gakona. Karstens won. McGonagall would rest a few days before starting with the second mail shipment. They planned to meet and swap loads near the head of the Delta River. Karstens left Fort Gibbon on December 5 with a sled laden with one sack of mail, tent, stove, dog food, dog pans, and provisions. He reached Fairbanks ten days later, where he added two more bags of mail. Now, near winter solstice, with the days barely four hours long, each day's journey began and ended in darkness. The four-hundred-mile return trip went well, the subzero temperatures keeping the trail hard-packed and fast. He reached Gakona without incident just as the first in a series of big storms broke. The mail shipment relayed over the new route eventually reached Valdez in sixteen days, well within the twenty-five days stipulated by contract.

After a day's layover in Gakona, Karstens switched loads with another musher up from Valdez. Accompanied by two trailbreakers hired by Fish, Karstens started back toward the head of the Delta, where he was to exchange loads with McGonagall.

Just before Karstens set out for the pass, a sudden deep snowfall buried the trail leading to Isabel Pass. On snowshoes, the Seventymile Kid and his helpers took turns breaking trail. Wind-driven sleet that afternoon pounded them. En route to the camp that Karstens had established at the head of the Gakona River, one of his trailbreakers, Normile, steering the sled from the gee-pole, plunged through the ice, soaking one foot. He said nothing until reaching camp, where he complained that he could not wiggle his toes and that his foot felt "like a club." Fearing the worst, Karstens wrenched off Normile's iced-up moccasins and socks and exposed a foot frozen stiff to the instep. "We did everything we could to bring life back in the foot using slush snow and then rubbing with bacon grease," Karstens recalled. Their remedies were fruitless, the damage done. Normile writhed in agony throughout the night, his cries keeping everyone awake.

The next morning, Karstens left Normile in the tent next to the stove, a pile of wood within reach. Accompanied by the second trailbreaker, he then snowshoed to the head of the Delta to meet McGonagall. Yet another blizzard had buried the trail, concealing or scattering the willow markers. At dark, after a long, hard day floundering in snow, the two men reached the prearranged rendezvous site but McGonagall was not there. Casting about in the fading light, Karstens found sled tracks out on the moraine. Somehow McGonagall had missed the camp, or had failed to await rendezvous, and his tracks led southeast and away from the trail.

Like Karstens's first mail route from Eagle to Tanana Crossing, the new trail through Isabel Pass lacked shelters of any kind. Where the trail traversed the high alpine tundra, there wasn't even firewood. Without firewood or bedding, the two men spent a miserable night in their unheated tent. For dinner, they gulped a can of "liquid bread," a mixture of flour and baking powder.

Early the next morning, they headed back to the Gakona camp and the injured trailbreaker. From a prominence above the camp, they saw a black dot working its way toward them. It was a man and two dogs pulling an almost empty sled. "We hurried over to camp and we got there a little before him. It was Mac and he was a sight," Karstens remembered. "He had tried to make a crossing farther down the divide and got in an awful mix-up."

McGonagall's errant turn had led him into deep snow. Instead of the team pulling him, he ended up dragging them. The dogs gave out one by one until only two were left. By accident, and as a result of snow blindness, he burned his snowshoes while trying to deice them. To save his life, he had chopped off the sled's handlebars and started a fire, which he fed with green willow branches. The smoke only worsened the pain in his eyes. As a remedy, McGonagall brewed tea leaves and tied them over his eyes.

To survive, McGonagall had dug a hole in a snowbank and crawled in to huddle with his dogs under his sleeping robe. His bivouac was horrendous, the situation tenuous. When Karstens found him the next day, McGonagall's sled was empty except for mail and sleeping robe. "He was the wildest looking man I ever saw," Karstens recalled. "It was lucky I was camped there or I'm afraid Mac would have been done for."

After a short night, with little sleep, the men loaded Normile into Mac's sled. Karstens added one of his dogs to McGonagall's remaining two and helped the three men start south for Gakona.

With their relay plan now a shambles, Karstens pushed north alone with six dogs pulling a loaded sled. Over the fresh-packed trail, he made good time to the upper Delta and continued on downstream thirty miles or more, much of it on glare ice. The sky cleared, and by dusk the temperature had dropped far below zero. In dense woods Karstens stopped for the night and hastily pitched his tent. Exhausted and nearly hypothermic, he decided to cook the dog food on the stove instead of on an open fire. He stoked the stove full, pulled off his heavy trail moccasins and socks, and hung them up to dry. While waiting for the dog food to cook, Karstens dozed off. Sometime later, he awoke to intense heat, the tent engulfed in flames. Frantically he beat out the fire, but the damage was extensive, his critical footwear and mittens reduced to ashes. "I should have known better [than to fall asleep] but I was too tired to care much," he explained.

He salvaged what he could, including enough of the tent to piece together as a shelter, and at about four in the morning, mushed off down the trail wearing two pairs of socks on his hands and just two pairs of socks, insoles, and light moccasins on his feet. Inadequately dressed, only rigorous effort would keep him warm.

"It was a hard grueling trip," he recalled. "Glare ice helped out a good deal but then I would pay for it by breaking trail and dragging the load along until it seemed I could do no more. My one hope was that someone would be camped at the mouth of the Delta."

Karstens, fighting exhaustion and fearing the loss of his team, likely tied one wrist to the handlebars. His life depended on his lead dog finding and staying on the trail. Karstens had gone almost seventy-two hours without any real sleep. If he had blacked out, or otherwise fallen from the sled, he would have frozen to death where he fell.

About five miles from the Tanana River, his dogs picked up a hard-packed trail. Soon they scented a camp and broke into a run with Karstens barely hanging on for the final sprint. He vaguely remembered someone helping him into a tent, where he fell into a deep, black sleep. Karstens awoke many hours later to find his dogs fed and rested. He owed his life to his lead dog and the miners who took him in. Later, he downplayed the incident, telling a friend that he survived because he'd had "a darned good set of underwear." His rescuers provided spare clothing and footgear for the final run into Fairbanks. In town, Karstens reoutfitted and a few days later, broke trail all the way to Fort Gibbon, where he delivered the mail.

In a lifetime filled with myriad wilderness challenges and battles with the worst that the northern winters could conjure, that night of the tent fire resonated loudest. Ten years later, on a mountain to the west, another accidental fire would test Karstens's perseverance, the success of an epic expedition resting on his ingenuity.

The frigid, demanding wilderness transformed the inexperienced young Karstens into one of the toughest of the tough. Harry Karstens's redoubtable reputation was made hauling the mail. Throughout his life of varied and storied challenges, the Seventymile Kid considered pioneer mail hauling as his most perilous undertaking. "The difference between the general travelling public is the mail has to go regardless," he later explained. "Ever since the winter of 1903–04, Mac and I figured we were living on borrowed time."

James A. Wickersham donning vital summer gear—the mosquito headnet—
on the bank of the Tanana near the mouth of the Kantishna, 1903

5. Judge Wickersham's Wall

JUDGE JAMES A. WICKERSHAM STOOD on the bluff above the boom-town of Chena at the confluence of the Tanana and Chena Rivers, "cogitating," as he phrased it, on the mountain looming in the distance. From the first moment he saw the mountain, he had burned with the desire to set foot on its summit, carrying the urge in the same way that prospectors yearned for gold. "The oftener one gazes upon its stupendous mass, the stronger becomes the inclination to visit its base and spy out the surroundings," he declared in his memoirs. "Could we blaze a new trail into a distant mountain, extend geographic knowledge? . . . I began to organize a party for the trip."

Wickersham's trail to Mount McKinley was long and circuitous. He was born in Patoka, Illinois, on August 24, 1857. Although he had only an eighth-grade education, he passed the Illinois bar exam in 1880 and soon married Deborah Susan Bell. Four years later, the couple moved to a small crime-ridden town, near Tacoma in Washington Territory, filled with gambling halls, bordellos, thirty saloons, a brewery, and seven churches. With thirty other lawyers already in practice, Wickersham worked as a carpenter to make ends meet. He eventually served as probate judge and Tacoma's city attorney, and later was elected to the Washington State House of Representatives. A large American Indian population in the area required Wickersham to develop innovative decisions integrating their customs with white man's laws.

An avid outdoorsman, Wickersham took his family on extended hiking and climbing trips into the Olympic and Cascade Mountains. He climbed all of the major peaks in the Olympics, walked the entire peninsula, and was the first to champion an Olympic National Park.

On June 6, 1900, an act of the US Congress overhauled the Alaska criminal and civil codes, dividing the Territory of Alaska into three judicial districts with headquarters in Sitka, Nome, and Eagle. One week later, acting on the recommendation of US Senator Addison G. Foster, President McKinley appointed Wickersham judge for the Third Judicial District. Within two weeks of his appointment, Wickersham, his family, and legal entourage set out for Skagway.

Instead of a hard slog over the Chilkoot Trail, Wickersham and his company rode in style to Whitehorse on the newly finished White Pass and Yukon Route railroad. In Whitehorse they caught a stern-wheeler to Dawson, explored the town and mines, then went on to Eagle, the newly designated seat of civil government for Interior Alaska.

Wickersham's Third Judicial District sprawled over a three-hundred-thousand-square-mile wilderness stretching from the Arctic Ocean south to the Aleutians and Prince William Sound. His constituency included Iñupiat, Athabascans, and fewer than fifteen hundred white residents. In the entire district, there were no roads, schools, courthouses, jails, or other public buildings, and no money to build them. US currency was almost nonexistent, fur and gold the measure of trade. Wickersham and his staff waited inordinate periods between their own meager paychecks. Congress provided no funding for the construction and operation of the court, but authorized the collection of mercantile and saloon license fees to support operations. The competent manner in which Wickersham turned his backwater post into a position of integrity remains an enduring legacy.

Eagle consisted of dozens of cabins, two mercantiles, two churches, a hospital, two restaurants, and five saloons. Fort Egbert, on the edge of town, provided military control over the Yukon River. In many ways, Wickersham's years in Tacoma uniquely prepared him for what he found in Eagle. Not only did he have experience dealing with pioneers and Native Americans, he was no stranger to hard labor.

Although most of the community greeted Wickersham and his entourage cordially, their arrival provoked little celebration. Area residents, many of them veterans of the Klondike stampede, were an independent lot and viewed the government with suspicion and open disdain. To them, Wickersham represented the federal government's unwanted attempt to establish civil authority over a territory viewed by inhabitants as a bastion of freedom and independence.

When introduced to the new judge, the proprietor of a roadhouse replied, "Well, this *was* a good country before the shyster lawyers and grafting marshals began to come through it with their damned law books . . . but it's going to hell now as fast as it can go."

Professionally, the new judge was challenged by one enduring trait of Alaskans—they tended to resolve breaches of "sourdough law" themselves. Anyone could call a miners' meeting to decide a serious issue, with the group's decision irreversible. Miscreants were handed a "blue ticket"—a one-way passage out of the territory—which was ignored only at great peril. Consequently, when official juries were impaneled, many refused to return indictments except in the most grievous violations.

Karstens and Wickersham met during a suicide investigation, becoming respectful acquaintances. Their paths crossed repeatedly over the years. At least once, Wickersham attempted to persuade Karstens to accept the position of US deputy marshal. Karstens declined.

Rather than being disappointed in his position, which some people saw as a "backwater," Wickersham seemed to take pride in it. "My family had been backwoodsmen for two hundred years—ever since my first Quaker ancestors settled on wild land . . . and began to people the western wilderness," he explained. Wickersham promptly built a log house for himself, wife Deborah, and son Howard, then seven years old. He quickly laid in a supply of moose and caribou meat, and even found time to do a little prospecting. Above all, his concern for the comfort and safety of his wife, who suffered with tuberculosis, and young son, seemed paramount.

Wickersham soon set to work, settling mining disputes and collecting saloon license fees, a whopping $1,000 per year. In midwinter, Wickersham left Eagle on a thousand-mile round-trip dogsled journey to Rampart to resolve a claim-jumping dispute. The stark reality of winter thundered home when the temperature plunged to fifty below and stayed there for long days. After forty-five days on the trail, his musher and guide described Wickersham as a tireless worker, a cheechako endowed with considerable strength and stamina equal to the hardships of the trail.

In 1901, a corrupt judge, politicians, and lawyers helped turn the great Nome gold fields into riotous anarchy. In mid-September, Wickersham was ordered to replace the district's corrupt judge. Many of his rulings, even his tenure, proved controversial, but he carved law and order out of chaos and reestablished confidence in the legal system.

Wickersham buried himself in work to assuage his longings for his family back in Eagle. In March 1902, a telegram brought stunning news—his son Howard had died two months earlier from typhoid fever. "His death almost killed his mother and quite destroyed one half of my life—hopes and happiness," mourned the grief-stricken judge.

Prospector Felix Pedro's fabulous gold strike near the confluence of the Tanana and Chena Rivers soon transformed Wickersham from a minor federal judge into the czar of Alaska's Interior. After leaving Nome and vacationing Outside with Deborah, Wickersham returned to Alaska, sold his furnished cabin in the abruptly deserted town of Eagle, and joined the stampeders headed down the Yukon. Wickersham temporarily located his new headquarters at Rampart on the Yukon River, but soon moved to the new boom camp named Fairbanks.

In the three years Wickersham had been in Alaska, the urge to climb Mount McKinley only intensified. It seems he was hooked from first sight. His love of climbing made his obsession predictable, but he also may have wanted to do something to honor his benefactor, President McKinley, the man he called a "martyr." Politically ambitious, he knew that a successful first ascent would bring him wide acclaim. In the spring of 1903, with court not due to reconvene for several weeks, Wickersham began organizing his attack on the mountain.

When word got out that the judge planned to climb the mountain, he was besieged with applicants. Wickersham chose longtime
acquaintances: Charley Webb, a rough-hewn packer, boatman, and
hunter from Eagle; lawyer Morton I. Stevens, an all-around athlete;
and his stenographer and secretary, George A. Jeffery.

Wickersham also recruited John McLeod, the twenty-six-year-old
son of a Hudson Bay factor at Fort McPherson. McLeod was born on
the Liard River and spent most of his life on the lower Mackenzie River.
He immigrated to Alaska by canoe over the Rat River Portage to a tributary of the Yukon and ended up in Circle City. His gold claims on nearby
Birch Creek yielded disappointing results. McLeod spoke several Indian
languages and dialects, and his success as a trapper-trader stemmed in
part from his ability to communicate. "We have accepted him as a philol-
oger, philosopher, and friend," Wickersham declared. Two additional,
but essential, members of the expedition were the hired pack mules,
Mark and Hannah, named for Ohio Senator Marcus A. Hanna.

Wickersham was pleased with his chosen companions. None had
climbing experience, but all were trail-hardened men accustomed
to Alaska's harsh climate. Wickersham trusted them to follow his
lead, no matter the difficulties encountered. In mid-May, a crowd of
well-wishers from the two rival boomtowns of Fairbanks and Chena
cheered the expedition team as it departed aboard the stern-wheeler
Tanana Chief.

The northern approaches to the mountain were then unknown.
River men told Wickersham that the Kantishna, a tributary of the
Tanana River, drained the highlands at the base of McKinley. Although
the judge studied accounts of Alfred Hulse Brooks's 1902 expedition
along the north side of the Alaska Range, his approach from the north
would be a pioneering affair. Brooks's government-funded expedition
had pushed cross-country from Cook Inlet in the south, through the
Alaska Range, and eventually into the northern foothills of Mount
McKinley and the central massif of the range. The mapping and geological discoveries of the Brooks Expedition rank it as one of Alaska's
most successful early scientific investigations.

Ice jams at the mouth of the Kantishna prevented the *Tanana
Chief*'s upstream passage. While waiting for the ice to clear, McLeod

salvaged a derelict but well-built sixteen-foot boat, big enough to carry the entire outfit, less the mules. They dubbed their new vessel *Mudlark*. The very next day, the ice quit running and the *Tanana Chief* churned upriver into what Wickersham described as "splendid virgin country." Here the river meandered through thickets of white spruce, birch, and cottonwood. The river traversed vast swamplike meadows called "muskeg."

Thirty miles up the meandering Kantishna, low water forced the *Tanana Chief* to unload and turn back. From there, Webb and McLeod rowed and poled the *Mudlark* upstream while the two lawyers, Jeffery and Stevens, rode the mules cross-country. Wickersham steered the boat and "commanded the navy." Lining and poling was backbreaking work; low water and sudden groundings added to the labor. Compared to the boaters, the riders had a relatively easy-going journey.

The two groups rendezvoused at intervals along the river. Supplied only with typical prospecting rations—bacon, beans, salt, sugar, and flour—the expedition lived off the land. They spent two days in one encampment, smoking and drying the meat of two bull caribou that McLeod and Webb had shot. McLeod killed fish by shooting into the water and stunning them. "What would Izaak Walton say to that?" the judge asked.

Twice the boatmen encountered trappers floating downstream with bales of fur. They met Athabascans and visited their villages. Wickersham recorded place names and a lengthy creation story. He said that the Natives called Mount McKinley *Dee-na-thy*, their word for "father." One prominent summit in the nearby hills, the people called *Chet-siah*, or "Heart Mountain." After Wickersham explained his plan to climb McKinley, a chief said something that provoked rude laughter. McLeod translated for Wickersham: "You are a fool."

While forging upriver, Wickersham employed the American tradition of ignoring Native place names and replacing them with the names of friends and politicians. He named several landmarks for each of his companions. His "Alma Lake," named in honor of Mort Stevens's sister, later became well known as Wonder Lake. Wickersham named McLeod Creek for his friend "on account of the fact that it does things early and late." He named the 17,400-foot peak west of

McKinley Mount Deborah, "in honor of my good wife, whose pure clean mind and heart are fairly typified by the white snow ever resting upon its 16,000 feet." (He was unaware that it had already been named Mount Foraker after an Ohio senator. Another peak to the east of Mount McKinley now honors Deborah's memory.)

Wickersham hired Native guides to lead the way, but once the expedition left the river and started overland, they were on their own. En route, while McLeod and Webb went hunting, Stevens, Jeffery, and Wickersham climbed to the 3,862-foot summit of Chitsia Peak. The view south was mesmerizing. Low hills and open tundra rolled toward the mountains shouldering into the azure sky. Beyond the piedmont, the swan-white summits of the Alaska Range stretched endlessly toward the southwest. Immense rivers of ice wound down from the heights and guarded every approach. Mount McKinley towered over the ocean of summits, its North Face offering one of the highest vertical rises from basal terrain of any mountain in the world. Wickersham and his cohorts could only stare at the mountain's stupendous bulk and wonder if the Indian chief was right.

The next day, while Wickersham helped Webb and McLeod preserve the meat of the caribou they had killed, Stevens and Jeffery prospected Chitsia Creek and found gold. Wickersham staked the discovery claim while his companions staked claims above and below, eleven claims in all for themselves, family, and friends. This find near "Two Bull Moose Gulch" would have a far greater significance than any of them could have imagined, gold the least of it. "When we filed our notices [in Rampart] in the following July, we also filed a map as part of our description, showing the general location. . . . It was immediately copied by numerous prospectors and the next year a horde of these hardy men explored every creek in this height of land for gold, and actually located rich placer diggings on our Webb (Moose) Creek . . . it became the center of the rich Kantishna mining district," Wickersham later explained.

The great icebound mountain loomed ever closer as the expedition left the hills behind and crossed the open, rolling tundra of the McKinley River valley. Wickersham found the country compelling despite the legions of mosquitoes hatching under the warm summer sun. "A more beautiful game country does not exist than this fine large mountain-backed mountain meadow region . . . with a background of Switzerland magnified 100 times," he wrote. His comments would be avidly absorbed by sportsmen already piqued by Brooks's reports of the region's abundant wildlife.

Unfortunately, tensions were building among Wickersham's men. Although the woodsmen, McLeod and Webb, tested the judge's leadership, his old friend George Jeffery posed an unexpected challenge. Jeffery and Stevens had formed a mutual admiration society and their undisguised contempt for McLeod and Webb undermined the expedition's already tenuous cohesion. Stevens and Jeffery seemed to delight in belittling the rough-hewn woodsmen, and Webb and McLeod were growing resentful of the condescending attitude of their companions.

For days, and despite the judge's disapproving glare, Stevens and Jeffery had teased and taunted the rustic McLeod. They knew McLeod was afraid of bears and told him countless horror stories. Time and again, they warned him that mules could suddenly turn vicious and deadly. McLeod avoided the mules as if they were grizzlies. He threatened to quit a dozen times, but each time the judge persuaded him to stay on. As the expedition approached the mountain, tensions within the party boiled over. "Johnnie McLeod has cold feet and is going to desert us," Wickersham confided to his diary. "He has been entirely scared out by the Indian stories about the inaccessibility of the mountain."

Near the very base of the mountain, the undercurrent of dissension exploded. "Hells to pay," Wickersham wrote. "Webb got mad at Stevens this morning, packed up and left us . . . [but he soon] came back and asked me for a statement which I gave him in this form: 'Mount McKinley, June 17, 1903: To whom it may concern - Very much to my regret Mr. Charles Webb has this day voluntarily left my party to go home. Respectfully, James Wickersham.'" After long negotiation, the judge convinced Webb to remain, but the expedition was close to implosion.

With tensions still simmering, the expedition pressed on. During the arduous cross-country approach, the judge stopped several times to study the mountain. He recognized that the towering ice wall ahead, which Brooks had described, was an insurmountable obstacle and veered course slightly to the southwest. After crossing the wide gravel bars of the McKinley River, he appears to have followed a tributary, the Muddy River, to a ridge at the terminus of Peters Glacier. From a base camp at about 4,000 feet, Wickersham scouted for a route up the mountain. Even in early summer, snow covered the rocky slopes and ridges to about 6,000 feet.

At ten o'clock on the evening of June 19, Wickersham set out for the summit with Webb, Jeffery, and Stevens, leaving McLeod behind to guard camp. Armed with alpenstocks, ropes, and knapsacks filled with four days' worth of chocolate, bread, and caribou jerky, the climbing party attacked the Peters Glacier. Five miles up the glacier, they roped up and ascended a side glacier—now named Jeffery Glacier—to a high spur on McKinley's western slope. The roar of giant avalanches the previous night had awakened them, and they moved cautiously. "Immense masses of snow and ice high on the mountainside broke loose with the report of a cannon," Wickersham wrote. "It sent a shiver of fear down every back and warned us to keep clear of the avalanche path."

Wickersham led, picking his way around crevasses, over tenuous snow bridges, and across icefalls. His experiences in the Cascades were invaluable on these volatile slopes. On the brink of a tremendous precipice at 8,100 feet, the expedition's summit attempt abruptly ended. "Our only line of further ascent," Wickersham said, "would be to climb the vertical wall of the mountain at our left, and that is impossible." (Sixty years later, a group of Canadian mountain guides were the first to top the 14,000-foot Wickersham Wall.)

Under summer's heat and thunderstorms, the peaks pulsed avalanches at an alarming rate. "Avalanches . . . by the hundreds and hardly a moment goes by without the thunderous noise of one tearing its way down the mountain sides," Wickersham wrote. "We recognize that we are inviting destruction by staying here."

The climbers returned to camp on the summer solstice. With their food running out, the summer term of court at Rampart rapidly approaching, and the mosquitoes simply hell, the men held a council that concluded with a unanimous decision: further effort was futile.

Wickersham seemed undaunted by his truncated attack. "We returned to our labors without any feeling of failure but with a glow of satisfaction that we had done so much with so little."

Rather than being a failure, Wickersham's assault is a tribute to the party's daring. The men pioneered the northern approach to the mountain, navigated the Kantishna River, explored a route up Peters Glacier, and, even though they did not know it then, their low-grade claims on Chitsia Creek provoked gold exploration in the Kantishna hills that would serendipitously spark the movement to establish a Mount McKinley National Park. They also proved without a doubt that summer, the peak avalanche season, was *not* the time to attempt a climb of Mount McKinley.

On a cloudless June 22, the expedition broke camp for the return trip. They discarded excess clothing, food tins, and gear. Under a rock, they cached a large can of table salt, thinking they had plenty for their return journey. Less than three months later, a ragged, almost desperate, band of five white men found their camp and salt cache. This expedition to climb Mount McKinley, led by Dr. Frederick Cook, had left the Native village of Tyonek on Cook Inlet almost on the very day that Wickersham turned back. Neither party was aware of the other's attempt.

Instead of retracing their steps, Wickersham and his men cut cross-country for the McKinley River narrows, planning to build a raft to float down to the Kantishna River. Under the relentless attack of countless mosquitoes, the boggy tundra slowed their withdrawal from the mountain. They surprised a cow moose and, despite dwindling rations and Wickersham's protests that the meat would spoil in the heat, McLeod shot it. By now, the judge had endured enough. "It was a brutal waste of a big fine animal by a man who ought to value them for he lives on them from year to year. It will be wasted and was a wanton exhibition of his brutal savage nature."

A short distance above Eagle Gorge, they built a crude log raft and loaded their supplies. Wickersham scouted ahead and eyed the whitewater with trepidation. Not willing to trust the raft, he and Jeffery took the mules overland. Undaunted, Webb, Stevens, and McLeod loaded their gear and pushed off. After a brief run, the raft smashed into the rocks and came apart, hurling the men into the plunging river. They scrambled to shore safely, but much of their gear was lost. Gone were Webb's gun and ammunition, the bedding and cooking utensils, two axes, and all of their provisions except for a two-day supply of flour. "McLeod was nearly hysterical after the wreck—laughing and crying—he lost all his little belongings except his gun—and this seemed a ray of sunshine to him for without it he is lost, but with it never. He sleeps with it, never allows it beyond reach of his hand, and is now cleaning and talking to it," Wickersham wrote.

Jeffery sided with Stevens, and the two lashed out at Webb, blaming him for the disaster. When Stevens boasted of his own skill and nerve, Wickersham exploded. He said Stevens's nerve was wholly in his mouth. The expedition was close to falling apart.

Every wilderness venture, no matter how successful, has its share of wrangling and conflict, an elemental truth of human nature. The long trail brought out the best and worst, in the men, untempered by the constraints of polite society. The judge himself, despite his quick wit and playful sense of humor, was not easy to get along with. "James Wickersham is no saint. . . . A man as impulsive, hot-tempered and combative as he, is sure to make mistakes. . . . But his faults are of that sturdy, rugged character that rather endear him to an Alaskan," wrote one acquaintance.

McLeod refused to set foot on the repaired raft again, and accompanied Wickersham and the mules overland. Undaunted, the others continued by raft. On the muskeg flats, the riders wound around willow thickets, waded or swam countless watercourses, and fought their way out of quicksand. Without McLeod's wilderness skills, they would have gone hungry. He cooked bannocks, shot a goose, and called hares into rifle range by mimicking their sounds. In the mutual struggle, under clouds of pestering insects, the two renewed their unlikely friendship.

One rendezvous produced an unexpected feast. In some of the best moose habitat in the world, Webb had killed a bull moose. Now the kill was pragmatic—shoot or starve, even if some waste was inevitable.

Just before the expedition had separated again, Stevens had warned McLeod, who alerted the judge, that he would wait at the next downriver rendezvous site for only two and a half days. By then he and the others would be out of food. If Wickersham and McLeod did not show up by then, he would leave them. "I realized that if they deserted us," Wickersham wrote, "or putting it more liberally, if we were unable for any reason to find them at the mouth of the Kantishna, we would be 150 miles in the bush and wilderness with no boat or raft and no means of making one."

Alarmed by Stevens's comments, Wickersham and McLeod insisted upon taking the guns, ammunition, and ax with them on the mules. "I felt they would be more careful and certain to wait if we kept the guns . . . and events proved that we did right . . . for they informed me plainly when we found them below the mouth of the Kantishna that they had intended to wait only 10 hours or 8 hours [more], before leaving us," Wickersham said. "We had not been gone from them but 24 hours. . . . I hate a deserter!"

Reunited at the final rendezvous, McLeod, still distrusting the raft now being repaired by the other men, built himself a canoe out of spruce bark. The next day, another violent quarrel broke out between Stevens and Webb, but the judge intervened. Farther downstream, they recovered the *Mudlark* and their meager cached supplies. They loaded the mules into the *Mudlark* and rowed on, McLeod paddling ahead.

Late on July 5, they reached Belt and Hendricks's trading post near Manley Hot Springs on the Tanana River. "We have been starving for eight days—four days on moose meat, straight . . . the last four days on flour and beans straight without meat or salt."

After nearly foundering on a huge meal and a brief sleep, Wickersham hiked fifty miles overland to Rampart, arriving late the next evening. Before greeting his beloved "Debbie," he bathed and dressed in clean clothes borrowed from a friend. His friend then stepped "gingerly to the bank of the Yukon and threw my cast-off clothing, with my hundred-dollar gold watch . . . into the river." The loss of the timepiece marked an ironic end to an expedition whose most enduring legacy was the incidental discovery of gold.

On his return, Judge Wickersham told reporters that "no one would get to the top [of the mountain] except by flying." But he felt no defeat, later saying, "We acknowledge our unpreparedness, both through inexperience and want of equipment, but at least we blazed a trail to the mountain's great base, mapped its approaches, the trail and rivers, and bore back to prospectors the hint of gold in Chitsia gravel bars. . . . No lover of nature, of mountains and glaciers, and high places, can have any sense of defeat after such a journey."

Frederick Cook on the north side of the Alaska Range, 1903

6. The Enigmatic Dr. Cook

WITH A FUSILLADE OF ROCKS and jabbing sticks, the men drove the reluctant packhorses into the churning, muddy river. Most of the animals bore toward the far shore, but the few that turned back were met with a withering barrage of stones. One horse, weakened by overwork and insect harassment, washed downstream toward a pile of driftwood and certain drowning. Somehow, the terrified horse avoided the tangled logs and stumps and safely staggered ashore downstream.

Once the heavily laden horses were across, the men followed, swimming for all of their worth. Seasoned by previous crossings, they knew how to use the current, and successfully dragged themselves shivering up the far bank, welcomed by black clouds of ravenous insects.

Later, drying by a choking smudge fire, the men roundly cursed their leader, who had gone ahead by boat.

In early July of 1903, as Judge James Wickersham was reuniting with his wife in Rampart, a six-man expedition, led by Dr. Frederick A. Cook, a Brooklyn physician, was struggling cross-country toward Mount McKinley from the south, intent on making a "first ascent." The expedition consisted of Cook, photographer Walter Miller, botanist Ralph Shainwald, journalist Robert Dunn, prospector John Carroll, and horse wrangler Fred Printz. None of them, including Cook, had any real climbing experience, a serious shortcoming for an attack on an unexplored mountain the size of McKinley. Only Carroll and Printz had experience in the Alaska wilderness. The previous year, in 1902, Printz had been over Cook's intended route when he wrangled horses for the US Geological Survey led by Alfred H. Brooks; he was afterward praised by Brooks as "the most powerful member" of that expedition.

Frederick Albert Cook, however, was a veteran of four polar expeditions, member of the Explorers Club, and a founder of the American Alpine Club. He was born on June 10, 1865. His father, a physician and Civil War veteran, died five years later. Cook worked his way through medical school, graduating from New York University in 1890. After losing his first wife, Libby, and baby from complications of childbirth, he volunteered for Robert E. Peary's expedition to northern Greenland.

Cook's flair as a lecturer led to financial and professional success that allowed him to develop his passion for polar exploration. He distinguished himself while serving as medical officer on a Belgian expedition to Antarctica. En route to the continent, the expedition's vessel was trapped in pack ice and imprisoned for the winter, earning them the unintended distinction of being the first humans to overwinter in Antarctica. While stranded in the ice, Cook and Roald Amundsen, the expedition's first officer, climbed an island peak in the Antarctic zone. After the long polar night, Amundsen praised Cook for his steadfast manner and medical professionalism. "He, of all the ship's company, was the one man of unfaltering courage, unfailing hope, endless cheerfulness, and universal kindness," Amundsen wrote. Prior to his Mount McKinley expedition, the Antarctic ascent appears to be the sum total of Cook's climbing experience.

In 1901, Cook joined a rescue expedition to Greenland to locate Robert Peary, who had disappeared. After a brief search, the rescuers found the sick and starving explorer on the northwestern edge of the island. Peary credited Cook for restoring him to health. By the time of his 1903 expedition to Mount McKinley, Dr. Cook had earned wide respect as both an explorer and ethnologist.

On June 27, the expedition left the Native village of Tyonek on the west side of Cook Inlet. Three weeks later the men were only a third of the way to the north side of the mountain, which Cook believed would be the best side to ascend.

Alaska Natives and prospectors considered it madness to try to access Interior Alaska from Cook Inlet in the summer season. The great basin drained by the Susitna River and its tributaries is a mosaic of muskeg, impenetrable alder and willow thickets, countless small watercourses, and thousands of lakes and ponds, all dominated by long periods of poor weather and ravenous insects. An optimist at the outset, Robert Dunn said in his remarkable book, *The Shameless Diary of an Explorer,* "I believed that to reach our mountain was just the old, old act of hitting the trail, hitting very, very hard, and staying with it."

Their trail followed in part the route taken by two previous expeditions. In 1899, US Army Lt. Joseph S. Herron crossed from the head of navigation on the Yentna River, a western tributary of the Susitna, through Simpson Pass to the north side of the Alaska Range, Herron's five-and-a-half-month, thousand-mile-long wilderness trek ranks as one of Alaska's most unheralded exploration epics.

In May 1902, Alfred Hulse Brooks's seven-man US Geological Survey (USGS) party left Tyonek bound for the unexplored northern slopes of the Alaska Range. This well-planned and organized expedition used packhorses to carry food and supplies for 105 days, sufficient to prevent the starvation and privation that plagued earlier explorers.

It took Brooks and his men seven weeks to reach McKinley's northern base. In early August, while camped on Slippery Creek, Brooks climbed a spur of the mountain to about 6,500 feet to study its geomorphology, in so doing becoming the first known person to set foot on the mountain itself. On the way down, he built a cairn and cached an expended rifle cartridge with a note rolled inside containing a brief account of his hike and party roster. (Fifty-two years later, Grant Pearson, a park ranger, and J. C. Reed, of the USGS, recovered the shell and note.)

Brooks's expedition measured the height of the mountain, which confirmed it at over 20,000 feet, and recorded its various Native names. In three and one-half months, the expedition covered eight hundred miles of uncharted wilderness, amassing an impressive catalog of discovery and information. Topographer D. L. Raeburn's plane-table survey of the entire trip is considered one of the grandest achievements of northern exploration. Like many others before and after them, the USGS party suffered the usual hardships of the sub-arctic wilderness. Less than half the expedition's horses survived the arduous trek.

Brooks himself did not view his endeavor as particularly incredible. On the northwest side of McKinley, he found a blazed trail, prompting him to ask: "Who were these lonely travelers of this wild region? Often they make journeys that would put to shame the . . . explorations of many a well-equipped government expedition. . . . Many a life has been lost on these hazardous journeys, and only too often are bleaching bones the sole record of un-proclaimed and unrewarded heroism."

In 1903, the National Geographic Society published Brooks's plan for climbing Mount McKinley, information used by both Wickersham and Cook. He detailed and promoted the mountain's northern accessibility. By comparison, the south side of the mountain experienced the worst weather, offered the poorest lowland approaches, and was surrounded by massive glaciers and a sea of lesser peaks. Brooks's survey convinced Cook that an assault on the mountain from any direction but the north was too demanding and dangerous to attempt.

Cook planned to follow Brooks's route from Tyonek, up the tributaries of the Susitna River, through the Alaska Range to the headwaters of the south fork of the Kuskokwim, then along the northern piedmont to the mountain proper. The expedition split into two groups for the first two-hundred-mile leg of the journey, with Dunn leading the horse party overland while Cook and Miller went by boat to a rendezvous selected by Printz on the Kichatna River.

Fred Printz's experience with Brooks the previous year proved invaluable in the arduous cross-country trek. Constant rain, water crossings, and thickets of alder and devil's club sorely tortured the men and horses, the latter constantly floundering in muskeg swamps. Halfway to the mountains, the horses were nearly hairless and bleeding from countless insect bites and small injuries. On the grueling trek, the men excelled at the favorite Alaska pastime—cursing the country and mosquitoes. Exasperated, Printz blurted, "I'd like to see [Cook] a-draggin' his behind off across these swamps."

Though crazed by insects and haggard by the brawl with swamps and weather, the overland party reunited with Cook at the pre-arranged rendezvous. From then on, the expedition traveled together through a dense mixed spruce and birch forest. Some of the trees were immense, giants of the sub-arctic forest, from seventy to ninety feet tall. The undergrowth, as throughout the trek to the mountains, was a tangle of willow, alder, ferns, flowering plants, and nasty clumps of spiny devil's club. The tangle shredded clothes and horsehair alike.

As the expedition slowly climbed out of the forest and swamps and neared the gleaming spires of the Alaska Range, twenty-five-year-old John Carroll played out from illness. Cook diagnosed Carroll as suffering from pleurisy, an inflammation of the lining of the lungs and chest. Until his illness, Carroll had been a tireless, yet unpaid, worker, lured along by the chance to prospect a rich creek that Cook had described to him.

Carroll struggled on as far as he could, sometimes lagging far behind the others. On the west side of the Alaska Range, five weeks out from Tyonek, Cook declared "that we must leave Carroll behind— with grub of course—till we come back this way." Robert Dunn took exception. There was no real plan, certainly none that guaranteed the expedition's return over the same route

"The risk of sending any sick man across that dismal pass alone, to swim and re-swim that mad river and raft two hundred miles, seems revolting and inhumane," Dunn exclaimed in his book. While Cook appeared sympathetic, Dunn thought he seemed uncaring and anxious to jettison the sick man. At first, Cook balked at even supplying Carroll with a horse. At Dunn's prodding, he finally gave Carroll one of the weaker horses and ten days' worth of food. Carroll knew the danger he faced alone. While lost in 1898 on the illusory Valdez Glacier trail to the Klondike, his partner had starved to death, Carroll's own survival a matter of luck.

When reported, the story of Carroll's abandonment infuriated pioneer Alaskans. Abandoning a sick or injured comrade on the trail violated the sacred tenets of the prospector's code. In a territory filled with prospectors and those living off their efforts, this event widely sullied Cook's reputation. Sketchy and unreliable reports of Carroll's survival did not mollify Cook's Alaskan critics.

On the northwest side of the Alaska Range, with their food nearly gone and their clothing and gear in tatters, the remaining members of the expedition were anxious to secure game. They had counted on living off the country, a mistake according to experienced Alaskans. Most prospectors always carried staples like bacon, beans, and flour, only supplementing with game meat. Every old-timer and Native knew the scarcity of game and the risk of starvation. Luckily, the north side of the Alaska Range supported abundant wildlife, and the men soon feasted on fresh meat.

Although the northern slopes of the Alaska Range get less rain than the sides hemming the Susitna Basin, the tundra and muskeg is still wet and soggy. The underlying permafrost holds the moisture at the surface, creating foot-and ankle-sucking quagmires. Except for the higher and drier alpine tundra, little of it is good horse country, a fact made painfully clear to Cook and his men on a daily basis.

The expedition's horses suffered terribly, not only from limited grazing, insect harassment, and overwork, but from unchecked mistreatment. Dunn's richly detailed book exposed both the unrelenting cruelty of the trek as well as a picture of Cook as a self-absorbed man oblivious to or uncaring about the festering cruelty.

Cook also appeared to be unaware of the conflict constantly riling his companions. "I think he would face death and disaster without a word, but through the insensitiveness of age and too much experience, rather than true courage," Dunn wrote. "I cannot believe he has imagination: of a leader's qualities he has shown not one. . . . I no longer ask him to show quality. I wish he'd show something."

In Dunn's opinion, a good leader gets up first, starts breakfast, leads tirelessly in every job, and gives orders when necessary, a role Dunn often took on for himself. Cook neither led nor ordered. Dunn loathed Cook's dreadful combination of stubbornness and indecision, and tired of being a "mind-reader to draw him out."

In his book *To the Top of the Continent*, Cook described life on the trail and around the campfire as one disclosing "the manly character."

In his florid prose, he offered a thinly disguised commentary comparing himself with Dunn. "If a man has been an artist, with system and order in the daily routine of his home life, he is sure to get a large measure of admiration from his comrades . . . but the haphazard chap who has run the life of a literary hack bewails his misfortunes, makes copy, secretes his observations of interesting things, and makes life tiresome by his egotism."

Without doubt, Cook and Dunn were an odd pairing. Robert Steed Dunn, the son of a wealthy eastern patrician, had graduated cum laude from Harvard in 1898, then promptly stampeded for the Klondike. The aborted trek via the Edmonton Trail claimed the lives of a quarter of Dunn's party. As a journalist, Dunn had traveled the world, covering wars and natural disasters, befriending the likes of Jack London and other luminaries. Cook invited Dunn to Alaska at the urging of the editor of the *New York Globe*, and to secure the funding offered by Dunn's aunt. In confidence, Dunn's editor told him that he distrusted Cook and to hold nothing back in reporting.

Cook hoped that Dunn would chronicle his rise to prominence as a mountaineer. Dunn's writings, however, were brutally honest without any attempt to sugarcoat anyone's failings or shortcomings. He vividly recounted his own anti-Semitic badgering of Shainwald and his sometimes petulant face-offs with Cook. In that era, expedition chronicles glossed over even the most egregious conduct and avoided anything that portrayed participants in an unflattering light. Dunn's magazine stories, and later his book, included all the squabbles, cruelty and folly, and a scathing appraisal of his vexing, detached leader.

On August 16, after almost fifty days of arduous struggle and fully two months after Wickersham had departed the mountain, the Cook Expedition camped at the terminus of Peters Glacier. The discovery of Wickersham's camp, the salt cache, horseshoes, and discarded clothing provoked an argument. Who had been here? Indians or a survey party? The possibility of a rival climbing expedition never crossed their minds.

Instead of energetic preparation, a strange lethargy seemed to afflict Cook. A week later, Dunn grumbled that Cook "is not trying his best to climb the mountain [but] making half-hearted tries to escape our judging him a quitter." Perhaps his opinion would change in the assault to come, but his continual second-guessing did not abate.

On August 25, following brief observations of the mountain made through breaks in the clouds, Cook led his team up the Peters Glacier. Avoiding the great ice wall on their left, the climbers ascended the middle of the glacier, unaware they were following in Wickersham's footsteps.

Over millennia, the glacier had ground out a fairly narrow canyon at the foot of the mountain. As the climbers marched upward, McKinley's North Face towered over them. On their right, the glacier was hemmed by sheer ice- and snow-covered ridges leading upward to the 10,568-foot Peters Dome. Soon after the glacier turned south, the surrounding heights rearing into a stupendous cirque of ice-encased rock.

Fred Printz, the real leader for much of the cross-country trek, led the way up the glacier, proving adept on ice and snow. By the time the climbers reached the magnificent Peters Amphitheater, the folly of Cook's ludicrous and naive stated goal to ascend the mountain "at a rate of 5000 feet per day" was obvious. According to Dunn, they lacked the skills, leadership, provisions, equipment, and weather to handle the challenges posed by this blindly chosen route.

With only three ice axes for four climbers, the lack of sufficient gear handicapped their movements and needlessly put at risk one man. While Cook and Printz chopped steps on a steep and treacherous slope, Dunn followed, flailing at the ice with a willow-stick tent pole. The climbers edged upward, taking more than ten minutes to cut each tiny step big enough for a boot toe and no holds for their hands. Imagine! *Climbing Mount McKinley equipped only with a willow tent pole!* The rest of their climbing gear was of little value. Because they had no training as a team and no climbing experience, they did not trust one another. Over much of the ascent, the men climbed unroped, unwilling to risk being pulled down by a falling partner. On a treacherous ice slope, Shainwald lost his balance and slipped. Printz caught him and pulled him to safety, saving his life. Printz, this "strange man," as Dunn described him, clearly was the pivotal and unheralded figure in the entire journey.

Headwall of Peters Glacier on the western edge of the Wickersham Wall

Despite Dunn's needless vulnerability, something about Cook's composure at altitude drew rare praise. "God! I admire the way you take this slope," he exclaimed. And he meant it. For Dunn, Cook would remain an enigmatic figure.

At 11,300 feet, beneath staggering 4,000-foot cliffs, the assault on the precipitous and icy Northwest Buttress ended, checked by steepness, avalanche threat, and worsening storms. The climbers turned back, unknowingly topping Wickersham's high point by 2,000 feet. "On a mountain this size, unexplored, yet unseen in its entirety, it was foolish to stake all on a dash up one questionable pinnacle found blithely in a ten days' storm," Dunn lamented. Dunn saw the climb as just another example of Cook's foolhardiness but had no one to reproach but himself for being a participant.

Now, a terrible dread descended on the men. On the north side of the Alaska Range, autumn advances rapidly, and by early September the signs of the looming winter are inescapable. Days grow short, the tundra blazes in crimson and gold, and the mornings turn frosty and cold. Preparatory to hibernation, grizzlies gorge on berries and moose battle for rutting dominance. Overhead pass immense flights of sandhill cranes and skeins of tundra swans, calling loudly as if to warn of the coming peril.

With food perilously low and the horses all but played out, retracing their route was impossible. Unwilling to forge north toward the Tanana River and deeper into the wilderness, Cook decided to press east for the headwaters of the Susitna River. The fear of being winterbound pushed the expedition along the piedmont and through the tundra passes to the East Fork River. Here Cook turned south toward the serrated peaks, gambling that he could find a way through the mountains. Leaving behind the route pioneered by Brooks, Printz led the way into unknown country.

Through blind luck, Cook and Printz found a high pass through the range, the only pass in an estimated 140-mile span usable by horses. On September 8, the expedition descended to the "safety" of the valley of the Bull River, a tributary of the middle fork of the Chulitna River, opening the way south to Cook Inlet.

Less than a week later, the men built log rafts for the float downstream to Cook Inlet. In what Dunn termed "a guilty conspiracy of silence" and "cowardice," the expedition abandoned its remaining horses. Deep snow and wolves doomed the pack animals to lingering death.

Cook described the abandoned horses as "fat and content," a gross exaggeration. He later offered a rosy and poetic description of them, a sharp contrast to his repeated disregard and lack of compassion. "We left seven of the finest and most faithful horses that ever traversed the wilds of Alaska," he wrote in his book, never mentioning the constant prodding and beatings that drove them forward. Two years later Cook claimed that the horses were still alive and well, a statement as absurd as the many others he made.

Three months after leaving Tyonek, the expedition returned to the village, completing a remarkable 750-mile traverse around the Mount McKinley massif. How this dysfunctional and inexperienced band accomplished such a feat is a wonder. Dr. Cook's writings offer no real insight into his leadership or strategy, nothing to explain how this almost rudderless ship made its way. A comment by Robert Dunn may offer the best and simplest insight: "Perhaps we were ill-equipped, incompetent. We did the best we could with the resources at hand."

Dance-hall queen Fanny Hall, outside a roadhouse on the Richardson Trail, was a well-known passenger on Karstens's sled.

7. Winter Traveler

LONG PLUMES OF SNOW BALLOONED off the summits of the 13,000-foot peaks west of Isabel Pass. From experience, Harry Karstens knew that the wind hammering the peaks would be worse in the narrow pass. At –20°F, the windchill would be daunting, maybe as much as –60°F. Exposed skin would freeze in minutes.

Karstens might have risked the pass alone, but with a paying passenger along, he opted for caution. Especially when the passenger was a comely and famous dance-hall girl bound for Valdez and the long steamer voyage to the States. Besides, to this point the trail down from Fairbanks had been hard and fast, putting his mail run ahead of schedule. After one last check of his dogs, Karstens retreated to the roadhouse for another round of coffee.

Boomtown Fairbanks and its golden creeks spurred construction of roadhouses and shelters along the northern segment of the Richardson Trail. Just one year after Karstens pioneered the mail route, several new roadhouses welcomed a growing number of travelers, their dogs, and their horses. Mail carriers still enjoyed special status, with Karstens's growing reputation earning him wide respect.

Despite increased traffic, which helped keep the trail open and passable, the route remained hazardous. As travelers knew, the strong cold could be murderous; the mining camps were rife with stories of gruesome accidents and people frozen to death. Old-timers bore scars from their jousts with the frost: blackened cheeks and missing toes, fingers, and parts of ears. Injuries included frosted lungs and frostbitten corneas. The thawing process is extraordinarily painful, inducing prolonged, almost ineffable suffering. Fear of the terrible agony of frozen limbs drove a few men mad. At least one isolated and incapacitated miner shot himself rather than freeze to death. So common were frost injuries that newspapers reported on "winter's grim harvest."

Karstens's segment of trail through Isabel Pass was subject to some of the worst weather on the entire 380-mile-long trail. Ground blizzards and sudden whiteouts could turn a routine crossing into a death-defying gamble. Even after the route was well established, with shelter tents in place, the pass was no place for the unwary. Karstens's boss continued to hire trailbreakers to help him though the pass.

In March 1904, Karstens and two trailbreakers where stalled by heavy sleet and forced to camp. The weather the next day turned bitter and one of the trailbreakers faltered. The mail run suddenly turned into a rescue mission. Karstens rushed the dying man to a cabin in time to save his life, if not his feet and legs. It seemed a terrible toll for a load of mail consisting of what Karstens described in one of his uncompleted biographical sketches as "a dozen letters and a few pounds of second class matter . . . with four or five sacks of old newspapers."

Harry Karstens, the Seventymile Kid, quickly become known as the person to hire if you needed transport or a trail guide. In just a few short years, he had developed into a recognized expert at dog mushing and winter travel. In the spring of 1904, Karstens led Episcopal bishop Peter Trimble Rowe to the village of Gulkana on the Copper River. There they planned to link up with another mail carrier coming up from the south with provisions for the rest of their trip. The carrier, however, got lost in a three-day whiteout and consumed all of the food before being rescued. Without their resupply, Karstens, Rowe, and Rowe's companion survived solely on a diet of snowshoe hares. It took Rowe twenty-four days of hard mushing to reach Valdez, normally a seven-day trip. Later, Karstens proclaimed Bishop Rowe "a prince. One of the finest fellows I ever traveled with." Of the third man on the trip, Karstens said, "[He] is too much of a cheechako to be on the Alaska trails in winter."

Fairbanks developed quickly, and quite soon "city people"—merchants, clerks, teachers, tradesmen—outnumbered the hardy, capable pioneers who opened the country. Many of these cheechakos were completely incapable of wilderness treks, never venturing far from shelter and a hot stove. The strong cold of winter intimidated—even terrified—some of them. "I have noticed," wrote Lt. Billy Mitchell in his book, *The Opening of Alaska*, "how little most of the residents really know about conditions in the winter time. This is because they 'hole up' for the entire winter and only go a short distance away from their houses." Consequently, winter travelers were held in high regard throughout the territory.

When mail loads were light, Karstens earned extra money by guiding travelers or hauling passengers, who always meant extra work and, often, grief. On one trip, Karstens broke trail in front of his team for three hundred miles and not once did his passenger offer to help. Each night the man made no effort to set up camp or help with the dogs. "I was so hungry I could have eaten the frying pan," Karstens recalled. "But I cooked for my passenger first. After that fellow had stowed away about a dozen hot cakes and showed no signs of reaching a limit, I said, 'No, brother, you watch me eat! I can't stand this any longer.'"

Some of Karstens's passengers, like Fanny Hall, the dance-hall queen, drew clusters of miners and trappers starved for female company to the roadhouses. Despite the fact Karstens spent most of his time in the wilderness, in town he always seemed to accompany comely young women.

For Karstens, the winter of 1904–05 was both tough and memorable. He hauled the mail and transported dance-hall queens, Klondike Kings, and church bishops. He survived howling winds, lethal cold, thin ice, and overflow—more than once, he fell though the ice or suffered frostbite on his face—all for which he was paid a hundred dollars per month. To earn that sum, he had to keep the schedule, turning back only when forced to. Karstens ran one particularly tough section of the trail "in three days averaging over forty miles a day."

In the howling wilderness, a man's life depended on his dogs, especially his lead dog. Karstens's first dog teams did not operate like well-oiled machines. He learned to keep his dogs well fed and healthy, but weak, injured, or reluctant dogs were his bane. Consequently, he was always on the lookout for good dogs. Some he bought to include in his team, others for breeding.

Freighters considered a team of five dogs a minimum, seven ideal. While larger teams could haul bigger loads, several factors limited the size of a team, the most important being the lack of available dog food in mining camps. A team not only had to pull a sledload of freight but their own food as well. Fifty pounds per dog was considered an appropriate load; loads topping a hundred pounds per dog were not uncommon. Heavy loads led to injuries, accidents, and slow travel.

Dog drivers of that era described four kinds of dogs: malemutes, Outside dogs, huskies, and Native dogs. According to Lt. Billy Mitchell, when the Hudson Bay voyageurs first went into the North, the Indian dogs "were very poor; small weedy things, descended from wolves . . . and used principally as pack animals." He described the importation of mastiffs, Great Danes, and Russian wolfhounds (which were bred with Indian dogs but never with wolves, as was often reported) to develop the 90- to 120-pound Mackenzie River husky, "the greatest sled dog man has ever seen."

"Outside dogs" were shipped to Alaska from the Lower 48. On their way north, desperate stampeders bought, or stole, any big furry dog they could get their hands on. The demand and premium prices for dogs sparked a trade that shipped hundreds of ill-suited animals north, most destined for brutal or tragic ends.

Newfoundlands, Saint Bernards, and other big, furry breeds were popular because of their assumed strength and durability in winter conditions. Most of these gentle, easily managed dogs were poorly adapted to weather extremes and lacked the stamina of northern dogs. In addition, their paws were tender and ill suited to the frigid trails; snow balling up between their toe and heel pads hobbled them. Frozen toes and pads were common.

Malemutes were Eskimo dogs brought inland from the Bering Sea and Arctic coast with a lineage born of several breeds of dogs, "and in every way inferior to the husky," Mitchell said. Most of the dogs he encountered along the Yukon River were either malemutes or huskies, the preferred type.

Prospectors and stampeders shied away from Native dogs. "His wolfish nature renders him rather dangerous on occasion when the team is obliged to travel through new-fallen snow, and the driver must go ahead on snowshoes to break trail. If the driver falls and flounders in the snow these native dogs become quickly excited and are liable to attack him, then he must be able to fight them off with a club or a whip to prevent serious injury from their fangs," Judge Wickersham wrote in *Old Yukon*.

"When we bought and used Indian dogs," Mitchell added, "they hated us. Even when we fed them, they were as fierce as wolves and would jump at us. We would have to knock them down with the stocks of our loaded whips."

Each driver nurtured a leader, usually a husky or an Outside dog, and taught the commands "gee," "haw," "mushon," and "whoa." (*Mushon* was the Americanized version of the French-Canadian voyageurs' command *to go*, which morphed into the Alaskan verb *to mush*.) A person with a dog team was called a musher, or, more frequently, a dog driver.

A loose leader, a dog set free to lead the way ahead of the team, was also taught the commands, "go on" and "come back." A good lead dog had to be the alpha, or dominant animal, in the pack, one that never backed down from a fight. More than one leader was killed by his teammates; more than one musher was attacked by his own dogs.

During his mushing career, Karstens developed two especially memorable lead dogs. Both were remembered as exceptionally intelligent and trainable. One, Bos'n, led a powerful team of seven brothers, closely matched in size and color. The wild nature of sled dogs was never far below the surface. Bos'n was killed by his own teammates.

Even the most dependable sled dogs could balk in low temperatures. Most dogs would work down to −30°F, but at −40° they didn't want to work at all. In strong cold, a musher absolutely needed a great lead dog to get a team going. In subzero temperatures snow takes on the consistency of sand, requiring extra effort to pull a sled. Dogs pressed too hard, or forced to run into bludgeoning wind, will quit and refuse to run, no matter the threats or inducements. Only the most exceptional dogs will run into stinging headwinds. Exceptional lead dogs could power a reluctant team through all but the very worst conditions.

On good trails, in moderate temperatures, a conditioned team could travel five miles an hour, faster in short bursts. Karstens considered three miles an hour good, but expected less in stormy weather or when breaking trail. In severe conditions, progress could be measured at under a mile per hour. Harsh punishment seldom made dogs run longer or faster than their conditioning allowed.

Well into the twentieth century, mushers carried whips, but the best mushers rarely lashed their dogs with them. Instead they relied on the loud *crack!* of the whip to keep the team moving. A grim legacy of the northern gold rushes was the cruel, inhumane treatment of animals. Many dog drivers beat their dogs unmercifully with chains, whips, even clubs, venting their own foul tempers rather than exacting greater speed or compliance from their animals. Some dogs were flayed, crippled, or even run to their deaths under the lash. Whip handles were weighted and used liberally to break up dogfights. Only the incautious drivers used their bare hands to separate those slashing jaws. Almost every dog driver bore the scars of dog bites.

For freighting operations, Karstens bought and modified a fourteen-foot hickory sled. The sled had high sides and was squared off in front to enable use of the gee pole. At the rear of the sled, he attached curved hardwood handles salvaged from a horse-drawn cultivator. His sled runners in the back were short, without extensions to stand on. His sled was designed to be steered from the front and pushed, not ridden. In subzero conditions, he bolted wooden "shoes" over the sled's steel runners, the wood sliding more easily than steel.

Selective breeding was rarely practiced. Breeding was left to chance with predictable results. The high cost of dogs and their upkeep hindered development of high-quality kennels. Although widely known for owning good dogs, it took Karstens almost ten years to raise and develop superior dogs. One man who sought out his advice and services was Deming Wheeler, described in the *Fairbanks Times* as the "mysterious musher of the Northland."

Wheeler, from a prominent and wealthy Indiana family, spent summers in the Lower 48 and winters in Alaska, a schedule that mystified most Alaskans. Sled dogs seemed to fascinate him. He studied and observed them and worked to develop sturdier and stronger dogs better suited for the harsh northern climate. When wolf pups were offered for sale, he bought them and announced his plan to own and drive a team of pure wolves. He quickly learned the folly of that notion. Over the course of several winters, Wheeler mushed throughout the Interior and as far west as Nome, perhaps becoming Alaska's first recreational dog musher. He later claimed to be the first person to circle Mount McKinley by dog team.

In the winter of 1913–14, Wheeler teamed up with Karstens on an epic seventy-day, fifteen-hundred-mile dog-team trip to the upper Kuskokwim River drainage. In temperatures to −40°F, they mushed from Fairbanks to Ruby, Ruby to Takotna, from there to the base of Mount Foraker and Mount McKinley, and back to Fairbanks. "The long trip was without incident of particular note or hardship," Karstens announced on their return.

For Karstens and other professional dog drivers of that era, dogs were work animals, not pets. Karstens, like all great mushers, always took care of his dogs first, his own needs second. His life, and that of his companions, depended upon it.

In early 1905, Karstens's boss decided to replace dog teams with horse-drawn sleighs, ending Karstens career as a mail carrier on the Richardson Trail. When looking back at his life years later, Karstens said that he considered hauling the mail the most hazardous thing he ever did. If he could survive that, he said, he could survive anything.

Karstens hauling mail and freight to the Kantishna mining
district during the winter of 1905–06

8. The Kantishna

JUDGE JAMES WICKERSHAM'S UNABASHED promotion of his gold strike on Chitsia Creek attracted the notice of prospectors far and wide. In October, just two months after his summit attempt, two miners from Nome spread electrifying news. They too had found gold near Wickersham's discovery, "bright and coarse, closely resembling Dawson gold."

Dawson gold! Their report and those two words heaped wood on the fire Wickersham had started. By twos and threes, prospectors slipped out of Fairbanks, Nome, and Rampart, bound for the Kantishna region, secrecy needed to avoid a larger stampede that might deprive the early arrivals of their chance to prospect for the best ground.

Throughout 1904, prospectors explored all of the drainages near the Wickersham claims but found only modest "colors." Slowly they moved south toward the Alaska Range, following the Toklat and Kantishna Rivers into the Kantishna foothills. Gravel and sand on every creek was sampled and tested. Intriguing, but limited, discoveries led the men farther into the wilderness.

On July 21, 1905, two prospectors hit the jackpot on the creek they named Eureka. A few miles away, and at nearly the same time, two others found gold on Glacier Creek. Two other men made another strike just upstream.

Fairbanks, well over a hundred miles away, was the closest place to record claims. It took several days for the first prospectors to arrive, but the samples of coarse gold they carried sparked intense excitement. "News of a gold strike has wings," old-timers said, and within hours, the rush was on. By late July, at least sixty poling boats loaded with men and supplies forged up the Kantishna River. By early August, the Bearpaw River, which led to the new strike, was lined with tents. *Kantishna or bust!* was the cry of the hundreds rushing into the hills. Almost every businessman in Fairbanks grubstaked prospectors or bought trade goods for the new camps. The initial rush led to Glacier Creek, the most publicized strike, but stampeders quickly fanned out to nearby Caribou and Moose Creeks.

Some of the first men to record their claims carried dazzling displays of coarse gold. One prospector arrived in Fairbanks with an eight-ounce can packed with nuggets. Goggled-eyed assayers proclaimed Eureka Creek "probably the richest creek the country has ever seen." In an era when even a mere rumor of gold could ignite a rush, the initial samples provoked a fevered response. Word of the new discovery sped out of the Interior to the Klondike and beyond. People came by boat and stern-wheeler and, after freeze-up, they came by foot and by dogsled. At the end of September, the Kantishna seethed with activity. Within a few short weeks, almost every creek and bench in the hills had been staked from source to mouth.

Placer mining here was labor intensive. Each miner wielded pick and shovel, gold pan and rocker. On the best streams, miners removed shallow overburden and then shoveled the foot or so of gravel above the bedrock into their rockers and sluices. On lower Eureka Creek, laborers moved countless boulders and rock slabs just to reach the gold-bearing gravels.

The Kantishna stampede peaked in late September when low water ended river navigation. A mining lull set in as the rivers and land slowly succumbed to winter. New boomtowns sprang up: Bearpaw, Glacier City, Diamond City, Roosevelt, and Eureka. Each settlement supported at least one trading post, restaurant, and saloon. Early in the winter of 1905–06, the tent camp of Eureka, on Moose Creek, bustled with as many as four hundred people. As in every other mining camp, a tent saloon and gambling hall entertained stampeders. A restaurant there charged four dollars and fifty cents per day for board alone, almost half a day's wage for laborers. According to Charles Sheldon, at least one prostitute, working out of a large tent, "absorbed a large share of the miners' wages."

As winter tightened its grip on the land, stampeders arrived by dog team and on snowshoes. The first winter travelers followed frozen waterways or made their own trails to the strike. By trial and error, good routes were found, cleared, and marked.

Food and supplies were scarce in the camps, and expensive. Flour sold for fifteen dollars per hundred pounds and salt pork between twenty-five and fifty cents a pound, inflated prices in those days. Fortunately, the isolated Kantishna District was located in some of the richest game country in Alaska. Domestic meat was not available, so hunters shot every moose they saw. Dall sheep abounded in the

Karstens, left, and miner Fannie McKenzie, on a spring mushing trip
on the south end of Wonder Lake

mountains, and caribou occasionally passed through in large numbers. The prized and flavorful sheep meat sold for fifty cents a pound, caribou for as little as fifteen cents, and moose from forty cents to two dollars a pound. Wildlife was so abundant that hunters eventually freighted sledloads of meat all the way to Fairbanks.

Harry Karstens and Charley McGonagall stampeded to the Kantishna in late autumn and staked a few marginal claims. Most of the richest ground was already claimed and the camps were perilously short of supplies. Food sold at extortionate prices; the whole scenario was all too familiar.

This time the partners saw an opportunity. Together they blazed a winter trail into the diggings and, at freeze-up, promoted an express service for passengers, mail, and light freight. They divided their responsibilities. Karstens had soured on stampedes and McGonagall wanted a break from freighting. They agreed that McGonagall would work their claims, while Karstens ran the freight business, spelling each other as necessary. At each town, Karstens arranged for a post office and set a fee of twenty-five cents per letter. In each postal location, he also established a small library, bringing books and periodicals from Fairbanks. Karstens later wrote that he started his mail service in the fall with a dog team and $1,000, ending in the spring with "five hundred dollars and a lot of knowledge."

While freighting, Karstens saw dozens of sheep carcasses hauled into the camps from the nearby mountains. Professional hunters reported thousands of these animals feeding on the hills and mountains. In the foothills, he found sheep in unusual locations, a sign of their then remarkable abundance. These simple observations would impact Karstens's life in an unexpected way.

Even after freeze-up, with temperatures plunging well below zero, a few prospectors continued the search for gold. As the winter deepened, dozens of others called it quits and returned to Fairbanks. Some vowed to acquire a new grubstake and return in spring. Most simply gave up. By February 1906, some miners began to describe Eureka and Glacier Creeks as "freak formations," predicting that even the best claims would quickly play out. The mining district would prove its worth after spring breakup, or go bust.

Owners of the best Kantishna claims greeted the spring thaw, and running water it provided for the sluice boxes, with high expectations. May and June saw frenzied activity on the diggings. By fall, the truth was known. Small sections of Glacier, Eureka, and Friday Creeks were exceptionally rich; other creeks proved worthless. The richest creeks drained from two neighboring peaks, Glacier and Spruce. A few people would spend their lives looking in vain for the mother lode.

Less than a dozen men struck it big. Dozens of others were paid only in deprivation and danger. The Kantishna strike, which engendered high hopes of another Klondike bonanza, fizzled rapidly as the pockets of gold played out. "The whole thing was a bust," Karstens said.

Karstens left the Kantishna District in the summer of 1906 with little regret. He saw the stampede as unremarkable, no different from many others that cycled from boom to bust. McGonagall stayed behind, seemingly content to work for grubstake wages and a home in those spare, rolling hills.

Whatever Harry Karstens had planned for that summer is unknown, but it was his good fortune to be free and available when a unique opportunity beckoned.

On July 11, 1906, a well-dressed traveler arrived in Fairbanks on the steamboat *Seattle No. 3*. Quickly the newspapers reported the arrival of Charles Sheldon, "the millionaire hunter from the East Coast" bound for the Kantishna region. Stories of the game-rich country spread by Alfred Brooks, Frederick Cook, and James Wickersham had brought Sheldon to Alaska. Before leaving home, he had visited geologist Brooks in Washington, DC, and quizzed him about the area's Dall sheep.

In Fairbanks, Judge Wickersham greeted Sheldon and freely offered his knowledge and advice. Wickersham recommended that Sheldon hire Bert Webb, a well-known market hunter, to guide him in the Kantishna. After meeting Webb, Sheldon declined and said, "This man . . . would not do [and] so I employed 'Kid' Karstens and I like him very much." Sheldon's favorable first impression of Karstens proved accurate. "I recall no better fortune than that which befell me when Harry Karstens was engaged as an assistant packer. . . . He is a tall, stalwart man, well poised, frank, and strictly honorable . . . peculiarly fitted by youth and experience for explorations in little-known regions, he proved a most efficient and congenial companion."

As events unfolded, Karstens's knowledge of the country at the foot of Mount McKinley proved to be indispensable. The sheep carcasses that Karstens had seen while mushing and hunting in the Kantishna, excited Sheldon, his destination now confirmed. Karstens, an inveterate explorer, fell easily into the role of hunting guide.

On July 14, Sheldon and Karstens boarded a chartered steamer, *Dusty Diamond*, bound for the Kantishna River. They also brought aboard a guide Sheldon had hired in Dawson City, Jack Haydon, and a string of packhorses Sheldon had purchased. Sheldon had dropped off Haydon and the horses a few days earlier at the mouth of the river to await his return. Now, after rendezvousing with Haydon, the steamer continued up the Kantishna.

The *Dusty Diamond* plowed upstream in tranquil, quiet waters, a sharp contrast to the previous year when stampeder boats and stern-wheelers flailed wildly against the current. They passed Bearpaw City, already a ghost town, and reached Roosevelt without mishap. The town's entire population of six men and two women met them at the landing.

The next day the pack string, with Karstens leading the way, struck out for Eureka, thirty miles away. The mining camp, at the confluence of Eureka and Moose Creeks, consisted of twenty tents and a few cabins. Karstens introduced Sheldon to the miners and they toured the diggings.

A day later, on the ridges above Wonder Lake, the clouds broke and Sheldon got his first close look at Mount McKinley. "I can never forget my sensations at the sight," he wrote. "I have seen the mountain panoramas of the Alaska Coast and the Yukon Territory. . . . I had viewed St. Elias and the adjacent mountains, but compared with the view now before my eyes they seemed almost insignificant."

If Karstens had harbored reservations about the cheechako hunter, they were quickly dispelled. From the very outset, Sheldon seemed comfortable and relaxed outdoors. Instead of futile complaining, Sheldon quietly coped with the clouds of attacking mosquitoes. He had spent parts of the previous two years hunting and studying Stone sheep in the Yukon, developing obvious skills with horses. He had been respectful and friendly to the miners they had met at Eureka; he treated his hired help like friends. He even did his share of camp chores!

Sheldon later compared the prospectors he met to America's western pioneers, explaining, "[The prospector] does not have to contend with hostile Indians, but he must face and conquer more serious conditions—those of a barren country, intense cold, long winter darkness, and still more, the danger of starvation and disease."

Charles Alexander Sheldon was unlike anyone else to have ventured into the Kantishna. In sharp contrast to the somewhat desperate men who had stampeded to the creeks, or the hardy few who hung on to their claims, Sheldon was not interested in mineral wealth but cared deeply about nature, wildlife, and hunting. Self-effacing to a fault, he preferred to be called Sheldon, or Billie. "Sheldon was personally a most attractive man," a friend said. "He possessed great sweetness of nature and was friendly, frank, and forthright."

Sheldon, the oldest of six siblings, was born on October 17, 1867, into a hardworking family involved in marble quarrying and manufacturing. Sheldon attended Andover preparatory school and graduated from Yale in 1890. Through family contacts, he was hired as assistant superintendent of the Lake Shore and Michigan Southern Railroad. From there, he moved to Mexico and in 1898, became general manager of the Chihuahua-Pacific Railroad. In just four short years, his investment in one of the richest silver and lead mines in Mexico secured his financial future, allowing him to retire at age thirty-five.

Sheldon's conservation career began in 1904, when he offered to collect specimens and make field observations for the US Biological Survey. A lifelong hunter, Sheldon prized North America's wild mountain sheep more than all other game. He first hunted desert sheep in Mexico's Sierra Madre and then pursued bighorns in the Rocky Mountains. Stories of the so-called "thinhorn" sheep of the northern wilderness attracted his attention. His love of these "noble and splendid" animals eventually landed him in Alaska in search of Dall sheep, then the least known of the four species of America's wild sheep.

From the moment Sheldon left Fairbanks, he began taking notes on people, wildlife, habitat, and terrain. He explained that "the main object of my trip was to study the life history of sheep and incidentally to gather as much information as possible about other mammals."

Karstens described Sheldon as dedicated and "very thorough," stopping at camp only long enough to care for specimens. "We collected every type of animal and bird in the area," Karstens wrote, "preserving the hides and skulls and taking measurements and stomach contents and all useful data for the Biological Survey." For nearly three months, Sheldon's party roamed the piedmont and spiraling peaks. Sheldon collected everything from shrews to bears. He even attempted to tame a grizzly cub for transfer to the Bronx Zoo. Dall sheep, however, remained the focus of his efforts.

Some people today view Sheldon's killing as excessive and repugnant. Sheldon without a doubt relished the hunt, but he also was an astute observer and chronicler of nature. His journals are full of detailed accounts of hunting, wildlife, and exploration. On a brilliant, cloudless day in late July, Sheldon climbed the lower

A banner ad for Karstens and McGonagall's private freight service, opened in the aftermath of the 1905 Kantishna gold stampede

slopes of McKinley. "I kept on over the ridges east of Peters Glacier, determined to climb the lower slopes of the great mountain," he said. He found Wickersham's 1903 camp near the glacier, and debris left by Frederick Cook on the glacial moraine. Sheer slopes checked his own ascent at 8,900 feet. For four blissful hours, he soaked in the dazzling view of the icy slopes raining avalanches into the basin below.

The idea of climbing the mountain never seemed far from Sheldon's mind. From a point he called "Bog Hill" (today's Stony Hill), he studied the mountain, identifying the twin summits, Harper Glacier, and Muldrow Glacier. "I believe that if the top of this glacier can be reached along its south edge the mountain can be ascended," he wrote. Sheldon thus appears to be the first to correctly identify the key route to the summit.

Time and again, Sheldon described the mountain's impact: "Denali in all its magnificence and imposing grandeur reared its massive snowy bulk toward the sky. . . . It ever dominated the landscape, glorifying that mountain world . . . the vision can never fade, and the ecstasies produced by such long intimacy with it will linger vividly throughout my life."

From a camp near the upper forks of the Toklat River, the tireless Sheldon hunted sheep, caribou, and bear. He made a solo camp on the Teklanika River and each day, weather permitting, hunted the big rams that he sought. "Not only did I long for solitude in this wonderful wilderness, but when completely alone, undisturbed by the numerous little diversions of camp life," Sheldon explained, "I had always been able to put more energy into the hunting."

While Sheldon joined with the country, its mountains and wildlife, he also bonded with his assistant guide, Harry Karstens. That this sophisticated, wealthy easterner bonded so closely with this tough, rugged frontiersman is somewhat surprising. America's class structure in those years was often as rigid as that in Europe. The American gentry mixed rarely, often awkwardly, with common people. The chasm in income was staggering. Two percent of the population controlled 60 percent of the nation's wealth. The annual average family income was $500. Although Sheldon was considered "New Money," his social circle included the so-called American Royalty. His friends included Theodore Roosevelt, Gifford Pinchot, Carl Rungius, Alexander Graham Bell, and Richard Byrd.

Even a casual examination of the Karstens and Sheldon friendship reveals common traits conducive to mutual admiration. Both men were resourceful and experienced outdoorsmen who viewed the challenges of the wilderness as obstacles to overcome but not fear. Neither was a complainer, braggart, or loud talker. Each let his accomplishments speak for themselves. Sheldon and Karstens possessed strength and endurance beyond ordinary for men their size, each about five foot ten inches and 170 pounds.

Karstens, then twenty-eight, possessed one trait that made it possible for him to live and work in harmony with Sheldon: "He knew when to keep quiet and leave Sheldon to himself," Karstens's son, Eugene, explained years later. When Sheldon and Karstens met, the Seventymile Kid was already famous in Interior Alaska as a man who always kept his word and could be counted on in any circumstance. Sheldon would frequently declare that Karstens was the best outdoorsman he had ever known and certainly the best dog musher.

When Sheldon returned to Fairbanks from his sixty-five days in the mountains, reports of his hunting success spread quickly. Karstens paid him the highest tribute, describing him to a reporter as "one of the best men he ever roughed it with." He told his peers that Sheldon often left camp in early morning and seldom returned before ten or eleven o'clock at night. Karstens reported that Sheldon relished "plain fare and hard travel" and always helped in setting up camp, so much so that "it would have been hard for an outsider to figure out which of the three of us was [on] a pleasure trip."

For his part, Sheldon considered his 1906 expedition satisfying but only partially successful. He wanted to collect several specimens of moose and caribou, but those he saw were still in velvet and their antlers not fully developed. More importantly, he had secured only the minimum number of rams requested by the Biological Survey. Sheldon believed that to complete a life history of Dall sheep, he needed to view them in all seasons. Even before the trip's culmination, he began plotting another expedition with a larger scope.

Although to outsiders the expedition may have appeared a pleasure trip, the results would be far grander. "The success of the New Yorker is significant to historical work in Alaska," one reporter declared.

"During the months we roamed over a good part of what is now Mount McKinley National Park gathering specimens," Karstens wrote years later, "Sheldon was so taken with the beauty of the area and the amount of game . . . that he decided to try and have this area set aside for a game refuge and park. If he got my encouragement he said he would be back the following year and stay a whole year using horses in the summer and my dog team in the winter."

Just before Sheldon said good-bye to Karstens and the wild Toklat, he vowed to return. "When we shook hands," Sheldon said, "I felt as though I were departing from a good friend."

New York City crowds greet Dr. Frederick A. Cook (third from right) in 1909 after his claim to have been the first to attain the North Pole.

9. Cook Claims the Summit

IN THE SPRING OF 1906, Frederick Cook was back in Alaska, preparing to attempt Mount McKinley again, even if it took, as he said, "a siege of five months." This time, instead of the long, draining traverse to the north side of the Alaska Range via Rainy Pass, Cook planned to forge directly through the Alaska Range east of his previous route. His entire plan hinged on the discovery of a new pass, a shortcut, which would open directly onto the north side of the range. Again, at Tyonek on Cook Inlet, he off-loaded twenty horses to carry supplies overland, and a motorboat specially designed to ascend the Susitna and Yentna Rivers.

Unlike the disparate crew Cook had assembled in 1903, his new expedition consisted of an experienced group of ten that included Herschel Parker, an expert alpinist; Belmore Browne, artist and out-doorsman; Russell Porter, topographer; Walter Miller, photographer, and Fred Printz, chief packer (both veterans of the 1903 expedition); and Ed Barrill, assistant horse packer.

Parker, a physics professor at Columbia University, was the expedition's coleader and one of its funders. A life member of the Canadian Alpine Club, the independently wealthy Parker was a Swiss-trained technical climber with several first ascents to his credit, including Mount Lefroy and Mount Hungabee in the

Canadian Rockies. In Europe, he had climbed Mont Blanc and the Matterhorn, among others.

Twenty-six-year-old artist and naturalist Belmore Browne was no cheechako. He had been a member of the 1902 American Museum of Natural History expedition to northern British Columbia, serving as hunter and artist. Afterward he explored Southeast Alaska in the company of famous naturalist/explorer Andrew Jackson Stone. The following year he returned to hunt and work in the Kenai Mountains from where he saw Mount McKinley for the first time.

Parker and Browne had met the previous year in the smoking parlor of a westbound Canadian Pacific train. The two struck up a conversation, sharing tales of climbing and exploration, the beginnings of a friendship that lasted forty years. After Parker described his plans to climb Mount McKinley the following year, Browne jumped at an invitation to go along.

Russell Porter knew Cook from previous Arctic expeditions. Inspired by a lecture by Robert Peary, Porter joined Cook's voyage to Greenland in 1893, serving as surveyor and artist. Three years later Porter accompanied Peary to Greenland, and to Baffin Island the following year; then he stampeded to the Klondike in 1898. Additional Arctic explorations followed, and in late 1905, Porter eagerly accepted Cook's invitation to Mount McKinley.

Why Walter Miller and Fred Printz agreed to return to Alaska with Cook after the blunders and deprivations of the 1903 expedition is baffling. Perhaps time had dulled their memories of toil and suffering, or maybe the inexplicable lure of Alaska had them firmly in its grasp. Or maybe their reasoning was hindered by the lure or promise of fame should the expedition succeed.

Even more confounding is Cook's decision to attack the mountain from the boggy, perpetually soggy southwest when clearly an approach from the north offered the fewest obstacles. Instead of a repeat of his previous withering summer-long battle to reach the north side of the range, Cook could have shipped all of his supplies to Fairbanks and hired a riverboat for transport to a point within a reasonable distance of the mountain. Why struggle again through all the swamp, impenetrable bush, and river crossings just to reach the perimeter ring of mountains and glaciers guarding the south flank?

Cook's remarkable 1903 circumnavigation of McKinley had failed to satisfy him, because he had a bigger agenda. His life's goal was clearly to reach the North Pole, and he apparently believed that a conquest of Mount McKinley would help finance a potent polar expedition. His first McKinley attempt drew enough attention to fund a second attempt on the mountain, but only a successful ascent would attract the needed polar funds. *Harper's Monthly Magazine*, businessman Henry Disston, and Herschel Parker had funded the 1906 expedition, but any polar expedition would require a wider net of financial support.

"Geographically Mount McKinley seems to have been placed in the most inaccessible position obtainable. It lies just north of 'sixty-three' in the geographical center of the great wilderness," Browne wrote. "The problem of *reaching* the mountain offered as many difficulties as climbing the mountain itself, and it was this perplexing problem that we determined to solve."

Once again Cook divided his company in two parts: one group forcing horses and supplies overland; the other boating to a rendezvous point high up the Yentna River. Reunited, the full company would plunge into an unexplored swath of the Alaska Range in search of a pass suitable for a pack string of horses.

The overland journey from Tyonek to the mountain turned into a predictably brutal slog. Printz and his packers found themselves badgering reluctant horses and cursing the merciless swarms of mosquitoes that rose in dense clouds from the thickets and muskeg, 130 miles of hellish toil and suffering. After a torturous trek, the packers linked up with the boat party as planned.

In early July, after a fruitless search for a pass through the glacier-hung mountains, Cook abandoned his original plan and redirected the expedition eastward on a reconnaissance of the wilderness foothills on McKinley's southern flank. Dutifully the company pressed on into another blank spot on the map, aiming for the base of the mountain seventy miles away. Again the packers forced the tormented and starving horses into swamp and thicket.

After almost three weeks of grueling effort, the expedition penetrated the outer ring of peaks by forging up the flank of the Tokositna

Glacier. Unobstructed views of the mountain finally revealed the enormity of the task at hand. "At the head of the Tokositna River, Cook, Professor Parker, and I climbed a high mountain west of the glacier that gave us an unobstructed view of the southern and western faces of Mount McKinley. At the first glance we all saw that the scaling of the peak was a hopeless undertaking," Browne later declared in his book *The Conquest of Mount McKinley.* Cook agreed: "The climb of Mount McKinley was now put down as a hopeless task."

On July 25, after over two months of battling rugged wilderness, the demoralized expedition headed back to the coast. En route, Porter broke off to finish his survey. Back at tidewater, with a second attempt on Mount McKinley out of the question, Parker, the climbing expert, left for home. Cook's plans for the autumn suddenly changed when his sponsor, Disston, canceled a hunting expedition he had scheduled as a prerequisite of his sponsorship. Probably a fortuitous decision, as most of Cook's horses needed for the hunt were dead or lost in the wilderness. Starved and abused horses would be one indisputable legacy of Cook's two Alaskan expeditions.

With winter rapidly approaching, Cook decided to devote the rest of the season to exploration rather than hunting or climbing. "As a final task of our season's work," he explained in his book, "I now determined to explore the river systems and glaciers to the east of Mount McKinley . . . for a route to the top of the mountain for a future ascent."

Browne thought the decision odd because Cook had already explored a significant portion of the Susitna drainage. Cook rebuffed Browne's request to go along, instead sending him east to collect trophy animals for Disston. Cook then dispatched Printz and Miller to the west on a similar errand.

In late August, Cook left the coast with just two men, horse wrangler Edward Barrill and John Dokkin, a prospector. Neither assistant had any climbing experience. Before departure, Cook contradicted his earlier statements, dispatching a telegram Outside that read, "Am preparing for a last, desperate attack on Mount McKinley."

The upriver boat trip went smoothly, unhindered by high water or mechanical failure. Cook plowed steadily up the Susitna to its tributary the Chulitna, then up the Chulitna to the mouth of the Tokositna

River, where he finally encamped at Alder Creek, a feeder stream at an elevation of 600 feet. With the boat secured, the three men set out for the Ruth Glacier. After a few miles, Dokkin turned back to start work on a winter prospecting cabin. Cook and Barrill were now alone. Each man carried a forty-pound pack, a load appropriate for exploration but woefully inadequate for an attack on a mountain whose summit loomed nearly 20,000 feet higher and more than forty rugged miles away.

Once again, Cook reversed himself. "Our intentions, however, were not to climb to the top," Cook explained. "We hoped only for an opportunity to discover a route that would permit a future ascent."

As the two men explored the Ruth Glacier, a massive river of ice rimmed by a chain of dizzying peaks and summits, Cook later said that he identified a route to the summit of McKinley. Dodging avalanches and yawning crevasses, and exploiting breaks in the weather, Cook and Barrill pushed quickly upward. Just four days after leaving the Alder Creek base camp, Cook claimed he camped "in a ditch" at 14,000 feet. On the sixth climbing day, with the temperature well below zero, according to Cook, the two climbers left their next camp at 16,300 feet and pushed on. "Our legs were of wood and our feet of stone," he explained. "After prodigious efforts we were forced to camp at 18,400 feet with not enough energy left to talk or eat." What transpired next is mired in legend and controversy.

Less than three weeks after leaving the coast, Cook returned with the astonishing news that on September 16, 1906, *he had climbed Mount McKinley!*

Cook's announcement, telegraphed south, electrified the country and then flashed around the world. The press hailed America's newest national hero, the conqueror of Mount McKinley.

The summit claim astounded and dismayed expedition members. Belmore Browne was incredulous. A thirteen-day round-trip from Alder Creek to the summit? *Impossible!* "I knew the country that guarded the southern face of the mountain," he stated, "and knew that the time Dr. Cook had been absent was too short to allow his even reaching the mountain."

After meeting with Cook, Browne was even more confident that he was lying. For Browne, the physical evidence was obvious. First, Cook and Barrill had carried no ice creepers (metal cleats worn over footwear to provide traction on ice). Second, Cook claimed that he and Barrill were roped together over the last stage of the climb, but Browne and Parker had discarded the climbing ropes as unsafe. More importantly, the summer's exertions had amply demonstrated that Cook and Barrill were physically unfit for strenuous climbing. Barrill, a blacksmith and packer, had no climbing experience at all. Furthermore, according to Browne, Cook lacked the instruments needed to verify the altitudes he claimed. All the details of the "ascent" were simply wrong.

At the first opportunity, Browne took Barrill aside. The two had become friends, and Browne expected Barrill to tell him the truth. In private, he asked Barrill for corroboration. "I can tell you all about the big peaks just south of the mountain, but if you want to know about Mount McKinley go and ask Cook," Barrill replied. Browne interpreted the comment as an admission of fraud. In the face of Browne's prodding, Cook said that he had not planned to climb the mountain at all, but once he discovered a way to reach the summit, he changed his mind. He offered no satisfactory explanation for his earlier contradictory telegram. "I found myself in an embarrassing position," Browne explained. "I knew that Dr. Cook had not climbed Mount McKinley."

When the indomitable topographer Russell Porter reunited with Cook and Browne, he, too, expressed skepticism. Porter had just finished a survey of a three-thousand-square-mile region and knew all too well the weather, terrain, and obstacles that would prevent a short dash to the summit.

Back in New York, both Browne and Herschel Parker rejected Cook's claim. They knew beyond reasonable doubt that two inexperienced climbers could not have made the ascent in less than two weeks as claimed. According to Parker, once Cook's original plan proved unfeasible, "It was perfectly understood that after the misadventure all further attempts were abandoned for the season."

In private, Browne and Parker voiced their doubts to the American Geographical Society but were rebuffed. They muted their public comments, believing it unseemly to challenge Cook, one of the founders of the American Alpine Club and member of the Explorers Club.

"Our knowledge however did not constitute proof," Browne wrote, "and I knew that before I could make the public believe the truth I should have to collect some facts . . . we were willing to give Doctor Cook every chance to clear himself." The fair-minded Browne and Parker were products of their era and social milieu—statements by gentlemen of Cook's standing were not publicly challenged. Branding a fellow gentleman as a liar was a serious breach of decorum.

Climbers unfamiliar with Alaska and McKinley did not see the eight-day climb as unreasonable. If Mont Blanc in the Alps, at 16,000 feet, could be climbed in a few days, why not Mount McKinley?

By the time Cook returned to New York in late November, he had moved into the first rank of the world's explorers. The American public feted him as a hero. His 1908 book, *To the Top of the Continent*, received wide acclaim. Most of the book offers a rich description of the 1906 expedition, but is vague in describing the summit route and details of the alleged climb. Included are pictures of Barrill holding a flag atop what Cook labeled "the summit of Mount McKinley." Browne and Parker scrutinized every detail, finding "misstatements that we knew to be downright falsehoods." The published photographs did not match reality, and the two men described them as "irrefutable proof of the deception." One photo of the alleged summit contained a damning flaw: visible in the distance was a *higher* peak. Once again, Browne and Parker maintained a public silence.

A few Alaskans praised Cook but most condemned him as a fraud. Prospectors familiar with McKinley's south side sneered at his story. Episcopal Archdeacon Hudson Stuck, a relative newcomer to Alaska but an avid reader and collector of adventure literature, proclaimed Cook "an ass [who] will never climb Mount McKinley."

Unless Frederick Cook recanted his story—or at least until another expedition climbed the mountain and returned with irrefutable proof of a hoax—he would be forever credited as the conqueror of Mount McKinley.

Karstens freighting Charles Sheldon's wildlife specimens from the
Toklat River to the Nenana trading post in 1908

10. Hunting the Toklat

EARLY IN THE WINTER OF 1906, Harry Karstens and his new partner, Ed Bunch, opened a fast freight service from Fairbanks to the upriver boom camps. The rich gold strikes north of Fairbanks propelled exploration of every stream pouring into the Tanana River. Prospectors made several new strikes: Tenderfoot, Banner, Buckeye, Richardson. New camps and new diggings; same faces and same gold fever. If nothing else, stampeders and prospectors were consummate optimists.

Under pressure from impatient miners clamoring for supplies, Karstens and Bunch were on the river with their dog teams soon after freeze-up, chancing the "first ice." Together they made their initial trips in daylight hours, marking the trail around thin ice and open water. Initially the obvious hazards were easy to spot, but the first snows hid them, creating a gauntlet of perilous traps. Ice fog drifting from open leads warned of danger, but patches of thin ice, covered by light snow, gave no warning.

Darkness compounded the risk. Near the winter solstice, the sun rises late and sets early in the North, with the Tanana Valley in December receiving less than four hours of daylight. The only illumination available to pioneer mushers was a lighted candle placed in a tin can, a small opening directing light onto the snow. A headlight it was not. The best a musher could do was to stop the team, light his candle, and cast about for a lost trail. Mushers placed trust in their lead dog to feel or smell out the trail ahead. No more deadly trap awaits a fast-moving dog team than the combination of thin ice, extreme cold, and darkness.

As the days shortened and slowly got colder, trail conditions improved. Except for a few channels of swift water, which would remain open all winter, the ice thickened and the trail set up hard and fast. Accumulating snow allowed the mushers to relocate much of the trail off the river.

In early December, with the thermometer stuck at −40°F, Ed Bunch fell seriously ill. The doctor in Fairbanks sent word to Richardson Roadhouse for Bunch to stay put and not come to town, judging his condition too risky for transport. When Bunch's condition improved slightly, the partners ignored the doctor's advice and decided to chance it. In late afternoon, Karstens loaded Bunch in his sled, wrapped him in fur robes, and mushed for town.

Not far from the roadhouse, the trail dropped onto the river and into an unexpected headwind. The wind is usually calm in extreme cold, but sometimes local gusts whip through canyons, down inclines, and along narrow river channels. The dogs hesitated, not liking the cutting wind. Somehow, Karstens coaxed his team on and soon they were in the timber again, running slowly but steadily into the gloaming.

After several miles, the trail again cut onto the river and into the wind. Karstens pushed his dogs as hard as he dared. Now was no time to force an unrealistic pace. He let his leader set the team's speed. Even the best-trained dogs balk in the face of frigid headwinds. Karstens ran behind the sled to keep himself warm, pushing all the way.

Slowly the wind subsided and the miles slipped by. In the last feeble light of day, Karstens stopped his team and rewarded the dogs with chunks of dried salmon. He soon had them moving again, picking up speed in the calm, frigid air.

Then, in near total darkness, disaster struck.

Without warning, the ice broke beneath the heavy sled, plunging Karstens into deep water. The sudden shock brought an involuntary gasp. Karstens flailed at the numbing water and current. In short minutes, he'd lose muscle control and the ability to swim or tread water.

The current here was weak; the bottom beyond touch. As he struggled, the ridge of ice around the hole broke away in handfuls. If he washed under the shelf of ice, he would die. Karstens bled adrenaline; the areas of his wet, unprotected skin began to glaze with ice. Just as the strength ebbed from his flailing legs, he found purchase and hauled himself from the water, his clothes icing up almost instantly.

He fought to stand up, look around, and orient himself. The ice had been just thick enough to support the dogs, which kept going, yanking the heavy sled onto firm ice. They had stopped just yards away. Bunch was yelling something as Karstens staggered toward the sled. Everything he knew screamed, *Build a fire!* But Bunch's condition alarmed him, complicating things. An occupied cabin a short distance away offered shelter. Shivering, muscles seizing, he made an all-or-nothing decision. He ran to the dogs stopped on the ice and cracked the whip.

Now he pushed as hard as he could, life and limb squarely on the line. If he missed the cabin or had misjudged his location, he could die. Both of them could die. Soon the dogs scented woodsmoke and picked up speed. Light from a cabin window beckoned from the riverbank. In minutes, both men were inside, the occupants hurriedly stoking up a roaring stove. Stripped of his icy clothes, Karstens took stock. His feet and hands were fine, but his face was not. Brilliant red welts and blisters rose from his frozen cheeks, his nose swelling as it thawed.

As soon as possible, Karstens was under way again, completing the remainder of the rescue run without mishap. In all, he made the sixty-three-mile run from Richardson Roadhouse to Fairbanks in sixteen hours, a record dash. He later told a reporter in his laconic way that "he felt as though a rest wouldn't hurt him any." Only after Karstens delivered his partner to the doctor did he seek treatment for his frostbitten nose and cheeks.

The following month, during another prolonged cold snap, Karstens and his friend Charley Smith left Fairbanks for the head of the Toklat River. Traveling light with just Karstens's dog team, they carried only a month's supply of food. Karstens and Smith told their friends that they were going sheep hunting, but no one seemed to believe them. Old-timers traded knowing winks, because Smith had previously prospected on the Toklat and found good prospects.

Two months later, without word of any kind from Karstens and Smith, friends began to worry. Two severe cold spells could have delayed their return, or they might have run into serious trouble. Other men had recently disappeared in those same lonesome hills.

Even back then, a city more isolated than Fairbanks was hard to imagine. Surrounded on all sides by hundreds of miles of wilderness, it had grown in less than six years from a single isolated trading post to an area population of ten thousand. There were no trains, planes, or automobiles, and for seven months of the year, the only supply route was the Richardson Trail to Valdez. Tidewater, offering the only escape to the outside world, was as much as three weeks of hard travel away. In summer, forty or fifty riverboats, some rivaling in splendor those plying the Mississippi, transferred provisions, equipment, and people. For some residents, brought north by commerce or family, the wilderness was a fearful place, the bludgeoning winter an ominous reminder of human frailty and nature's power. The idea of people moving about on snowshoes and dog teams, seemingly unaffected by the extremes, was confounding, a toying with death—or so it seemed to the city types.

On April 11, 1907, fully three months after leaving Fairbanks, Smith and Karstens mushed into town, men and dogs fit and well. At the head of the Toklat River they had hunted, trapped, and prospected, with very little to show for their efforts except for one prized silver fox fur. Again, old-timers exchanged looks: "Three months: one fox skin."

That spring, Karstens received a wire from Charles Sheldon that read, "Prepare for a year's trip." Karstens dutifully began gathering equipment and purchasing supplies. Sheldon was slightly vexed when Karstens did not respond to a planning letter. He followed up with another telegram: "No letter received: will you go with me?" For some reason Karstens did not respond, but Sheldon left New York anyway. He trusted his friend.

Sheldon and Karstens reunited in Fairbanks in late July. After visits to the bank and Judge Wickersham, Karstens laid out his plan.

Once again, a chartered steamer would carry them up the Kantishna River. From the head of navigation, two hired packers, using horses and mules, would assist in transporting a year's worth of supplies and equipment to the upper Toklat. At timberline, they would build a cabin. The pack animals would return to Fairbanks. One man would remain behind to assist Sheldon while Karstens acquired and trained a new dog team for winter operations, collecting specimens for scientific study and inclusion in the Smithsonian Institution.

Sheldon was impressed with Karstens's careful planning, adding only a few odds and ends to the assembled supplies and provisions. Attention to detail was wholly typical of Karstens. Prior to every trip, he wrote long, detailed lists, leaving nothing forgotten or overlooked.

On an "insufferably hot" day in mid-July, the expedition left Fairbanks aboard the heavily loaded steamboat *Luella*. En route to the Kantishna, miner Tom Lloyd, one of a few additional passengers on board, regaled Sheldon with vivid stories of the gold rush and his own hunting exploits in the Kantishna Hills. Lloyd, a veteran of the Klondike, was well established in the Kantishna mining district, with numerous claims and holdings. Gregarious almost to a fault, Lloyd loved to tell stories to friends and anyone else who would listen.

The journey up the Kantishna River to the mouth of the Bearpaw River was routine, but low water on that stream abruptly halted navigation far short of the intended destination, Glacier City. With no other alternative, Sheldon and his crew reluctantly off-loaded their mules and supplies. It took six days of backbreaking labor, under the relentless attack of swarming mosquitoes, to relay the entire outfit ten torturous miles to Glacier City. From there, it took almost three weeks to pack everything the forty miles to the Toklat River.

The cabin site was located on the west side of the river at timberline. A short distance upstream, where Divide Mountain shouldered skyward, the Toklat forked, the two branches traversing a wide gravel plain lined with willow thickets. Alpine passes on either side of the plain were used by migrating caribou, foraging grizzlies, and foxes. The high winds that frequently roared down from the serrated summits cleared the slopes of snow, creating ideal winter habitat for Dall sheep, the main focus of the expedition.

Sheldon had picked his location the year before. "No more ideal spot for a timberline cabin could have been found. It had abundant water . . . protection from the wind, and surrounded by mountains where sheep were almost always in sight. A grove of straight dead spruce . . . provided not only abundant fuel, but logs to construct the cabin," he remembered.

In less than two weeks, the cabin was almost complete, the provisions cached, and the equipment organized. With only the interior left to finish, the packer left for Fairbanks with his mules and Karstens left for Glacier City.

Sheldon eagerly began his explorations. He hunted little and began his observations of Dall sheep pre-rutting behavior. On a solo jaunt, he found one of Alfred Brooks's 1902 USGS camps, the date and names of the expedition members still legible on a peeled section of a spruce tree.

Charles Sheldon spent much of October by himself. His book *The Wilderness of Denali*, published posthumously, recounts in vivid detail his remarkable stay in the mountains. "Alone in that remote section of the Alaskan wilderness, I had a strange feeling of complete possession of these wilds. . . . The wind had ceased and complete quiet reigned; not even the sound of the river running under the ice could be heard. . . . Denali, rising in a brilliant golden sky was before me; the north sky was banked with clouds of purest pink, deepening above to the dark blue of the ether; and later, the gold behind Denali was replaced by crimson." (Unlike Frederick Cook and Belmore Browne, who thought McKinley a proper name for the mountain, Sheldon preferred the Athabascan name, *Denali*.)

On his forays, he located several different bands of sheep, identifying individual animals by their unique horns and recording their behaviors. In all, he saw sheep "in all their hundreds." Each day passed with camp chores and long tramps and climbs in the mountains. A complete naturalist, nothing escaped Sheldon's attention. He trapped voles and shrews and prepared study skins. After each new snow, he tracked hares, wolverines, foxes, lynxes, weasels, and the few grizzlies wandering before hibernation. His only "neighbors" were the gray jays that greeted him whenever he stepped outside. He shot a ewe sheep and preserved its hide and bones for study. By early November, the temperature had dropped to thirty below and the river had all but frozen over save for a few stretches of open water.

The treasured solitude ended in early November when two miners mushed into camp on a meat hunt, one of them having been without meat for over two months. Harry Karstens returned the next day with his new five-dog team.

Karstens's mushing skills quickly impressed Sheldon: "He always took the best care of his dogs, taking no end of trouble to prepare ample food, and arranging the best available spots for them to rest. He always insisted however on their strict attention to work and never permitted one to shirk. In case of failure on the part of any dog the discipline was severe." One dog, Silas, was so attached to Karstens, Sheldon said, that "even after my kind treatment throughout the winter the dog refused to follow me."

Under clear, calm skies, a deep cold settled on the mountains. Somewhat ironically, the Dall sheep rut occurs during the very heart of sub-arctic winter. In severe cold and near darkness, rams battle for dominance and jealously guard ewes in estrus, expending critical reserves of strength despite months of winter still ahead. Given their beauty and grace, coupled with their marvelous ability to survive in exposed and extreme conditions, it's not surprising that Sheldon and Karstens admired them.

The short, brutal days of late November and December did not keep Sheldon and Karstens cabinbound. Each day brought new adventures and observations. No doubt Karstens's admiration for his employer grew in part out of respect for Sheldon's indefatigable pursuit of his goals. Day after day, no matter the cold and darkness, Sheldon hunted, collected specimens, and continued his sheep study. Karstens supported Sheldon's solo excursions, packing in the horns, hides, and meat.

Sheldon and Karstens paused numerous times to study Mount McKinley shouldering into the frigid azure sky. Every morning and evening, the low sun bathed the peak in sherbet hues of magenta, crimson, and gold. "To view Denali towering in a sky of unimagined splendor evokes a state of supreme exaltation," Sheldon declared.

More than once the two discussed climbing the massive peak. Karstens encouraged Sheldon: "With time and careful study we can do it like a charm . . . in my opinion you're the man." What either man then thought of Dr. Cook's claim was not recorded, but they likely shared the belief that he lied. (Later, Sheldon denied providing an appendix that appeared in Cook's book and was attributed to him.)

To facilitate his studies, Sheldon spent part of November in a tent near the forks of the Toklat. Some days he tramped twelve hours or more, in semidarkness and bone-chilling cold, to observe sheep behavior or secure specimens. Despite the privation, he reveled in the beauty of winter: "Only the creaking of my snowshoes broke the stillness," he wrote one day. "Denali, rising in a brilliant golden sky, was before me; the north sky was banked with clouds of purest pink, deepening above to the dark blue of ether; and later, the gold behind Denali was replaced with crimson."

Day after day, the specimens and hunting trophies piled up: skins, skulls, and bones of bears, lynxes, wolverines, and foxes; hides, horns and antlers of sheep, moose, and caribou; specimens of birds and small rodents; rocks, spruce cones, and dried plants. In one day alone, Sheldon shot five bull caribou and two moose, preserving the meat for the dogs and saving the antlers and hides for study. Sheldon's collection grew and grew. He also killed animals for himself, collecting rams in winter and spring pelage.

Sheldon was not the only person hunting the Toklat. Hungry miners living off the land were one thing, market hunters were another. A fusillade of distant rifle fire broke the silence of a late winter day. "The winter market hunters were there," Sheldon wrote, "and the following day Karstens saw numerous tracks of ewes and lambs that had been driven across the divide." The next day four hunters mushed into Sheldon's camp. "They had killed more than twenty ewes and lambs," he noted, "but since they had been there for some time their dogs had consumed so many that they did not have the desired loads of meat to take back to Fairbanks." Sheldon estimated that an average-size sheep provided five dogs with two meals, and one caribou fed the dogs for a week.

Nothing disturbed pioneer conservationists like Sheldon more than commercial hunting, or what was called "market hunting." American conservationists had witnessed the slaughter of tens of thousands of bison for their tongues and hides, the decimation of the passenger pigeon and wading birds for their decorative feathers, and the destruction of beaver populations for their fur to make hats. Such wasteful hunting was anathema to Sheldon and his peers, something to abolish once and for all.

At that time, however, market hunting in Alaska and the Yukon Territory was a way of life. Without a domestic livestock industry, the only meat available, other than summer shipments by riverboat, was wild meat. People had to hunt in order to live. Without market hunting, the swarm of people that stampeded to Fairbanks in the winter of 1902 would have starved.

Sheldon knew that Karstens had on at least two occasions been a market hunter. Just the previous winter, Karstens and Charley Smith had camped on the Toklat with plans to haul sheep meat to Fairbanks They had not explained to friends in town what they had intended to do in the mountains, but killing sheep for sale had been their main goal. "A young friend and I went out for a six-week hunt at the head of the Toklat River. We had two sleighs and seventeen dogs," Karstens later wrote his sister. John McLeod, who had been with Wickersham, rendezvoused with them and joined them on the hunt. "The cache you see [in the picture] is loaded down with wild sheep and caribou. We were ready to load up and return to Fairbanks when a terrible mountain blizzard came up and snowed us in for two weeks. After the storm we killed fifty more sheep and the same thing happened storming and blowing . . . we had to feed our game [to the dogs]." In all, the hunters did this three times before finally pulling out for town with nothing to show for three months in the mountains, other than one silver fox skin.

Karstens may not have told Sheldon the details of that hunt, but it seemed not to have affected their friendship. Sheldon was a pragmatist. "One has to shoot a great many animals to feed the dogs," he wrote his friend Frederick Selous, the famous African hunter.

Hunter-conservationists of that era pushed hard to outlaw market hunting, an effort Alaskans resented as a threat to basic survival.

The first Alaska game laws limited sport hunting but did little to curb market hunting. Sheldon thought it illogical and unfair to control sportsmen like himself. "I paid no attention to the game laws. Why should there be laws in that country," he told Selous, "only to exclude a poor sportsman and allow animals slaughtered by hundreds for the market and men who live a mere existence?" This statement, if made public, would have infuriated Alaskans, who viewed all attempts to set aside game reserves and protected areas as the work of "Eastern elitists" who wanted the areas for their own trophy hunting but objected to meat hunting.

Although Sheldon and Karstens lived on wild meat and fed it to their dogs, they each knew the risks of commercial hunting. Both of them had seen what unrestricted killing could do. Even then, wildlife around the bigger Alaskan and Yukon mining camps had been exterminated. The buffalo and elk slaughter on the western plains of the Lower 48 revolted Sheldon, and he pondered ways to protect Alaska's wildlife from the same fate.

In mid-December, with temperatures at –23°F, Sheldon and Karstens left the cabin on an extended dogsled trip to the Muldrow Glacier. From a tent camp near the Muddy River, they explored the surrounding terrain. In the ensuing days, Sheldon made several long climbs near the base of McKinley, including a solo ascent of a 6,000-foot peak overlooking the Peters Glacier. In an icy wind, he spent four hours on top studying the colossus.

Early in the morning on Christmas Eve 1907, Karstens set out with his dog team for the mining camp at Eureka Creek to spend the holiday with his friends. Sheldon opted to stay behind, reveling in the solitude. For him, the ensuing days were magical. Spending New Year's Eve alone at thirty-five below zero, at the base of Mount McKinley, was ineffably joyous for Sheldon. "Each night the sky was highly illuminated with the radiance of brilliant auroras," he wrote. "I would go outside the tent and watch the moving dancing paths . . . as they flashed across the star-sparkled heavens. Often the lights circled from north to south and sinking behind Denali faintly illuminated it . . . the year died as the heavens were flashing with auroral fire."

Although hunting and wildlife dominated Sheldon's life, wilderness and mountains ran a close second. The mountain enthralled him, as did the wildlands and wildlife around it.

While camped alone at the base of the mountain, Sheldon's vision of a wildlife sanctuary jelled. He envisioned a national park where wildlife roamed undisturbed in the shadow of the great peak. In mid-January, he jotted notes about setting aside the region as a park and preserve. "When Denali National Park shall be made easy of access," he wrote in his diary, "with accommodations and facilities for travel, including a comfortable lodge at the foot of the moraine of Peters Glacier, as it surely will be, it is not difficult to anticipate the enjoyment and inspiration visitors will receive. They will be overwhelmed by the sublime views of Nature's stupendous upheaval."

Shortly after Sheldon penned those words, he and Karstens broke camp for the return to the Toklat. At Glen Creek, they stopped to visit Tom Lloyd at his cabin. Also there were Karstens's old freighting and prospecting partner, Charley McGonagall, and Lloyd's mining partner, Billy Taylor. Taylor held placer and hardrock claims of his own in the Kantishna District, and was partners with Lloyd and McGonagall in others as well. Another miner, Pete Anderson, worked for Lloyd and Taylor, and owned small, largely unproductive claims on adjacent streams.

"From the crest of the high ridge behind Lloyd's cabin extended a magnificent unobstructed view, reaching along the Alaska Range east and west of Denali," Sheldon wrote in his journal. "While standing there with Tom Lloyd, I told him of the double ridge summit and of the great ice fall descending easterly from the basin between them; and asserted my belief that if no technical difficulties should be found on the upper areas, the great mountain could be climbed from the ridge bordering the north side of the glacier."

The Muldrow Glacier was in fact the best route to the summit, but in one important detail, Sheldon was wrong. The north ridge, now called Pioneer Ridge, was not the best access ridge. Instead, the south ridge of the Muldrow, now named Karstens Ridge, was the one that opened the way. The notion of climbing Mount McKinley may not have been fermenting in Lloyd's brain at this date, but Sheldon's comments would prove useful to Lloyd in the near future.

In March of 1908, Karstens loaded his dogsled with part of Sheldon's collection and headed for Duke's Trading Post at the confluence of the Tanana and Nenana Rivers for later transfer to Fairbanks. One month later, Fairbanks buzzed with news: *Harry Karstens had frozen to death.* A rescued man, suffering with badly frozen feet, spread the word that Karstens had died and had been buried in the Kantishna. He said that Karstens was suffering from some malady when he started on the trail and, weakened by it, had succumbed to the cold. The story rapidly spread, morphing to include grisly details—shocking friends and the community at large.

A week later, a fur buyer arrived from Duke's Trading Post and scotched the wild rumors, which he labeled "laughable." Karstens had delivered Sheldon's trophies without mishap, he said, and had gone back to the Toklat. For the second or third time in a year, the Seventymile Kid had been rumored dead—victim of the lethal cold. Quite likely, his growing reputation as a winter traveler, coupled with his long absences, provoked speculation by townspeople awed and intimidated by the cosmic cold.

Charles Sheldon saw and did many remarkable things during his winter in the Alaska Range. On two occasions, he saw a lynx kill a Dall sheep. He compiled a list of sixty regional birds, and amassed enough hides, skulls, skeletons, and study specimens to fill many gaps in the Smithsonian's collection. He had accomplished his main task of observing Dall sheep in all four seasons.

In Sheldon's day, the golden-horned, all-white sheep had been known to American science for little more than forty years. Rather than behavior or ecology, most early research focused on taxonomy, the classification of animals. Sheldon's work helped establish the link between Stone and Dall sheep as a single species.

As a by-product of his two trips, Sheldon had spent more time viewing and living close to Mount McKinley than any other person from Outside. His observations of the mountain were largely accurate and his judgments astute. If not for one unforeseen development in his life, Sheldon may have returned for a summit attempt.

As the days wound down and his winter in the mountains came to a close, Sheldon treasured each day as if it were his last. "Karstens, as planned, left . . . and I remained to enjoy the last few days in undisturbed possession of this, my wilderness."

My wilderness—a telling remark, for Charles Sheldon had fallen in love with the wild Alaska Range. On June 11, Sheldon left his Toklat cabin, never to return. "No words can describe my sorrow and regret as I led the horse out of the woods from the cabin. . . . I was leaving forever this region in which I had lived and hunted with a feeling of complete possession."

Safely back in Fairbanks, Sheldon began to resupply for an autumn trip with Karstens to the Koyukuk River. A flurry of telegrams from New York brought dire financial news. Sheldon had to return home at once or risk ruin.

Sheldon left Alaska determined more than ever to see his game paradise become a wildlife sanctuary. In the coming years, he would enlist his influential friends in the battle to create a Mount McKinley National Park. If, and when, his dream became reality, Sheldon had one man in mind to become the park's first ranger—Harry Karstens.

Charles McGonagall, left, and Tom Lloyd, on the Muldrow Glacier, 1910, using their unique alpenstocks with steel points and hooked tips

11. Sourdough Summit

NOW JUST THE THREE OF THEM—Charley McGonagall, Billy Taylor, and Pete Anderson—remained at high camp. Their leader, the fifty-year-old flabby and alcoholic Tom Lloyd, had retreated to base camp, defeated at 10,700 feet by his age and condition.

At two in the morning, with the sun soon to crest the northeastern horizon, the novice climbers packed their knapsacks for the day's climb toward the summit of Mount McKinley. Dressed in bib overalls, moose-hide mukluks, cloth "parkees", fur hats, and oversize mittens, the trio looked exactly like what they were—prospectors and dog mushers. The only specialized equipment they carried were long pike poles fitted with steel points and hooks, and crude metal ice creepers. Coal shovels took the place of specialized snow shovels. Their knapsacks were filled with candles, an ax, a camera, film, cotton rope, minimal clothing, most likely extra mittens or gloves, and food, by one account just thermoses of hot chocolate and six doughnuts apiece. They also carried a six-by-twelve-foot American flag and a fourteen-foot spruce pole that weighed about twenty-five pounds.

More than once, they must have considered leaving that unwieldy spruce pole behind but without it, their flag would be useless. They had a clear goal: gain the summit of Mount McKinley, once and for all proving that Dr. Frederick Cook had lied about his climb, and leave the flagpole as irrefutable proof of their first ascent. Because they believed the pole could be seen from Fairbanks with a powerful telescope, it was indispensable. They traded turns carrying it.

No one knows for sure what they planned when they set out on the morning of April 3, 1910, the temperature −40°F. Was this to be an all-out summit bid? A last gasp try for the top? Or was this an exploration, a route-finding move? Without instruments, they had no way of knowing their elevation or even the actual height of the mountain. No one had ever come this way before, or climbed so high on Mount McKinley. They thought their camp was at 15,000 feet, or roughly three-quarters of the way to the top by their reckoning. In truth, they had camped at a point where the Muldrow Glacier dead-ends at the Harper Glacier icefall, just slightly more than halfway to the true summit of 20,320 feet. According to McGonagall, in an account offered forty years later, the climbers had previously cut a staircase up the ridge to 14,600 feet. We know that they were running short of food, and the dogs and sleds that had transported much of their gear were back in base camp with Lloyd. It appears they planned to summit, but with all the lies and tall tales told in the wake of this incredible day, we will never know.

Although inexperienced climbers, the men were facing conditions familiar to them—almost routine. Together they possessed decades of experience with ice, snow, and killing cold. Tempered and honed by life in the northern wilderness, these frontiersmen were not only inured to hardship, but undaunted by wilderness, and fit beyond the meaning of the word. Charles McGonagall, at forty years old, was a veteran prospector and dog team mail carrier; William "Honest Bill" Taylor, thirty-three years old (according to the 1910 US Census and contrary to his obituary, which stated his age as twenty-seven at the time of the climb), an experienced musher and miner; Pete "the Swede" Anderson, forty-two years old, a prospector and explorer like the rest, and a man his contemporaries considered one of the strongest men in all the Far North. None of the three, with the possible exception of the Swede, had any climbing experience. The party had looked to Anderson for direction and advice as they had moved up the Muldrow Glacier to their high camp—Tunnel Camp—which they dug into a snow slope. He soothed them with calm responses to the grinding and moaning of the glacier and the thundering avalanches that swept the slopes. He reacted placidly to each alarm.

Modern climbers would be appalled by the men's simple clothing and rations, but their outfit was tried and trail tested. These were trail-savvy men, witnesses to frostbite and frozen limbs, unlikely to head into the unknown without taking extra gear. In light of the modern pastry, much has been made of their ration of "doughnuts." Here's Jack London's description of the prospector's version:

> "The pride of the Klondike cook in his bread is something which passes understanding. The highest commendatory degree which can be passed upon a man in that country, and the one which distinguishes him from the tenderfoot, is that of being a 'sourdough boy' . . . Next to bread a Klondike cook strives to achieve distinction by his doughnuts. This may appear frivolous at first glance, and at second, considering the materials with which he works, an impossible feat. But doughnuts are all-important to the man who goes on a trail for a journey of any length. Bread freezes easily, and there is less grease and sugar, and hence less heat in it, than in doughnuts. The latter do not solidify except at extremely low temperatures, and they are very handy to carry in the pockets of a Mackinaw jacket and munch as one travels along. They are made much after the manner of their brethren in warmer climes, with the exception that they are cooked in bacon grease—the more grease, the better they are. Sugar is the cook's chief stumbling-block; if it is very scarce, why, add more grease."

Cooks often mixed dried fruit and nuts, sometimes cooked meat, into their doughnuts, making a high-fat-content trail food perfect for the frigid northern extremes.

On that brutally cold, calm morning, the temperature unremarkable to these men, the early light glinting off the snow and ice, the party shouldered their gear and headed up the northeast ridge, now known as Karstens Ridge, a 30- to 40-degree snow and ice incline that bypasses the icefall.

How these men came to be on the climb was a classic northern tale, the result of a barroom wager. Alaskans viewed previous summit attempts with a mix of amusement and disdain. These tough, proud, self-made men, who labored for a few flakes of gold to support a hardscrabble life, tended to view the cheechakos who came north to climb McKinley as frivolous, privileged "sports." The local antipathy toward mountain climbers had festered since 1906, when Frederick Cook, accompanied only by a blacksmith, of all people, telegraphed the news, "We have reached the summit of Mount McKinley." Alaskan readers devoured Robert Dunn's 1907 book, *The Shameless Diary of an Explorer*, and excoriated Cook. When Cook's own account, *To the Top of the Continent*, came out, many Alaskans labeled it fiction. His summit claim infuriated old-timers, who thought he had garnered headlines for efforts that the average prospector would consider commonplace.

Tom Lloyd's Mount McKinley expedition grew out of his loud, intemperate chatter. One night in December 1909, Lloyd, who was in Fairbanks buying mining supplies for his Glen Creek claims, paid a visit to the notorious Washington Saloon. He bragged to its proprietor and friend, "Big Bill" McPhee, that he knew that McKinley could be climbed, and that miners could do it.

The saloonkeeper scoffed at the notion. Lloyd swelled and blustered that his "boys" could do it and that for two cents he would do it himself, just to prove that it could be done. McPhee said that Lloyd was too old, and too fat, even to try. He offered $500 for expenses if Lloyd would make the trip and disprove Cook's claims. A rival saloon owner, Gust Peterson, pledged a like amount. Hearing the news, E. W. Griffin, a merchant in the small town of Chena, also kicked in $500 and provided a flag, with his name on it, to fly from the summit. Lloyd accepted the challenge. Later, McPhee accepted a bet of $5,000 that one of Lloyd's men would reach the summit before July 4.

Lloyd claimed that he wasn't out for fame or glory. All he wanted to do was prove his strength and health and "to give the Cheechakos 'the laugh' by proving that what the Easterner brags about . . . the sourdough [old-timer] does as a part of a day's work," Lloyd told the *New York Times*.

At midday on winter solstice 1909, the expedition members, less Pete Anderson, who had left Fairbanks earlier, posed for photographs in front of the Pioneer Hotel. Lloyd, Taylor, McGonagall, Robert Horn (forty-five), Charles A. Davidson (thirty-six), and William "Billy" Lloyd (fifty-nine) set off to wild cheers. By one account, Harry Karstens would have joined them, but he was somewhere in the Alaska Range and couldn't be reached. He later lamented his lost chance to join what he called the "dash to the summit."

Hampered by the brutal cold, it took nearly all of January for the men to relay the climbing and mining supplies the approximately 175 miles to Glen Creek on the south flank of the Kantishna hills. The trail led down the Tanana River, across the Nenana River, then through spruce forest and across frozen muskeg. Daily lows in those short, dark days of midwinter varied from −40°F to −60°F. The horse-drawn sleds and dog teams struggled over packed trails and bogged down in unbroken snow. For the most part, the men endured in silence.

Glen Creek was home to all but two members of the expedition. The creek was one of the last placer finds in the Kantishna District and the site of several hardrock prospects, a search for the "Mother Lode" that had eluded miners since the '05 strike and stampede. Judge Wickersham, intrigued by the undiscovered jackpot, bought claims #3, #4, #5, and #6 on Glen Creek, his investment inspired, in part, by Tom Lloyd.

Mining partners Tom Lloyd and Billy Taylor employed McGonagall and Anderson on their claims. Originally, Lloyd had hired Horn and Davidson to survey his claims, but he soon invited them along on the climb. Billy Lloyd would maintain the base camp while the others challenged the mountain.

Glen Creek offered ideal views of Mount McKinley. It was from the ridge above it that Charles Sheldon had described to Tom Lloyd a route up the Muldrow Glacier and a bordering ridge to the summit. Wickersham also must have passed on what he knew.

The "Glen Creek boys," as they were called, enjoyed several advantages over cheechako climbers, foremost being their northern experience. All of them were undaunted by severe conditions and knew the country intimately. While prospecting a fork of Cache Creek at the base of the mountain, McGonagall had emerged at a pass open-ing onto the Muldrow Glacier, unaware that he had just discovered the door to the summit. He found no gold, "just a lot of snow and ice and rotten granite." Pete Anderson had pioneered a shortcut through the range from Broad Pass to the Kantishna. Two years earlier, Tom Lloyd had followed Anderson's route through the range. Later, Anderson guided McGonagall and Taylor through the pass that would one day bear his name. In all, the Swede had crossed the range eleven times. Finally, unlike other expeditions that began in unstable late spring and summer weather, Lloyd's group began the climb in late winter, a time of stable weather offering a realistic promise of success.

The men outfitted themselves with their everyday trail clothes. For footwear, they chose their usual shoepacs with felt insoles; at very cold temperatures, they could swap these for knee-high canvas or animal-skin moccasins. For bedding, they took caribou hides, wolf-fur robes, sheepskin sleeping bags, and down bags. McGonagall designed their ice creepers (crampons) and steel-tipped pike poles and had them made by a Fairbanks blacksmith.

They also took their snowshoes, which proved indispensable. After their climb, Lloyd told the *New York Times* that the mountain's gla-ciers could not be crossed at any time of the year without snowshoes. That Dr. Cook had made no mention of snowshoes was proof enough for Lloyd that Cook had not climbed the peak.

Old Billy Lloyd, who came to the Yukon in the 1880s, helped cook the prospectors' traditional trail rations: bacon, beans, doughnuts, and bread. He made and prepackaged meat stews, and cut caribou steaks to cook over open fires or on a stove. He gathered and packed butter, coffee, chocolate, sugar, and dried fruit.

In mid-February, the men set up a relay camp in the last timber on the McKinley River, near the site of Alfred Brooks's 1902 US Geo-logical Survey camp. By month's end, they had established base camp, dubbed "Willows Camp," above timberline near Cache Creek. Billy Taylor used his dogs to haul spruce poles to be hewn into hundreds of trail markers. He also gathered stouter poles for bridging crevasses.

On March 1, the temperature –32°F, Anderson and McGonagall hiked ten miles up Cache Creek, through what they named "McPhee

Pass" (now McGonagall Pass), and out onto the Muldrow Glacier, which they called the "Wall Street Glacier" for the stupendous walls of rock and ice rimming it. At last, they were on the highway to the summit.

The expedition progressed up the glacier unroped, a dangerous practice. Instead of ropes, they relied on the poles they carried to arrest a sudden plunge into a crevasse. Many years later, when asked by an interviewer, Norman Bright, why they went unroped, Taylor replied, "Didn't need 'em. We took our chances independently."

For the first four or five miles, the men saw no visible crevasses, most blown full of snow. Then, at a slight turn in the glacier, danger yawned before them. "The next eight miles are terrible for crevasses," Lloyd wrote in his newspaper account. "You can look down in them for distances stretching from a hundred feet to Hades or China. Look down one of them, and you will never forget it . . . most of them appear to be bottomless."

Charles Davidson, the youngest of the climbers and the only one with a scientific bent, quit the climb on March 2 at Willows Camp, due to a bad knee that had hobbled him through much of the winter. One apocryphal story has it that Lloyd and Davidson got into an angry row that degenerated into a fistfight.

In retrospect, the loss of Davidson, a photographer and surveyor and later surveyor-general of Alaska, was a serious blow to the expedition. He had been designated to map the route and keep track of elevations, and without him, the climb was reduced to a "sporting" ascent. Two days later, Lloyd compounded the problem by losing the aneroid barometer that Davidson had lent him. A day's search proved futile. From that point on, altitude reckoning was guesswork.

While Taylor backtracked for dog food, Anderson, Lloyd, and McGonagall marked a route to a depression on the glacier about four or five miles above the pass where they set up their second relay camp, "Pothole Camp." Lloyd incorrectly estimated the new camp to be halfway to the summit, but in reality it was less than 7,000 feet.

Here they relied on Anderson's knowledge and nerve. At one point, when an avalanche appeared to imperil camp, Lloyd jumped up, "but the Swede, who had crossed many glaciers, paid no attention at all," he told the *New York Times* "He simply looked at me and smiled and said: 'It's just rippling a little below; it is safe here.'"

While waiting out periods of blustery snowstorms, the climbers cut trail markers and, when possible, built pole bridges over threatening crevasses. "In many places we had to put long poles across them, as they were too wide to jump over," Lloyd said. The men then shoveled snow onto the poles to form a bridge. After the snow hardened, they snowshoed across. "This was the theory upon which we attempted to climb Mount McKinley at the time we did," Lloyd said. When tentbound, they passed around their one magazine to read and reread.

Above Pothole Camp, the mountain walls, which Lloyd estimated at 10,000 feet, seemed to press in on them, the avalanche threat worsened by the snowy weather. Lloyd quickly came to the realization that warm summer weather would turn the route into a trap of deadly crevasses and avalanches.

When the weather finally moderated, Anderson and McGonagall, trailed by Lloyd, pushed ahead marking the trail. Taylor, who had rejoined the party with his dog team, ferried wood and freight up from Willows Camp. Some of his dogs eventually made it to a point just shy of their high camp at 10,700 feet. Dog team support was an innovation that would be copied by subsequent expeditions.

Each man escaped close calls. Taylor slipped on an incline and shot downhill "with the speed of an express train." He used his hooked pole to arrest his fall at the very edge of a precipice. McGonagall plunged into a crevasse but caught himself with his pole, "which held him suspended there, in snow up to his waist, with limitless space below him. He [pulled] himself out," Lloyd reported.

The men prayed for the temperature to drop, so it couldn't snow and the trail would remain firm. "We didn't want any weather above zero," Lloyd remembered. Despite the men's experience and preparation, the extreme cold exacted its toll. Anderson froze one of his toes. It "bled something fierce every night," Lloyd said, "but he never complained."

On March 18, the men established Tunnel Camp in a snow cave at the head of the Muldrow and near a notch in a ridge that offered a way upward and around the icefall. Anderson and McGonagall used their coal shovels to cut steps to the top of the ridge, but the waning days of March ushered in more snow and fluctuating temperatures. After each passing storm, the men had to clear fresh snow. Lloyd, possibly suffering altitude sickness, took the dogs down to Willows Camp, with Tunnel Camp his high point. What parting instructions or advice he offered his partners will never be known.

On April 1, the three remaining climbers—McGonagall, Taylor, and Anderson—headed up the ridge, but a storm forced them back. Two days later, they tried again, leaving in the predawn light of a frigid spring day.

Anderson led up the ridge, a route he had identified as the only practical way to bypass the Great Icefall. Step by measured step, they conquered the ridge and transitioned into a vast, snow-filled basin called the Grand Basin. There they made a crucial decision. The South Peak, the true summit, was to their left, the North Peak to their right. It appears they made their choice with little or no debate.

With a defined goal to unfurl their flag where they believed it had the best chance to be seen with telescopes from Fairbanks, they trudged to the base of the North Peak. Years later, Taylor explained to Norman Bright that "we set out to climb the North Peak [because] that's the toughest peak to climb."

Unroped, they inched up a steep, icy 2,200-foot couloir—later named Sourdough Gully—to the summit ridge. A few hundred feet below the North Peak, McGonagall turned back. Later he explained that he did so because he had completed his turn carrying the spruce pole; he did not mention altitude sickness or debilitation of any kind.

Grant Pearson, who summited Mount McKinley in 1932, and knew McGonagall, said that McGonagall was suffering from altitude sickness when he turned back. Harry Karstens recorded a different account of McGonagall's decision to turn back. "Five hundred feet from the summit McGonagall returned, being afraid that if he went further he might not be able to return," he wrote in his diary. "The other two went on and planted the flag pole. McGonagall was gone from camp sixteen hours: the others returned an hour or an hour and a half later. Lloyd was all the time in the glacier camp." Whatever his reasons, McGonagall's perilous solo descent of Sourdough Gully remains an incredible testimony to his strength and determination.

Taylor and Anderson pushed on along the knife-edged ridge to the 19,470-foot summit, which they marked by burying a coal shovel. No doubt, they congratulated each other and exulted in their grand achievement. They stood on the edge of one of the world's highest precipices, and for two and a half hours, though the temperatures reached −30°F, they soaked in the breathtaking views. To the south, the true summit rose another 850 feet into the flawless sky. Below them, the icy Wickersham Wall plunged over 14,000 feet to the piedmont below. From their spectacular vantage point, they could study their cross-country route from the Kantishna Hills and their home territory; peer at the forests surrounding Lake Minchumina; and speculate on the location of Fairbanks in the distant Tanana Hills. Though it was freezing (Taylor later commented to Bright, "I know it was colder than hell. . . . Mitts and everything was all ice"), they were reluctant to leave.

On their descent, in the last exposed rocks near where McGonagall had turned back, they planted their spruce flagpole and guyed it off with four cotton ropes. "We dug down in the ice with a little axe we had and built a pyramid of [rock] 15 inches high and we dug down in the ice so we had a support of about 30 inches," Taylor told Bright. At the pole's base, they placed a small piece of board preinscribed with the party's names and those of supporters Griffin, Petersen, McPhee, and the Pioneers of Alaska. They added the date and time. After a last look at their handiwork, Taylor and Anderson headed down, returning to Tunnel Camp just after ten o'clock that night. The summiteers had climbed 8,000 vertical feet in one incredible eighteen-hour round-trip. "We made it all in one day, by God!" Taylor later exclaimed.

Two days later, at Willows Camp, Lloyd heartily congratulated their triumph, their success inflaming his imagination. The four men returned to Glen Creek on April 6, welcomed with a bountiful dinner prepared by Billy Lloyd. After a day's rest, Tom Lloyd set off with his dog team for Fairbanks, and infamy.

The incredible tale that Lloyd told in Fairbanks met with a tumultuous welcome. He boasted that *all four* men had reached both the north *and* south summits. He fabricated events and descriptions of the upper mountain. He said the summit looked nothing like the photographs printed in Frederick Cook's book and he found no evidence that Cook had been anywhere near the summit. Ironically, his account was as fanciful as Cook's and his uncontrolled blathering would severely tarnish Taylor and Anderson's amazing accomplishment. But Lloyd could not rein in his tongue. He boasted that for $50,000 he would build a permanent trail to the summit, complete with lumber bridges across the crevasses and "fifteen or sixteen miles of handrails!"

In one detail, however, Tom Lloyd was wholly honest: "I wish to state emphatically that I, personally, could never have got any place if it hadn't been for Pete Anderson, Charley McGonagall, and Bill Taylor . . . they were far superior to me in ability at any stage of the climb." He singled out Anderson for special praise: "Mount McKinley must be 21,000 feet high, but that Swede is a wonder. If it was twice as high as it is I believe the Swede could go to the top of it."

The *Fairbanks Daily News-Miner* reflected the local delight: "Alaska will this summer be the Mecca of all the he and she mountain climbers of the world [and when they] are forced to sit down near the foot of the mountain [they will] gaze upward at the flag of the Pioneers waving above them." Some locals, familiar with Lloyd's barroom tales and lack of relative fitness, refused to believe the story without corroboration. Others wholeheartedly embraced the local and Alaskan triumph.

By newspaper and telegraph, Lloyd's tale flashed around the world. A flood of congratulatory telegrams, including one from President Taft, poured in. Once Lloyd's story made the world's newspapers and came under wide scrutiny, however, it came under attack. Perhaps in a subtle caution, one local headline described Lloyd's story as a "Proud Boast." When Lloyd's tale reached Glen Creek, his partners exploded in outrage.

In the East, Charles Sheldon, who knew Lloyd, McGonagall, and Taylor, cautioned the *New York Times* "not to encourage full credibility in the reports . . . until all the facts and details are authoritatively published. Only Tom Lloyd apparently brought out the report, the other members of the party having remained in the Kantishna District

150 miles away; so we haven't had their corroborative evidence." In private, Sheldon was atypically blunt. "Lloyd is a windbag and cannot climb," he wrote to colleague Edward W. Nelson. "If he climbed Mount McKinley (He is over sixty and fat and full of whisky pickled in it) any fifteen year old boy can do it."

Opinions varied. Edward Barrill, who had recently recanted his story of Cook's climb, declared flatly that Lloyd's party did not make the summit. A group of Fairbanksans countered with a bet of $100,000 that Lloyd's story was true. John Bradley, one of Cook's former millionaire backers, believed Lloyd and repudiated Cook.

But where was Lloyd's proof? On clear days, people in Fairbanks used binoculars and telescopes to look for the flagpole, but saw nothing. A Kantishna miner said that he had looked for the pole but also failed to see it. A reputable fur buyer then touring the Kantishna said he saw the flagpole twice, from two different locations, through his binoculars. As time passed, the public pressed for physical evidence. Now Davidson's withdrawal from the climb, coupled with the loss of the aneroid barometer and the corroborating evidence it would have provided, loomed enormous. In addition, the photographs Lloyd took on the mountain were worthless.

Amid growing controversy, Lloyd sent word to his partners and asked them to retrace their steps to the summit. Despite spring conditions and soft snow, Anderson, Taylor, and McGonagall dutifully set out again in early May, armed with a borrowed camera to take pictures of the summit and flagpole. Incredibly, they reached the 18,200-foot pass between the twin peaks before deteriorating weather beat them back. No details of this second ascent were ever recorded. What became of the pictures they took remains a mystery.

In June, newspapers reported the astounding news that on May 17, the prospectors had again climbed to the North Peak. According to the *Fairbanks Daily Times*, "Lloyd had asked the boys to get as near the summit as necessary to get a good picture and as they figured they could not get any nearer to the summit than the top, they just kept on climbing until there was no more mountain left to climb." Lloyd had again fabricated a story, robbing his friends of their rightful acclaim for the second attempt.

The 1910 Lloyd Expedition (clockwise from top left):
Charles McGonagall, Pete Anderson, William Taylor, and Tom Lloyd

According to climb historians, when summoned to Fairbanks later that month, Anderson, McGonagall, and Taylor signed a notarized statement, with Lloyd, that said "a party of four in number known as the Lloyd party" had reached the north summit. However, the statement does not say that. The curiously worded document states only that the party of four had unfurled and attached a United States flag to a flagpole on the north summit. Of course, such action implies that all four signers had made the summit, but the wording appears purposely vague, with plenty of room for interpretation.

Perhaps the men signed the statement to garner some credibility for their achievement, or maybe the simple pressures of their mutual business pursuits influenced them. To these men, loyalty to a partner was one of the most valued traits, but when applied in this case, such fidelity soiled them all. "He [Lloyd] was fine in his way, but he was lookin' for too much fame," Taylor told Norman Bright years later. "He conflicted his stories by telling his intimate friends that he didn't climb it and told others he was at the top."

Lloyd's contradictions eventually discredited the entire expedition. "[Lloyd] was the head of the party and we never dreamed he wouldn't give a straight story. . . . We didn't get [to Fairbanks] till June and they didn't believe any of us had climbed it," Taylor said. "I had implicit confidence in Lloyd so I never kept no data on it at all."

And with that, the Sourdough Expedition, as it has become known, seemed just one more northern tall tale. Though Lloyd's fakery caused many to doubt their accomplishment, the trio of climbers retained the support and belief of their peers. Certainly Harry Karstens never doubted his friend McGonagall's role in the climb. Those who knew the others never doubted their ability to make such a climb. Archdeacon Hudson Stuck described Anderson and Taylor as "two of the strongest men, physically, in all the North." Another trail-hardened pioneer described Taylor as "built like a packhorse . . . [and] one of the toughest of them all." He vividly described Taylor's ability to backpack 150-pound loads up a slope where another miner struggled with just 50 pounds.

The Glen Creek boys' ascent of the North Peak was an incredible achievement and a testament to the fortitude and courage of the northern pioneers. Instead of glory, however, their success was sullied by a blowhard's tale. Over the course of the next three years, they watched an array of climbers attack the mountain, each attempt stirring dark mutterings of past deception and fraud.

Herschel Parker leading on the first reconnaissance of the Great Serac at the head of the Ruth Glacier in the 1910 attempt to find a route to McKinley's summit

12. Dr. Cook's Summit Fraud

FREDERICK COOK ASTOUNDED THE WORLD again in 1909 by claiming to have reached the North Pole. After years of grim struggle and deprivation by renowned explorers to gain one of the world's last remaining geographic prizes, Cook, the self-proclaimed conqueror of Mount McKinley, announced that he had reached the pole on April 21, 1908. All America hailed its returning international hero.

The celebration did not last long. A week after Cook's announcement, Robert E. Peary returned from his own polar expedition with news that he had been first to the pole and that Cook had been nowhere near it. Claim and counterclaim generated headlines worldwide.

If not for Cook's polar tale, his claim to the first ascent of Mount McKinley may never have been challenged. The Cook-Peary controversy ignited an international uproar and reinvigorated doubters of Cook's McKinley story. Under questioning, Cook claimed that the hardships of "his long polar night" had affected his memory and that he could not recall the details of his climb without consulting his diary. In October 1909, Edward Barrill, Cook's Mount McKinley climbing companion, recanted his story and released his faked diary, which he said had been dictated by Cook.

Alaskans were quick to side with Peary and assail Cook as a liar. "Ever since Dr. Cook described his ascent of Mount McKinley,

Alaskans have been suspicious of the accuracy of this explorer," said one writer. "All of us who know anything about Mount McKinley know that Cook's story of his successful ascent of that mountain is a deliberate falsehood," Judge Wickersham added. "His story was so fraudulent, that one does not have time to talk about it."

On a very practical level, Alaskans knew Cook was lying about his polar trek. Cook claimed to have mushed dogs from Etah, Greenland, to the North Pole, a round-trip of eleven hundred miles, without resupply. Mushers knew that no sled dogs could travel such a distance without a resupply of dog food.

Overall, however, American public opinion favored Cook. Polling revealed overwhelming support. Disproving Cook's polar claim was nearly impossible. At that time, the poles seemed as remote as the moon, and as inhospitable. (By 1930, out of the one thousand people who attempted the North Pole, fully three-quarters perished in the attempt.) A growing number of people, however, suggested that if Cook had lied about Mount McKinley, he had lied about the pole, too. Critics speculated that Cook had faked his McKinley climb to win fame in order to finance his polar journey. Belmore Browne and Herschel Parker's case against Cook, thrust front and center by the polar controversy, suddenly took on powerful significance with sweeping consequences should they proffer solid proof of fraud.

Until Barrill recanted his story, Cook had threatened Browne and Parker with a slander suit if they spoke out publicly. The doctor's supporters attacked anyone who dared challenge their hero. "Originally our claims were really more or less private and personal," Browne explained in his book *The Conquest of Mount McKinley*. "Looking back on that remarkable controversy, I am still astonished at the incredible amount of vindictive and personal spite that was shown by the partisans of Dr. Cook . . . scarcely a day went by when we did not receive abusive anonymous letters."

Browne said that his disagreement with Cook was not personal but "simply a question of mountaineering ethics." He also declared that the "North Pole was an international prize that had claimed the heroic efforts and lives of the explorers of many nationalities for many years. There was no sport here—it was a question of international importance."

Barrill's affidavit helped Browne and Parker finance a new expedition to the mountain. Backed by the American Geographical Society and Explorers Club, Browne and Parker assembled a superlative team of scientists and experienced climbers to explore the south side of the mountain with three main goals: to reach the summit; produce the first reliable map of the region; and primarily to "duplicate Dr. Cook's photograph . . . settling once and for all time his summit and polar claims."

When the news broke that a group of Kantishna miners had reached McKinley's summit, Parker expressed open skepticism. He said the alleged ascent proved nothing as Lloyd had attacked from the north side of the mountain and not the south. Gloating Alaskans mocked Browne and Parker's "Egghead Expedition," then outfitting in Seattle.

Browne and Parker left Puget Sound in May 1910, unaware of a rival four-man expedition heading north. In Cook Inlet, they crossed paths with an expedition organized by the Mazamas Mountaineering Club of Portland, Oregon, vocal supporters of Cook. The Mazamas intended to prove Cook's story by climbing the mountain over his alleged route.

Wary of yet another cross-country ordeal, Browne and Parker used a powerboat to transport men and supplies to the mountain's base. Browne steered the remarkable boat of his own design almost to the terminus of the Ruth Glacier. Using Cook's published description and pictures as reference, the climbing team parsed out his route up the glacier. "Our mountain detective work was based on the fact that no man can lie topographically," Browne wrote. "In all the mountain ranges of the world there are not two hillocks exactly alike."

The central Alaska Range is a jumble of summits and peaks draped in ice and perpetual snow. Finding one otherwise unremarkable pinnacle seemed a daunting, almost impossible task, but incredibly, in late June, the explorers found what they called the Fake Peak, a mere 5,836-foot spire almost twenty miles southeast of McKinley's true summit.

Expedition member Herman Tucker, holding an American flag, posed for photographs on the peak, duplicating photos that Cook had claimed were taken on the summit of Mount McKinley. "After this discovery we no longer expected to find that the Doctor had actually climbed a high peak," Browne wrote. "Climbing with printer's ink was

Parker and Browne's 1910 Ruth Glacier camp, which they dubbed the "Big Basin," now known as the Sheldon Amphitheater

far easier." Browne proclaimed the discovery of the fake peak as "the end of the polar controversy."

After this stunning success, the expedition then turned toward the real summit. While Browne and Parker explored up the Ruth Glacier, the leader of the Mazamas floundered into one of their lower camps to report his expedition had run out of food and was quitting the mountain. They had found Cook's map inaccurate, his published route almost impossible. Instead of vindicating Cook, the Mazamas came away from their trek as doubters, stating that their "sympathies were no longer with the Brooklyn explorer." As Claude Rusk, the Mazamas' expedition leader, explained: "As we gazed upon the forbidding crags . . . at the point of Cook's and Barrill's farthest advance and realized that it would require perhaps weeks or months more in which to explore a route to the summit, we realized how utterly impossible and absurd was the story of this man, who carrying a single pack, claims to have [reached the summit in eight days]." Rusk concluded that "there is a thread of insanity running through the roof of [Cook's] brilliant mind."

Browne and Parker began their final push toward the summit in early June, almost two months to the day after Anderson and Taylor had scaled the mountain's North Peak. They knew Cook's story by rote, having scrutinized his book time and again. Although Cook's written account was a rich description of the 1906 expedition, it turned vague in describing the summit route and details of the alleged climb. In late July, Parker, Browne, and Tucker made it to the head of the west fork of the Ruth Glacier, where yawning crevasses and thunderous avalanches ended their quest at 10,300 feet. "This is the end! Our farthest North," Browne wrote. "Ten thousand feet does not seem much in the abstract . . . we have given all of our best efforts, we have actually won every foot of our way . . . and are proud in a small way of our work, for we have proved Mount McKinley un-climbable from the south side." Even with fifty more days of food, Browne said, the expedition could not have reached the summit, another hammer strike to Cook's tale.

Browne was not naive—he knew their expedition carried international significance because it would help expose Cook as a fraud. But the evidence offered by Browne, Parker, and the Mazamas failed to silence Cook's defenders. Instead of ending the controversy, the combined reports of the two expeditions only spurred Cook's defenders to new levels of absurd explanations and attacks. Despite overwhelming evidence disproving Cook's claim to the summit, the controversy has continued to simmer for over one hundred years.

The discoveries of 1910 did not placate Browne and Parker. "Immediately after our second failure to climb Mount McKinley Professor Parker and I began to plan a third attempt," Browne wrote. "We were through with the southern approach—and our next attempt would be made from the northern side of the Alaska Range." Subsequent study, reinforced by photographs taken by Charles Sheldon and conversations with Alfred Brooks, convinced the two that the best route to the summit was on the north side of the range, and east of Wickersham's ice wall. A 1911 attack on the mountain was postponed when Browne and Parker fell victim to gold fever and they stampeded to strikes in Prince William Sound.

Portrait of Hudson Stuck, Episcopal archdeacon of the Yukon,
dressed for the trail

13. Archdeacon "of All Outdoors"

"HOW MY HEART BURNS within me whenever I get views of the great mountain of the North!" declared one Alaskan. "Yet how its apparent nearness mocks me. . . . How many schemes I have pondered and dreamed these seven years past for climbing it!"

Clearly Alaskans were not immune to the lure of Mount McKinley, but this dreamer was unique—Hudson Stuck, Episcopal Archdeacon of the Yukon. No armchair adventurer when he wrote this, Stuck was long inured to the hardships of wilderness travel and weather extremes. During his seven years in Alaska, he had experienced much: the power of spring breakup along the Yukon, enormous herds of caribou, giant moose and bears, and winter's fearsome cold. Yet two sights never failed to move him: the northern lights hovering in the star-spattered sky and the vision of Mount McKinley beckoning mirage-like from the horizon.

Denali, as he called it, captivated Stuck from the moment he first saw it. The controversy swirling around Frederick Cook excited Stuck, because he, too, burned to be the undisputed first person to the summit.

The Alaskan frontier seemed an odd place to find a person like Hudson Stuck. Born on the outskirts of London on November 11, 1863, Stuck sorely tested his pious parents, who seemed unable to curb his rambunctious nature. Like all boys of his era and class, Stuck subscribed to *The Boy's Own Paper*, a periodical aimed at teenagers and filled with adventure tales, nature study, sports, and moral teachings.

Stuck was reared on British imperial adventure narratives. The exploits of missionary-explorer David Livingstone, the most popular hero of Victorian England, captivated him. He devoured Sir Martin Conway's books on mountaineering expeditions to the Karakoram, Spitsbergen, the Andes, and the Alps. By tradition and practice, British explorers published books of their ventures, successful and otherwise, to raise money for future endeavors, a point Stuck did not miss.

After graduating from King's College, Hudson Stuck settled into a brain-numbing office job in the port of Bristol. He befriended his employer's son, a kindred spirit hankering for adventure. Distant places and wide-open spaces called to them. A coin toss decided their destination—Texas. After a stomach-churning Atlantic crossing, they landed in New Orleans on April 1, 1885. With typical focus, Stuck ignored the tug of the port city and quickly boarded a train for San Antonio, arriving with just three dollars in his pocket.

Stuck eventually found work in San Angelo. For three years, he taught in small one-room schools and worked as a ranch hand. He began his church career as a lay reader in the local Episcopal church. In 1889, Stuck entered the theological school of the University of the South, at Sewanee, Tennessee. Stuck's arrogant and authoritarian demeanor brought him into conflict with school administrators and teachers, some of them Civil War veterans laden with antebellum prejudices.

After graduation, Stuck returned to Texas, becoming Dean of Saint Matthew's Cathedral in Dallas. Over the next ten years, he developed a school, a children's home, a home for the elderly, and shelters for the homeless. He waged a constant battle to protect those he considered downtrodden, fighting to limit child labor, lessen racial injustice, and improve the welfare of the disadvantaged. His brash, confrontational personality resulted in bitter jousts with city fathers and church hierarchy. Diplomacy was not his forté.

In 1901, Stuck met Peter Trimble Rowe, the first Episcopal bishop of Alaska, at the Episcopal General Convention in San Francisco.

Bishop Rowe administered the church's far-flung Alaska missions and was said to "know more about Alaska . . . than any other living man." Rowe sorely needed help, especially individuals capable of working alone in northern conditions. Stuck resigned from his Texas parish and accepted Rowe's invitation to serve as archdeacon for Interior Alaska. At thirty-eight, Stuck was older than most first-time missionaries, but the work was something he had long desired. He arrived in Fairbanks on September 1, 1904, and quickly discovered the enormity of the task facing him.

Alaskans of all stripes admired and respected Bishop Rowe. The Bishop's humility, charity, and nonjudgmental approach blended perfectly with Alaskan attitudes. His sermons were straightforward and fitted to a frontier people. He dressed in trail garb and did not look or sound like a typical preacher.

Well before the Klondike stampede, Rowe had climbed the Chilkoot Pass and floated the Yukon River to Alaska. Tall, lean, and powerful, Rowe possessed incredible outdoor skills and courage that impressed miners and Natives alike. He took tremendous risks to reach those in need, traveling alone through remote wilderness, defying storms and lethal cold. His grit and dedication won widespread respect and admiration. Harry Karstens traveled with Rowe and commented on his energy and willingness to take on any chore, calling him "a Prince."

Rowe and Stuck were opposites both in appearance and attitude. The youthful-looking archdeacon was described as an "obvious Britisher" and a "brilliant, refined gentleman." Often sarcastic and proud, the authoritarian Stuck demanded a lot from those around him. Plagued by insomnia, he was sharp-tongued, easily angered, and quick to the attack. "Impulsiveness seems to be his nature," sighed Bishop Rowe after one typical outburst. Stuck was "a very difficult, temperamental, exasperating, somewhat egocentric man," wrote his biographer. "Not always right and certainly not always likable, he affects the course of his times by his resolute opposition to social evils."

Uninhibited, rollicking Fairbanks immediately roused Stuck's ire. Gambling, prostitution, and drunkenness went unchecked, and the commonality of violence, unmatched even in Texas, shocked him.

His sputtering, and ineffectual, tirades on the evils of alcohol won him few friends.

Upon arriving in Fairbanks, and without sufficient funding or sanction from church headquarters, Stuck hired workers to finish construction of a new hospital and church. More than once Bishop Rowe had chided Hudson Stuck for his profligate ways. Stuck consistently exceeded his mission budget and spent into the red. He eventually owed Rowe several hundred dollars. Except for what it could do for his work, Stuck simply did not care about money.

In November 1905, with a "beat" of 250,000 square miles, the self-described "Archdeacon of all the outdoors" began preparations for a circuit of his parish. In contrast to Rowe's solitary, spur-of-the-moment trips, Hudson Stuck strategized and planned each journey well in advance. Instead of going alone, he hired a guide, a precedent that he maintained throughout the remainder of his life. Despite Rowe's protests over money "wasted" on a guide, Stuck adamantly refused to travel alone.

The archdeacon's first winter trek by dog team began the day after Christmas and looped through Circle City, Fort Yukon, Eagle, Bettles, Coldfoot, Rampart, and then back to Fairbanks. His guide picked the route, drove the dogs, and pitched camp each night. Stuck's job was trailbreaker, and as such he learned hard lessons—frostbite the unavoidable price of carelessness. He learned how to build a fire and how to cope with the fierce cold. His guide pointed out hazards, especially dangerous "blow holes" (thin ice or open water) and overflows. Stuck learned that you did not train *for* the country; you were trained *by* the country. Tutored by his guide, Stuck learned that dog drivers covered about twenty or more miles per day, most of it running or walking ahead of the dogs. Almost no one sat in the sled or rode the runners. As one of his friends later said, "To live here, you must *run*."

The cheechako minister stopped at roadhouses, isolated mining camps, and Native villages, dispensing religion, advice, and first aid in almost equal measure. Stuck's first circuit lasted sixty-two days and covered 1,480 miles, in temperatures averaging −32°F.

Long nights on the trail gave Stuck plenty of time to read tales set in the North. He read Robert Service and Jack London, sharing the dread of "To Build a Fire" and snorting at the nonsense of "The Wit of Porportuk." He also read John Muir, proclaiming *The Mountains of California* "the finest mountain book ever written."

The archdeacon's initial experience with the strong cold impressed him with its "irresistible power and inflexible menace." Throughout that first journey, a nagging unease haunted him. Like all cheechakos new to the trail, his fear was both real and warranted. "All devices to exclude the cold to conserve vital heat," he explained in his book, *Ten Thousand Miles with a Dog Sled*, "seem feeble and futile to contend with its terrible power."

Like other winter travelers, Stuck found the very power of the cold, and the dread that it inspired, also gave "a certain fearful and romantic joy to the conquest of it." Very few people ever felt totally at ease in the strong cold, or functioned at top form when out in it. "A man who has endured it all day, who has endured it day after day," Stuck wrote, "face to face with it in the open, feels himself somewhat the more man for the experience . . . feels an exultation that manhood is stronger than even the strong cold." He then warned that a man who succumbs to such conceits is a fool. "It waits, inexorable, for just such disdain, and has slain many at last who had long and often withstood it."

The following winter, Stuck made another circuit of his parish, this time covering twenty-five hundred miles. He hired a fourteen-year-old Native boy to lead him into the wilderness, their ultimate destination the Eskimo village of Point Hope on the Bering Sea. A bout of pneumonia delayed his departure from Fairbanks until November 27. During the week prior, the temperature seldom rose above −50°F. Under clear skies, snow was nowhere in the offing, the trails hard-packed. The two travelers left with a five-dog team and a sled loaded with five hundred pounds of food and gear.

Because he was still relatively inexperienced, Stuck was totally reliant on his young guide's skill and knowledge. Their trail led up and over the Tanana Hills to the Yukon River, where it then meandered across the Yukon Flats, a sixty-mile-wide and two-hundred-mile-long patchwork of forest, muskeg, watercourses, lakes, and ponds. According to Stuck, the flats constituted the most difficult and dangerous part of the entire Yukon River drainage. Braided channels led mushers

down dead ends or into dense thickets; snowstorms quickly obliterated trails on the landmark-less flats; uncertain ice, overflows, and
jumbles of house-size blocks of ice impeded travelers on the river trail.
Thin ice was an ever-present, and lethal, hazard.

Small mistakes and judgment errors marred the first few days on
the trail. No doubt, a certain tension developed between the demanding, irritable archdeacon and his young guide. Some village youths, in
the company of strangers, could go a whole day without saying more
than a dozen words.

At dusk one day, en route to a shelter cabin said to be somewhere
close ahead, Stuck stopped the team to confer with his guide. Stuck
had no idea where the cabin was, although his young guide claimed it
was just "only a little way more." Hesitant to pitch a tent if there was
chance of a warm cabin nearby, Stuck decided to lighten their load
by caching most of their supplies, including the tent and stove, and to
push ahead taking only the bedding and grub box. Through carelessness, their one indispensable tool, an ax, was left behind.

Long after nightfall, the temperature sixty-five below zero, they lost
the trail. Stuck again called a halt, their peril now vivid. The boy seemed
hesitant—perhaps the cabin was close-by, maybe not. Stuck was worried
that in the darkness they may have bypassed it. The dogs were playing
out and were only "stirred by the whip, heavily wielded." The cold seemed
almost a living, breathing thing, but without an ax, they had no way to
build a substantial fire or shelter. "Surely never men thrust themselves
foolhardily into a worse predicament," Stuck later admitted.

For some reason, perhaps to see the cabin or pick a campsite, Stuck
decided to climb the riverbank. Six steps from the sled, he plunged
through thin ice into waist-deep water. He cried out, flailing at the
stabbing cold. The moment he scrambled back onto solid ice, his
moose-hide breeches froze solid, but no water penetrated to his feet.
"Under Providence," Stuck wrote, "I owe it to the mukluks I wore tied
tight round my knees, that I did not lose my life, or at least my feet."
With no means for building a lasting fire, the only way to stay warm
was to keep moving. Hurriedly the men cut the dogs loose and ran
back up the trail toward their cache, unaware that the cabin was just
two miles ahead, occupied and heated.

Back at their cache, they built a roaring fire. Stuck warmed himself and dried his clothes. The two then pushed on into the darkness, running another eighteen miles to Circle City. Stuck and the boy had covered forty-four miles in twenty hours in temperatures from −52°F to −65°F. Unscathed, the archdeacon attributed his survival to divine intervention.

By early 1907, *Ginkhii Choo*, "the big preacher," as Athabascans called Stuck, had visited every mining community and Native village in the Interior. Over his sixteen-year career, Stuck estimated that he had trekked more than sixteen thousand miles by dog team. Stuck determinedly carried his ministry to isolated communities. "I could not endure Alaskan existence if I were tied to one place," he wrote, revealing his innate wanderlust.

Stuck's peripatetic forays included constant jousts with the implacable cold. In one three-week trip, the *mean* minimum was −38°F, several times falling to −50°F. On another occasion, the night temperature dropped to −72°F, with a *high* the next day of −64°.

In 1908, Stuck moved his church headquarters from Fairbanks to Fort Yukon. Although charged with the spiritual and physical welfare of both whites and Natives, he felt that Natives, "threatened by the steamroller of civilization," needed his help the most. He moved to the remote village to be nearer his chosen congregation. He said he wanted to create a "viable, Christian Native people, living in a traditional way, free of white influence." He thought it nonsense to encourage Natives to abandon all tribal and cultural traditions. By the standards of his day, Stuck was a radical. Missionaries worked to convert Natives to Christianity and assimilate them into white culture. Stuck adamantly opposed full assimilation. "The nobler ideal," he said, "is to labor for God-fearing, self-respecting Indians rather than imitation white men and white women." On behalf of his church, he became the champion of Native rights and welfare. He fought for aboriginal land rights and local control of commercial salmon fishing, and against efforts to teach Native children from standardized English textbooks that were largely written for urban schools and students. He lobbied also to maintain Indian names on the land. Asked years later why he left a comfortable position in Texas to work in the Alaska wilderness,

Stuck said, "When . . . I realize how long they [Alaska Natives] have inhabited this land in which God has planted them, a great wave of indignation swept over me that they should now be threatened with a wanton and senseless extermination."

The archdeacon also fought bitterly against liquor sales, which he thought were driven by "unscrupulous greed." Selling or giving alcohol to Natives was illegal, but the law was largely unenforced. He waged "fearful battles against the 'hooch-peddlers' and the degenerate riff-raff," and sought a territorial-wide ban on liquor sales. His support of Prohibition made Stuck many powerful enemies, but he never gave up. In 1918, two years before the nation enacted Prohibition, Stuck's work helped secure passage of the so-called "Bone Dry Law" outlawing liquor sales in the Alaska Territory. A Fairbanks crowd burned him in effigy.

In summers, Stuck ministered to his far-flung flock by boat, first by steamboat and canoe, then later with his own gasoline-powered launch, the *Pelican*, so named for its Louisiana benefactors. Due to perpetual poverty, the Episcopal Church's work relied largely on Outside funding. In the autumn of 1908, Stuck went Outside on a fund-raising trip, the first of what he called "begging trips," and secured enough money to order the shallow-draft vessel from a New York builder.

The cruise of the *Pelican* in 1909 put to rest Bishop Rowe's concern about its cost by proving to be the most effective way to reach missions, villages, mining, and wood camps along the Yukon River and its tributaries. European diseases—smallpox, diphtheria, measles, tuberculosis, and influenza—cut a terrible swath through Alaska Native people. When smallpox threatened villages on the Porcupine River, the *Pelican* proved invaluable in limiting the catastrophe. "In one summer, we have managed to vaccinate almost every native in the Interior of Alaska from Eagle down to Holy Cross, and on all the tributary rivers," Stuck exulted.

By mid-1910, Hudson Stuck was thinking of a spectacular way to publicize the Episcopal Church's upcoming twenty-fifth Alaska

Few men in Interior Alaska matched Karstens's reputation as a winter traveler. Certainly he had had his share of mishaps; it was impossible to trek the wilderness, summer or winter, without them. Yet he kept going back into the wild. Each near disaster, each near tragedy, taught lessons that he learned well, never repeating the same mistake twice. Like others schooled in the outdoors, Karstens saw the wilderness not as an enemy but a place to adapt to, a test of resourcefulness, knowledge, and pluck.

After a decade and a half in the northern wilderness, Karstens, the Seventymile Kid, had become an archetype, a style of Alaskan revered to this day. Rural or wilderness living demands proficiency in multiple skills. Writer John McPhee coined the term "man of maximum practical application" to describe Alaskans possessed of multiple talents. In the Siberian taiga, such men were described as having "the golden hands." Karstens was that type of man—expert dog driver, horse wrangler, hunter, carpenter, mechanic, and guide. He did everything well.

Harry Karstens, however, was not perfect. By nature he was combative and possessed of a volcanic temper. He suffered fools badly. He was a proud man, a self-made man, a man who did not like to be second-guessed once he took a course of action. He had supreme confidence in his own judgment. Notoriously thin-skinned, he took criticism personally.

In the North, a person's name, or pedigree, meant nothing on the trail. Ability was all that counted. In such conditions, in such country, among such men as resided there, the ability to persevere, to press on, to succeed, meant everything. *Meant life.* Such attributes brought admiration, respect, and stature unrelated to social position. In short, the skilled men were leaders, unquestioned.

Karstens had no climbing experience, but time and again, he had displayed the pure power of perseverance, the determination to never give up. Stuck believed that Karstens possessed the will to get himself—and anybody else along with him—to the summit of Mount McKinley.

Harry Karstens, the "Seventymile Kid," on a six-month-long hunting trip to the Toklat River drainage

14. The Long Leagues of Silent Places

HARRY KARSTENS DID NOT WANT TO CLIMB Mount McKinley with Hudson Stuck. He wanted to climb it with Charles Sheldon. He said his friend Sheldon "was very much taken with the mountain observing it from all angles and from what I knew later he picked the only way to make the climb, before leaving he asked me if I would join him if he decided to make the climb. I told him I would take a chance with him."

In New York on May 12, 1909, Sheldon married Louisa Walker Gulliver, an adventurous socialite famed for driving four-horse carriages. When Karstens heard news of the wedding, he saw his dreams of a climb with Sheldon evaporate. "Sheldon spoiled it by getting married," he lamented. For Sheldon, a return to Alaska was out of the question as he struggled to recover from the financial setbacks incurred during his winter on the Toklat.

Hudson Stuck knew of Karstens's interest in Mount McKinley. The two frequently crossed paths at roadhouses and shelter cabins, the long nights offering ample time for sharing stories. "Mr. Karstens and I discussed the proposed ascent as long ago as 1906 or '07 and I should never have attempted it without his cooperation," Stuck later said.

Since Charles Sheldon's trip to the Toklat in 1907–08, Karstens had been involved in several business enterprises, most involving transportation. Typically, these pursuits entailed winter travel and personal risk. The movement of gold from isolated creeks to banks in Fairbanks inevitably attracted the attention of thugs bent on robbery. Armed highwaymen stopped sleds and sleighs and took pokes of gold. In 1905, a mining engineer turned thief, Charles Hendrickson, known as "The Blue Parka Bandit," terrorized the trail with his brazen robberies. Bishop Rowe was a passenger on one stage that Hendrickson robbed. When the bishop identified himself, Hendrickson gave back his money, calling it a church donation. To deal with bandits like Hendrickson, claim owners organized heavily armed posses to make the rounds of the creeks and escort the gold into Fairbanks. For two winters Karstens, alone or with a partner, hauled bullion from Cleary Camp to Fairbanks without losing a shipment. Karstens once transported 190 pounds of gold, crossing those vast, silent places alone.

Mine owners had to keep tabs on their workers. Most of the claims near Fairbanks were labor-intensive operations, the easily recovered placer gold long gone. Dishonest laborers would pocket small nuggets or, when no one was looking, pan out a little gold to augment their wages. During spring cleanup, pilferage from the sluices was not unknown. (Each spring, after breakup, the gold-bearing gravels that had been excavated during the winter were washed through sluice boxes, the "cleanup" being the gold collected after sluicing.) At least two claim owners took advantage of Karstens's tough-guy reputation and hired him to oversee the sluicing operations and prevent stray nuggets from finding their way into pants pockets.

In the spring of 1910, Karstens's no-nonsense style was on full display in downtown Fairbanks. Karstens owned a rental cabin. On Second Avenue, just up from the steamboat dock, he accosted his renter, who was behind in his rent. A melee broke out, Karstens slugging it out with the renter and another man. A fourth man soon joined the fray, siding with Karstens. A patrolman broke up the fight, the angry combatants loudly calling for a rematch. After a quick court session, Karstens was fined thirty-five dollars for throwing the first punch; his antagonist was assessed fifteen dollars.

Karstens attempted to capitalize on his knowledge of the country and mining. In the spring of 1909, W. F. Whitely and Richard C.

Wood opened the R.C. Wood Company in Fairbanks, with Harry Karstens as treasurer. The three had met in 1905, when Wood and Whitely had staked claims in the Kantishna and hired Karstens to haul freight from Fairbanks. The new enterprise focused on claim transactions and mining properties.

Wood was a genuine Fairbanks pioneer. In 1903, he started the Tanana Restaurant and later worked as chief clerk for the First National Bank, earning the sobriquet of "dean of banking in the Tanana." A year after opening the new company, Wood turned over full management to Whitely and Karstens, "both of whom are well and favorably known here."

The new Whitely-Karstens Company emphasized mining properties, loans, collections, and accounting. The partners brought different but complementary skills to the business: Whitely managed the office; Karstens handled the field operations.

Karstens, third from right, poses in front of the R.C. Wood Company in Fairbanks, home to the Whitely-Karstens Company, circa 1910.

Whitely-Karstens also grubstaked claim owners, the claim itself serving as collateral for the loan. In winter, Karstens mushed to isolated diggings, like the Kantishna, and took orders for staples, tools, and supplies. Back in town, he would place the order and ship it as directed. Payment for the goods, plus charges, would come due after the spring cleanup.

Enormous sums were spent developing the claims in the foothills north of Fairbanks. Bedrock could be two or three hundred feet below ground. In winter, workers thawed the frozen ground with steam points, and sank shafts to bedrock. From the main shaft, they dug tunnels, called "drifts," from which they hoisted the gold-bearing gravels to the surface. All winter the gravel "dumps" grew high and higher, the true value of the mine unknown until spring cleanup.

Debt, foreclosure, bankruptcy, and legal tangles were typical of pioneer mining. To dodge their responsibility, some debtors hid out in isolated cabins. The Whitely-Karstens Company served as agents for aggrieved lenders. A company slogan was "Send us your collections. We get them." When the Seventymile Kid mushed in out of the howling wilderness and banged on a cabin door, the startled occupant handed over a poke of gold to settle up, or signed the appropriate legal documents.

The distant Iditarod mining district piqued the new company's interest. The Iditarod region was the site of Alaska's last major gold rush. It was the most productive strike in the vast "Inland Empire," which spread from Ruby on the Yukon River south into the Kuskokwim River drainage. Minor stampedes occurred in 1906 and '07. The rush to Iditarod and Ruby, between 1910 and 1912, attracted ten thousand stampeders.

In 1910, freeze-up on the Yukon River caught the steamboat *Minneapolis* at Lewis Landing, three hundred miles downstream from Fairbanks, trapping Harry Karstens and other passengers until conditions allowed overland travel. Karstens used the time to train and condition his dog team, extending each day's run so that by early November the team was hardened and ready to work.

In mid-November, Karstens started on the 107-mile-long "shortcut" to the Innoko River and the boomtown of Ophir, named by miners after King Solomon's source of gold. With just seven dogs, Karstens carried six hundred pounds of freight and two passengers, Mr. and Mrs. James Chronister. The two men knew each other from the Kantishna, where Chronister had been hailed as a "Kantishna King," one of the few miners to strike it big. He had reinvested his wealth in new claims in the Iditarod.

The trip over the unbroken trail to Ophir went rather smoothly, Karstens's passengers walking or breaking trail. Each night they found shelter in cabins or in a tent pitched in dense timber. The weather remained mild with little wind and they made good time. They stopped in Ophir for a brief rest before pushing on.

The ninety-mile-long trail from Ophir to Iditarod traversed flat ground through scattered spruce before gradually climbing into the Beaver Mountains. Thanks to the passage of freight teams, the first part of the trail was hard and fast. As the route wound into the foothills, the wind began to blow, quickly obliterating the trail and creating dangerous whiteout conditions. Howling winds, plunging temperatures, and darkness slowed the travelers, forcing them to bivouac in the lee of a high, sharp ridge.

Conditions deteriorated overnight, the treeless, nearly barren domes of the range disappearing in the total whiteout. When the storm broke on the third day, Karstens was under way at first light, searching for the trail buried by drifting snow. The three travelers took turns parsing out the route. In places the wind had scoured the trail to bare ground; deep drifts covered other sections. Karstens was forced to relay his freight over long miles of trail. Late that night, and just thirty-three miles from Ophir, the exhausted travelers stumbled into the shelter of a crude cabin.

The next day, under cold but clear skies, Karstens was again under way at first light. After cresting seemingly endless barren, rolling hills, the travelers entered the broad floodplain of the Iditarod River and began to pick up the pace. In early December, after nine days of hard mushing, Karstens delivered the Chronisters and freight safely to Iditarod, the *Iditarod Pioneer* noting the arrival of the "famous musher."

Iditarod, a corruption of a Native word meaning "distant place," was located at the nominal head of riverboat navigation on the Iditarod

River, and was the support and commercial center for the surrounding mining district. The town supported three hotels, six restaurants, eight saloons, sundry businesses, and, of course, a lively red-light district. In time, the surrounding district developed into Alaska's third-largest gold producer.

On behalf of Whitely-Karstens, Harry Karstens inspected claims throughout the district and transported bulging pokes of gold from the diggings to Iditarod. On one brutal 33-day, 240-mile-long trip, he transported $40,000 in gold (worth $4.5 million in 2012) from Iditarod to Kaltag, on the lower Yukon, keeping a sharp watch for bandits.

Earlier that fall, two masked men had held up the tramway between Iditarod and Flat, taking with them $35,000 in gold—and they were still on the loose. Karstens transported several consignments of gold from isolated camps but was never attacked. Maybe it was his reputation, or maybe it was the sawed-off shotgun and pistol that he carried. The Seventymile Kid seemed to enjoy being alone on the trail, or as one contemporary put it, to be out in "the long leagues of the silent places."

Karstens crossed paths in Iditarod with Archdeacon Stuck, accompanied by his trail helper, Walter Harper, the son of one of the North's legendary pioneers. As usual, whenever Stuck and Karstens met, the conversation veered to a discussion of climbing Mount McKinley.

After spring breakup in 1911, Harry Karstens bought his first gas-powered launch, the 30-horsepower *Snoqualmie*, and used it to haul freight and passengers to various mining camps. That spring, in peak mosquito season, he used his launch to push a heavily loaded barge up the Koyukuk River to the foothills of the Brooks Range, a round-trip of about 1,000 miles.

Karstens spent the winter of 1911–12 visiting relatives in Chicago and Charles Sheldon in New York, who, according to a Fairbanks reporter, proved to be "as good a guide there as Karstens was on Alaskan trails." He returned to Fairbanks in late March, upon arrival "looking fit and perhaps a little scrappy," according to the press, having hiked long stretches of the 311-mile trail from Valdez.

No one anticipated Karstens's return more than Hudson Stuck. Anxious to secure a commitment for the attempt on Mount McKinley, Stuck had written Karstens back in December. The first tentative plans for the climb had been discussed in the spring of 1911, and some preliminary assessments were made. Now Stuck wanted a firm commitment so that he might order climbing equipment and prepare for a spring 1913 expedition. "My heart is set on this attempt and having you with me," Stuck pleaded. "I should bring my boy Walter, who is a fine strong young fellow, and perhaps another man. . . . I don't think there is anyone who can take your place."

While he awaited Karstens's response, Stuck again obtained Bishop Rowe's permission for the climb and ordered climbing hardware, including a stipulation that the order could be canceled if Karstens backed out.

Karstens and Stuck finally reached an understanding. Stuck agreed to finance the venture, keep the records, conduct scientific observations, and share fully half of any profits accruing from the climb. The church was to have no interest in the venture. They agreed that Stuck would take care of the literary and financial affairs; Karstens was to furnish nothing more than the critically needed experience. Karstens also agreed to transport the expedition's supplies by launch to the Kantishna prior to freeze-up.

"I didn't feel I could afford to do it," Karstens later explained. "I had to make a living." But Hudson Stuck had repeatedly, and loudly, bemoaned the financial windfall Frederick Cook had accrued from his fake climb. Consequently, Karstens fully expected to make a handsome profit for his toil and leadership. The promise of a half share in profits finally convinced Karstens to commit. Theirs was a verbal agreement, and in that era, a handshake was considered as good as a written contract. "I was bound to stay on that mountain until we got to the summit," Karstens later said.

Karstens explained that he based his decision on several factors. Foremost was his genuine desire to climb the mountain. Next, he wanted to vindicate Charley McGonagall and prove that the Glen Creek boys had told the truth about reaching the top of the North Peak. He may have felt an obligation to his friend Charles Sheldon, who had expressed the value of an ascent as it related to his advocacy for a park. And, finally, Karstens told Sheldon, he was swayed by "Stuck's self-promotions and promises."

Charles McGonagall breaks trail while hauling mail on the
Richardson Trail, circa 1903.

Years later Harry Karstens elaborated on his thinking.

*"Bishop Rowe gave me permission to stop at any of their missions
and in this way I met Archdeacon Stuck. For six years previous to 1913 he was after me to join him in an attempt to climb
McKinley. I would meet him on the trail in different parts of the
country. He would try to get me under obligations to him by giving me things and doing things for me.*

*"I did not care to join him in such venture because he was not
liked very well by the gentry of the trail, but after the failure of
all those other parties I was very curious to know how come. So I
promised him I would join him the following spring."*

Harry Karstens was arguably the best man that Stuck could have chosen as the expedition's field leader. Not only was the Seventymile Kid trail-hardened and indefatigable, he at times seemed immune to winter's extremes. What he lacked in climbing experience, he made up for with good sense, toughness, and determination. How the two men would function as part of a team was still unknown. In the spring of 1912, two men stood in Karstens and Stuck's way: Belmore Browne and Herschel Parker, then back in Alaska and again approaching or on the mountain.

From Broad Pass, the 1912 Parker-Browne Expedition pushed into the Alaska Range in search of a pass to the range's north side and the base of Mount McKinley.

15. Storm Wracked

THROUGHOUT THE WINTER OF 1912, Hudson Stuck kept a worried eye on the Parker-Browne Expedition, then reportedly scaling the mountain. A successful, unchallenged first ascent would dash his plans for a place in history.

In fact, *two* climbing expeditions were then attacking the mountain, the second being an all-Alaskan team sponsored by a local newspaper, the *Fairbanks Times*. Stuck may have viewed the hometown party with a bit of amusement. The *Fairbanks Times* Expedition was bent on beating Belmore Browne and Herschel Parker to the summit, even though it consisted of three Alaskans who were novice climbers, led by a cheechako with minimal experience on the trail or in the strong cold. In comparison to the Parker-Browne Expedition, with its highly skilled alpinist and superlative leader, the Fairbanks crew looked farcical.

The ongoing saga of climbing Mount McKinley had enlivened countless winter nights in isolated Fairbanks. The tales of Frederick Cook and Tom Lloyd had simmered until early 1912, when the *Fairbanks Times*, still smarting from the journalistic blunder of spreading Lloyd's unverified tale, sponsored an expedition to the mountain. The party, led by Ralph Cairns, the newspaper's telegrapher, and climbers Martin Nash and George C. Lewis left Fairbanks on February 5, the temperature well below zero. Dog freighter Jack Phillips supplied and guided the four separate dog teams that transported the team to the base of the mountain.

Despite having had no experience on or near the mountain, Cairns had developed a plan based in part on Lloyd's still-suspect story. After establishing base camp on the McKinley River, Cairns intended to push through McGonagall Pass to the Muldrow Glacier and move upward following Lloyd's route. He then planned to ascend the North Peak first and then cross the saddle to the south and true summit of the mountain. Cairns believed that Browne and Parker were already on the mountain and he aimed to beat them to the top.

In mid-month the expedition arrived at Tom Lloyd's climb tent, which was still standing on the McKinley River and was now maintained by itinerant prospectors. Cairns discharged Phillips, who soon departed for Fairbanks, leaving behind one small sled and three dogs.

Martin Nash, a tough Klondike veteran and the expedition's putative and energetic field leader, quickly located Lloyd's "Willows Camp" on Clearwater Creek. Over the course of the next five days, while Nash explored approaches to the mountain, Cairns and Lewis used the dogs to move camp a few miles to the Clearwater.

Nash, unable to locate McGonagall Pass, let alone find the Muldrow Glacier, explored the Peters Glacier, the same route as followed by Wickersham and Cook in 1903. The map he used, based on sketches made in 1902 by geologist Alfred Brooks, showed the exact location of the lower Muldrow and moraine, but the upper section of the glacier was a blank spot on the map. The Peters Glacier segment was shown in detail.

Alone, Nash explored to the head of the Peters Glacier and saw no way to proceed. Cairns said that "it would be impossible for human beings to climb the north exposure," the Wickersham Wall. Nash next scaled the "northern, northeast ridge," now named Pioneer Ridge. Topping the ridge, he saw for the first time the Muldrow Glacier, confirming for himself the existence of Lloyd's "man-eating" Muldrow.

"Along this backbone we confidently expected to pick our way the remaining three miles or more to the mountain," Cairns explained. Cairns studied the ridge and planned a camp at 6,560 feet, a place now

Never-before-published photo of Martin Nash on Pioneer Ridge, during the 1912 *Fairbanks Times*–sponsored assault on Mount McKinley

called Gunsight Pass, and another "at an estimated 14,000' [where] we planned to establish a sort of dugout camp in a snow saddle."

The expedition never got that high. Delayed by storms, they ran low on food and fuel. Sheer pinnacles of ice, far beyond their abilities to scale, blocked them at 9,240 feet. While on the ridge, they studied the glacier and the parallel ridge to the south. They looked for movement but saw none. "Beyond that ridge somewhere we pictured the Parker climbers toiling among the crevasses in the glacier-strewn canyons," Cairns remembered. Cairns averred that the distant ridge, the route pioneered in 1910, looked climbable. "It appeared to us," he said, "that no more than ordinary mountain climbing obstacles would be encountered the remainder of the way to the summit."

Without mishap, other than snow blindness and a twisted knee, the Cairns expedition returned to Fairbanks on April 9, unaware that Browne and Parker had just then crossed to the north side of the Alaska Range. Cairns returned with one firm opinion, something Cook never learned and still others were yet to learn. "None of us

A rare departure shot of the *Fairbanks Times* Expedition,
with 2,100 pounds of gear in tow: Ralph Cairns, Martin Nash, George Lewis,
and musher Jack Phillips

think it practicable to climb the mountain," he said, "when the spring
and summer sun is getting in its work."

Harry Karstens grilled musher Jack Phillips, an old friend from the
trail, but likely learned nothing new. Karstens knew the Kantishna as
well as anyone, but Phillips may have provided some details of future
value. Nash, an old-timer, told Karstens everything that he had seen
and learned.

Belmore Browne and Herschel Parker left Seward by dog team
on February 1, 1912, bound for the north side of the Alaska Range.
Their route followed the cut of the defunct Alaska Central Railroad
through the Kenai Peninsula to the shore of Turnagain Arm. Near
present-day Girdwood, they cut into the mountains on a trail that

topped 3,500-foot Crow Pass before dropping down to the forested slopes of Knik Arm, just north of the future city of Anchorage.

Two weeks after leaving Seward, at the town of Knik, Browne and Parker rendezvoused with Arthur Aten and Merl LaVoy, teammates from the 1910 expedition who had preceded them with laden sleds. The two had just returned from caching the expedition's supplies far up the Chulitna River. From the cache, the expedition planned to forge north and find a way to cross the Alaska Range. The discovery of a pass was key to the success of the entire expedition.

In hindsight, Browne and Parker's plan seemed unnecessarily challenging. Instead of mushing all the way from Seward, breaking trail and relaying supplies, with their ultimate success hinging on an unknown pass, they could have shipped their supplies via the Richardson Trail to Fairbanks, 175 trail miles from the mountain. Geologist Brooks, who had coauthored the seminal "plan for climbing Mount McKinley," was baffled by their decision. "For some reason, which I do not understand," he wrote, "[Parker] has chosen to drag his outfit through the heart of the range, instead of approaching the mountain from the north side, which would be comparatively easy." Browne later explained that they knew that Fairbanks was closer but "it was our desire to explore the unknown canyons of the Alaskan Range east of Mount McKinley from where we could further elucidate Dr. Cook's claimed approach route." In practice, however, they almost never sidetracked from a direct route to Broad Pass.

From prospectors, Browne had heard rumors of a pass through the Alaska Range and he aimed to find it. It took weeks of hard mushing to relay their ton and a half of supplies up the Chulitna River to Broad Pass. There, in search of the mythic pass through the range, they veered west up an unnamed creek (now called Ohio Creek) that ended in a jumble of 6,000-foot peaks. "If there was no pass our expedition was already an absolute failure," Browne said, "for we would be forced to use our mountain food before reaching Mount McKinley."

After reconnoitering, Browne located a high gap in the range. Seventeen hard days later, they finished relaying their supplies to the gap and began lowering their sleds down a steep snow slope to the glacier far below. At the base of the slope they found themselves at the

Camp of the 1912 Parker-Browne Expedition on the
upper Muldrow Glacier

mouth of the prospectors' pass they had sought (Anderson Pass) but
did not recognize it as such. They were now but a short distance from
the Great Bend of the Muldrow Glacier.

Brian Okonek, a highly respected climber and former Mount
McKinley climbing guide, has been to the exact gap in the mountains
that Browne and Parker crossed, and was amazed by the difficulty of
the route and terrain and their ability to piece their way through without maps. "Finding Muldrow glacier meant a lot to us," Browne wrote
in his book *The Conquest of Mount McKinley.* "It made the first part of
our journey a success, from the point of view of an exploration."

The expedition set up camp beside the lower Muldrow, with a
view of Gunsight Pass in the distance. Two and one-half months of
hard travel had taken its toll and the men needed rest. A week later,
bolstered by fresh meat from a Dall sheep killed by Browne, the men
descended the glacier to the McKinley River and soon blundered into
Tom Lloyd's old tent camp, recently vacated by the Cairns party. Inside

they found a bundle of newspapers that included "some articles about our movements that amused us greatly," Browne said. "One of these stated that Tom Lloyd and a party were coming with dog teams to the foothills 'to watch us climb the mountain.' As I knew Tom Lloyd personally I could picture his facial expression on reading the item."

While Parker and Aten mushed twenty miles to the Eureka mining camp to buy supplies, LaVoy freighted their outfit to Clearwater Creek and Browne went in search of a route to the mountain. Browne quickly located McGonagall Pass and continued to reconnoiter. "I was overjoyed, as in one day's travel from camp I had actually prospected a route to an altitude of 12,000 feet on the big mountain," he said. "With a light heart I started down from the pass." Browne did not mean that he had actually ascended to 12,000 feet but rather had identified a possible route from McGonagall Pass to that elevation. In a little over fourteen hours, Browne had hiked thirty-five miles and climbed 6,000 feet.

While waiting for Parker's return, Browne prowled his "big game paradise," adding fresh caribou and sheep meat to the camp larder. "I spent all my time wandering through the mountains with my gun and camera," he wrote. "[It was] the most beautiful stretch of wilderness that I have ever seen and I will never forget those wonderful days when I followed up the velvety valleys or clambered among the high rocky peaks as my fancy led me."

April nights on the north side of the Alaska Range can be cold, but the lengthening days warmed enough to melt snow and sprout early wildflowers. Frozen rivers whispered with runoff, and the earth smelled rich and new. Bears stumbled from hibernation and the first birds winged in from the south.

While securing needed supplies in Kantishna, Herschel Parker met Charley McGonagall. We can only wonder what they discussed. Did McGonagall describe or sketch a route to his pass, or up the mountain? Did he offer insights that Parker later found to be accurate? Did Parker grill him for details or form a new opinion of the 1910 climb? No one knows, but according to Hudson Stuck, the men who took part in the 1910 expedition gave Parker and Browne "all the information they possessed."

After Parker's return to base camp, the climbers explored up the Muldrow Glacier via the route pioneered by the Glen Creek miners. Warm weather triggered countless avalanches. Snow squalls and hidden crevasses slowed their movement. The climbers marked the trail with willow wands as they progressed. Unlike Lloyd's party, which eschewed ropes, Browne, Parker, LaVoy, and Aten roped up, a practice that saved them, and the dogs, several times.

In early May, LaVoy and Browne drove their teams to about 11,000 feet, where they cached a total of three hundred pounds of food, fuel, and equipment. "For the first time we felt confident of conquering the mountain," Browne said. "We were not so foolish as to belittle the task ahead of us, although we could see no climbing difficulties that we did not feel able to overcome." Browne also felt their chances for success were "improving as the days were growing longer."

Despite their growing confidence, none of them seemed in a particular hurry to begin the actual climb. Browne and Parker freely admitted that they had underestimated the rigors of their trek and needed time to recover. Bone-weary, they descended to base camp, where in the ensuing days they hunted, mended gear, and explored the surrounding piedmont. Three wondrous weeks passed. *Three weeks* of stable weather ideal for climbing. In fact, Kantishna miners relayed word to Fairbanks that the "Parker climbers had to be successful due to three weeks of perfect weather."

On June 5, over four months after leaving Seward, Browne, Parker, and LaVoy finally headed up the mountain, leaving Aten behind to care for the dogs and guard their camp. The first night out, the climbers foundered in a heavy snowstorm, Browne lamenting, "we were dumbfounded by the turn the weather had taken." Huge avalanches checked their advance, and they waited for conditions to settle.

Under imminent threat from crevasses and avalanches, the three climbers moved slowly up the glacier to their high cache. Just above the cache, on what Browne called the "north-eastern ridge," they established a camp in a gap in the ridge, likely near the site of Lloyd's Tunnel Camp.

In the following days, they fought storms and the first symptoms of altitude sickness to relay supplies up the ridge. On June 22, they established Ridge Camp at 13,600 feet, a spot where the "ridge dropped away at a dizzy angle for 5,000 feet . . . and on the right it fell away almost straight for 2,000 feet; you felt as if you were flying."

By the time they reached the Grand Basin between the twin summits, "we were awful objects to look at," Browne said. "LaVoy and I were always more or less snow-blind . . . our eyes were swollen to slits and ran constantly; we were all almost black, unshaven, with our lips and noses swollen, cracked, and bleeding, our hands, too, were swollen cracked and bloodstained." The North Peak drew their attention. "On our journey up the glacier from below we had begun to study the North peak with our powerful binoculars," Browne said. "We not only saw no sign of the flagpole, but it is our concerted opinion that the Northern peak is more inaccessible than its higher southern sister." It was a damaging blow to the story of 1910.

Slowed by rapid, violent weather fluctuations, the climbers relayed supplies to their ultimate high camp at 16,600 feet. No previous McKinley expedition had established a camp so high. Everything seemed ready for a final summit assault, but the climbers began to suffer terribly. For food they had relied on canned pemmican, a mix of dried meat, fat, oats, and fruits, but that proved almost indigestible at high altitude. Without pemmican, they had only tea, sugar, raisins, bits of chocolate, and hardtack for sustenance. At that altitude, modern climbers try to maintain their energy and strength by eating twice as much food as usual. In comparison, Browne, LaVoy, and Parker had *cut* their previous intake by over half.

Early on June 29, in cold, calm silence, the three climbers launched their attack. Confident of success, but weakened by the altitude, diet, and fatigue, LaVoy and Browne traded the lead, chopping steps only where necessary, conserving their strength for the toil ahead. At 18,500 feet, they paused to celebrate setting what they believed to be the official American altitude record. Overhead and to the north, the cloudless sky seemed to stretch forever, but the wind began to rise as ominous clouds enveloped the southern horizon. Pushing beyond 19,000 feet, the climbers surmounted a rise and saw the summit in sharp relief. "It rose as innocently as a tilted snow-covered tennis-court and as we looked it over we grinned with relief—we *knew* the peak was ours," Browne exulted.

As they labored upward, the wind rapidly picked up force. Below the summit, gale-force winds pounded them and they battled to keep their climbing ropes taut. They fought on in subzero, whiteout conditions so intense that the last man on the rope could not see the first.

Each step, each breath was torture. Several times the men paused to pound life and warmth back into their numb feet and hands. They dared not stop for long, even to dig through their rucksacks for dry mittens; in that wind, exposed skin would freeze in minutes. Above 20,000 feet, the cold and the blasting wind exacted a terrible mental and physical toll. Here the diminutive, bear-tough Browne again took the lead. He saw the worry and fatigue etched on his partners' faces and knew they were nearing their limit, but he determined to press on. Perhaps a lull would allow them to claim the summit.

They struggled on, one agonizing step after another. Just below the mountaintop, they moved out of the lee of a low ridge and into the tempest. "I was struck by the full fury of the storm. The breath was driven from my body and I held to my ax with stooped shoulders to stand against the gale; I couldn't go ahead," Browne recalled. "As I brushed the frost from my glasses and squinted upward through the stinging snow I saw a sight that will haunt me to my dying day—*the slope above me was no longer steep!*"

On his hands and knees, Browne plowed forward a few short feet, then quit. At victory's door, the game was over. To continue was suicide. The climbers used their ice axes to chop out a hollow depression to sit in. Despite huddling together, they began to freeze. "The game's up," Browne yelled above the tumult, "we've got to go down." Parker offered to chop steps and press on, but LaVoy pointed to their back trail vanishing in the drifts. Without the trail to follow back to camp, they would die. The ability to maintain perspective in the pursuit of a long-held dream is a rare asset that marks a real leader. To go forward meant winning the summit; winning the summit meant death. Just 125 feet below the summit, an easy 200-yard walk in good weather, the beaten climbers began their perilous descent. Now their survival hinged on trust and teamwork.

Late that evening, the half-frozen men staggered to safety at their high camp. Although Browne and Parker would make one more attempt, their six-year-long struggle to reach the summit of Mount McKinley was over. "We reached camp at 7:35 PM after as cruel and heart-breaking a day as I trust we will ever experience," Browne wrote. By their most "conservative" estimate, they had fought through fifty-five mile per hour winds at −15°F, with a windchill of −54°F.

The defeat plunged Browne into "deep despair," the descent one of the blackest moments of his life. The constant strain of route finding, and the responsibility for his companions' safety, sorely tested him. In defeat, Herschel Parker's character shone its brightest. He knew this attempt would be his last, but on the retreat said only, "Perhaps I wanted it too much, but at least I had the privilege."

A few days later, Arthur Aten greeted the climbers' return to base camp with tears of joy. The planned two-week climb had taken a month, and Aten had begun to despair. The relief was mutual.

On July 6, a tremendous roar from the peaks roused the men from their tent. The earth trembled and the men fought to keep their footing. Trees whipped back and forth and their gear caches toppled to the ground. Fissures opened in the earth and filled with mud. A nearby lake boiled as if heated. "I can only compare the sound to thunder, but it had a deep hollow quality," Browne wrote in *Outing* magazine, "a sinister suggestion of overwhelming power that was terrifying. I remember that as I looked, the Alaskan Range melted into the mist and that the mountains were bellowing."

Minutes after the earth settled, Aten looked up and yelled, "Good God! Look at Brooks!" The others bolted from the tent to stare toward the peak they had just named for the geologist. "The whole extent of the mountain wall that formed its buttress was avalanching," Browne wrote. "The avalanche seemed to stretch along the range for a distance of several miles." They watched a white cloud of avalanche debris obscure the entire range and billow thousands of feet into the air. As the blast hurtled toward them at a mile a minute, they frantically braced the tent's guy ropes and rolled boulders onto the tent pegs. After the shock wave passed, the men emerged from the tent and found the tundra around them spotted with ice and snow from an avalanche *ten miles away*.

By a matter of days, the three climbers had narrowly missed certain death in that cataclysmic upheaval of ice and rock. Had they been anywhere on the mountain, or its glacial approach, their names would have been added to the long list of those lost to the wilderness.

Now began the arduous trek north to the Yukon River. Kantishna miners greeted them with typical hospitality. At the outset of the expedition, the five-foot six-inch Browne had weighed 145 pounds but now barely registered 125. His waist had shriveled from thirty to twenty-three inches. The others were equally emaciated, especially the lanky Herschel Parker. Miner Fannie McKenzie stuffed them with what Browne called "the most delicious meal that I have ever eaten."

As the expedition lingered on the claims, they by turns met Anderson, Taylor, and McGonagall. During these friendly encounters, Browne and Parker must have formed some opinion of these men and their story. Anderson's impressive size and strength was obvious. Surely they were told of Taylor's reputation for honesty. They must have compared experiences on the mountain and made some judgment. Parker later acknowledged that Anderson and Taylor had discovered the access ridge, but he remained skeptical. "Dr. Cook didn't have anything on the Lloyd party when it comes to fabrication," he said. Belmore Browne's only public comment on these encounters was noncommittal: "The lack of photographic evidence, added to the contradictory statements made concerning this climb, make it a difficult matter for an outsider to tell much about it," he explained in *Outing* magazine.

Browne and Parker owned their defeat from the outset. Given the way these men went about investigating Cook's claims, withholding public pronouncements until they had proof, it would have been beyond imagining for them to have conspired to falsely claim the summit. Judging by both public and private documents, it seems impossible that such an idea even crossed their minds. The incredible cross-country trek to the mountain, the honorable defeat, and the narrow escape from the earthquake—none of these achievements needed embellishment to rank their trek as one of the greatest expeditions in American climbing history.

Even though they failed to secure their prestigious prize, Browne and Parker's effort proved beyond reasonable doubt that Cook had not been to the top, and in the process, they pioneered a practical route to the summit. "If Mount McKinley is ever climbed to the final dome," Browne explained in his book, "the men who climb it will follow the very trail we pioneered, until, weather permitting, they walk the short distance to the . . . highest point on the continent."

Sooner than Browne may have anticipated, Harry Karstens and Hudson Stuck would prove him absolutely correct. News of Browne and Parker's defeat spurred Stuck to action, as he redoubled his efforts to raise money and order necessary equipment. A letter to Karstens detailed summer plans and confirmed the climb for the following spring.

Frieda Louise Gaerisch, just eighteen in this photo, married Harry Karstens on July 31, 1914, in Fairbanks. The couple began courting just prior to the 1913 attempt on Mount McKinley.

16. Gearing Up

HUDSON STUCK WAS FRANTIC. A mechanical failure onboard the *Pelican* imperiled the start of the expedition. For the climb to begin as planned in the spring of 1913, most of the supplies had to be cached somewhere on the Kantishna River the preceding autumn.

In late August, for the first time ever, the *Pelican* failed completely, broken down without a chance for immediate repair. In Tanana, Stuck desperately sought another boat but had no luck. Falling river levels threatened to put an early end to summer navigation. Without the *Pelican*, Stuck feared that he "might have to give up the entire enterprise." In desperation, he fired a flurry of telegrams to Karstens in Fairbanks, beseeching his help. *Serious mishap, Pelican. Delay; Greatly distressed; Buy grub 5 people two months; Misfortune dogs my footsteps; Go without us; Get fish [dog food] Nenana; Let me explain why you have to do everything alone.*

With no time for delay, Karstens jumped to work. First, he had to find a gas launch to use; his boat was already out of the water, engine fluids drained, and stored for the winter. After a friend agreed to lend Karstens a boat, he quickly gathered everything on his lengthy list except for a few items to buy later. Once Stuck's last minute additions were carried aboard the launch, Karstens, assisted by two Natives, cast off for the Kantishna.

The fate of the river trip was uncertain. Water levels in the Kantishna fluctuated quickly, rising and falling with each storm. Low water was typical in autumn. When Karstens left Fairbanks on September 20, the season for river travel into the mountains was almost over. Karstens, however, was determined to get the expedition's forty-five hundred pounds of freight as far up river as he could, even if it meant by manual labor.

Hudson Stuck could only sit and wait, the course of the expedition entirely in Karstens's hands. "This . . . hazard of the undertaking worries me very much," Stuck confessed.

To his great relief, Karstens found the Kantishna navigable to its confluence with the Bearpaw River. Turning up that stream, he retraced the route he had taken with Charles Sheldon, reaching the deserted boomtown of Diamond City without major incident. Once the supplies were safely cached inside a stout cabin, Karstens turned for home, beating freeze-up by mere days.

Safely back in Fairbanks, Karstens wired Stuck of his success—the caching of the expedition's outfit just forty-five miles from McGonagall Pass. "I do very greatly appreciate your faithfulness and resourcefulness and kindness," a relieved Stuck replied. "Please let me know if there is any expense you have had to bear."

With the supplies cached, the first phase of the plan was complete. Almost a year earlier, Stuck had outlined his scheme to Karstens: "My plan is to fill the *Pelican* full of grub and take her as far up the Kantishna as she can get." There they would select a site as a base camp and haul the boat out of the water for the winter. In early spring, they would use Stuck's dog team to relay their outfit to the base of the mountain. After the climb, they would launch the *Pelican* and motor down the Kantishna to the Tanana and back to town.

Pre-positioning the supplies made imminent sense. In so doing, they eliminated the arduous long-distance freight relays that had weakened and delayed previous expeditions. River transport also allowed easy transfer of heavy items and extra supplies.

For Hudson Stuck, an approach from the north was the only sensible one. "Strangely enough, of all the expeditions that have essayed this ascent, the first, that of Judge Wickersham in 1903, and the last, ten years later, are the only ones that have approached their task in this natural and easy way. The others have all burdened themselves with the great and unnecessary difficulties of the southern slopes of the range," he explained.

From almost the very moment the *Pelican* broke down, the verbal agreement between Stuck and Karstens began to fall apart. With Stuck's enforced absence, Karstens took on sole responsibility not only for transporting the expedition's outfit, but also for the purchase and assembly of their entire outfit. The archdeacon would fire off a telegram and Karstens would respond as required; thus the "equal partnership" came to resemble that of an "employer-employee" arrangement. The seeds of future discontent were sown early.

Even with two and a half tons of gear now stored at Diamond City, a hefty portion being dog food and a poling boat, several hundred pounds more would come later by dog team. The previous spring, Stuck had placed a special order with Abercrombie & Fitch in New York for two light silk tents, down quilts that could be fastened into sleeping bags, two ice axes, alpine boots, silk rope, and sundry alpine supplies. The order came too late to go by boat, with half of it missing. The silk tents did not arrive; the purchased ice axes were worthless; and the hobnailed alpine boots were too small to use.

Jim Johnson, a local blacksmith, built stout ice axes with heavy hardwood stocks from the model provided by Stuck. Ice creepers, or crampons, were also locally made. To replace the alpine boots, Karstens bought six pair of shoepacs and several pairs of Indian trail moccasins. Seventy pounds of food—figs, sugared almonds, milk chocolate, China tea, and *erbswurst* (long a staple ration of the German army)—were imported for high-altitude work. These items would all go by dog team.

Before and after the emergency boat run, Harry Karstens spent long days going over lists and checking details. With Stuck tending to his missionary duties, Karstens filled the role of purchasing agent, expediter, organizer, and packer. The two would not meet face-to-face until February 18, less than a month from their planned departure.

In large measure, the success of the climb depended on preparation. In a first ascent, overcoming the fear of the unknown—what lies ahead—is one of the great challenges. Any first ascent includes some mortal risk—a threat that Karstens well knew could be minimized by meticulous planning. To gather and use the wisdom and experience of preceding expeditions, Hudson Stuck wrote long query letters to Charley McGonagall and Herschel Parker. Parker and Browne both replied, the latter generously supplying a lengthy climb narrative and Parker providing sketch maps of their route. Browne's magazine story of the climb had just been published and offered additional information. By reaching out to the Glen Creek miners and the explorers of 1912, Stuck and Karstens took giant strides in understanding the task ahead. One huge question still loomed, however: did they have the right team for the job? Karstens, now thirty-five years old, was the critical member of the team. Several times Stuck had said that he would not even attempt the climb without him. "With the full vigor of maturity, with all this accumulated experience, and the resourcefulness and self-reliance which such experience brings," Stuck explained, "he had yet an almost juvenile keenness for further adventure which made him admirably suited to this undertaking."

Harry Karstens made no pretense of being a mountain climber. Hudson Stuck, on the other hand, was an avid student of climbing and claimed wide experience. Stuck, however, was no Herschel Parker, a Swiss-trained technical climber. As a boy, Stuck had hiked three 3,000-foot peaks in England's Lake District and later trekked in the Swiss Alps. He had camped at 12,500 feet on Blanca Peak in Colorado's Sangre de Cristo Mountains, and claimed the summit of Mount Rainier in Washington State. The attempt on Mount McKinley would soon reveal his actual experience and ability.

Stuck, now fifty years old, was described by an acquaintance as "energetic but frail." He needed a trusted partner to lean on, so he chose his trail assistant and protégé, Walter Harper, whom he described as "a fine strong young fellow." Stuck's judgment proved accurate. After the climb, Stuck wrote that Harper "ran Karstens close in strength, pluck,

Summer freighters at the McCarty telegraph station on the Richardson Trail where it crosses the Tanana River

and endurance ... his kindness and invincible amiability endeared him to every member of the party."

Harper had notable parents. His father, Arthur Harper, was hailed as one of the three "fathers of the Klondike." Born in Ireland in 1832, the elder Harper immigrated to America at age eighteen and spent the remainder of his life following gold stampedes in the American West and Far North. In 1872, he came north with a party of Yukon-bound prospectors who wintered in the heart of the northern wilderness. For two years, he prospected alone on the upper Tanana River before joining in a trading concern with L. N. "Jack" McQuesten and Alfred Mayo. Theirs was not an easy life; only thirty-two whites then lived along Alaska's three major Interior rivers, and the three partners spent most of their time just staying alive. Harper's kindness and fair dealing won the respect of local Natives.

In 1878, Harper and Mayo ascended the Tanana for two hundred miles and "saw the great ice mountain to the south." Three years later, Harper and two others crossed from the Yukon drainage to the Tanana River. In a moose-hide boat, they floated five hundred miles downstream to the Yukon, the first trip down Alaska's third largest river.

Harper's trading company moved its main post to the mouth of the Fortymile River in 1886, switching focus from fur trading to mining support. In response to each new strike, the partners established, or moved, a trading post to support the new find. By offering a reliable source of supply, the three pioneer traders were credited with opening the North to prospectors.

In 1896, Arthur Harper helped stake the new town of Dawson City, at the mouth of the Klondike River. The next year, Harper, ill with tuberculosis, left Yukon Territory, seeking a cure in Arizona's dry desert heat. He died there, in virtual penury, on November 14, 1898, at age sixty-six.

Arthur Harper greatly admired the superb adaptation of Alaska Natives to the rigors of the northern wilderness, and embraced much of the Native lifestyle. He married a respected Indian woman, *Seyndahn*, or Jennie Albert, in Nulato on the lower Yukon River. By one account the couple spent their honeymoon poling a boat up the Yukon 1,050 miles to Fort Selkirk. Arthur Harper provided his wife and their eight children with genuine love and respect, sending his older children to school in California. Being away from her children bothered Jennie, however, and led to a separation between herself and her husband.

Walter Harper, the youngest child of Arthur and Jennie, was likely born in a village at the confluence of the Tanana and Yukon Rivers. He was just four years old when his father died. Jennie raised Walter in traditional Athabascan fashion, teaching him to always speak the naked truth. Gentle and unobtrusive by nature, Harper was sixteen when he attended school for the first time. On enrollment at St. Mark's Episcopal Mission in Nenana, he spoke little English and could not read or write. In his first year, he made swift and remarkable progress.

Walter Harper was a child of the strong cold. "Adept in all wilderness arts . . . ax, a rifle, a flaying knife, a skin needle with its sinew thread—with all these he was at home," Stuck wrote. "He could construct a sled or a pair of snow-shoes . . . and could pitch camp with all the native comforts and amenities as quickly as anybody I ever saw."

Hudson Stuck employed several Native youths in his traveling ministry. When he first met Walter Harper in 1909, he saw the perfect combination of interpreter, guide, dog driver, and operator/mechanic for the *Pelican*. Stuck came to admire Harper's self-reliance and ingenuity, by-products of a traditional Native lifestyle.

Constant travel, almost two thousand miles a winter by dog team, kept Harper away from formal studies for weeks at a time, but his education proceeded apace. Stuck taught him mathematics, literature, history, and writing. Each night on the trail, Harper read aloud the classics, from *Treasure Island* to *Hamlet*, the Bible to the *Inferno*. In his diary he wrote lists of US presidents and states, the books of the Old Testament, and the names of the week from Norse and Latin mythology. Stuck praised Harper's character: "The lad possessed a modesty, a courtesy, a deference, that marked him a gentleman in any company." He offered his young apprentice the best education he could. Theirs was a complex father-son, teacher-student, employer-employee relationship that lasted nine years. By the spring of 1913, Stuck and Harper had been together for three years. Hudson Stuck clearly understood that his sole chance for the summit relied on a blend of Harper's strength and assistance blended with Karstens's wilderness savvy.

For the fourth member of the expedition, Hudson Stuck had his eye on a US Army Signal Corps officer stationed at Fort Gibbon, 2nd Lt. Howard C. Tatum, twenty-five, of Fort Worth, Texas. During the Spanish-American War, Tatum had fought in the Philippines with the rank of first sergeant. After officer training school in Kansas, Tatum was posted to Alaska. In Fairbanks in 1910, he married Margaret Sophia Funk.

Because maintenance and support of the telegraph line required Tatum to be afield in all seasons, he acquired winter skills with a reputation for courage in daunting circumstances. Perhaps Tatum's insistence on discipline and duty among the troops also impressed the archdeacon, who had long railed against the unsavory "fraternization" between soldiers and Native women.

When the army refused Lt. Tatum's request for leave to join the expedition, Stuck invited another officer, 2nd Lt. Delos C. Emmons, twenty-four, of the 30th Infantry, to take Tatum's place. Barely two weeks before the start of the expedition, he too was denied leave. (Both officers went on to distinguished careers. At the rank of lieutenant colonel, Tatum served in France as chief of military intelligence for the 90th Infantry Division led by Major General Henry T. Allen, famous for his 1885 Alaska explorations. Emmons later transferred to the air force and enjoyed an illustrious career, rising to the rank of lieutenant general.)

By happenstance, Lt. Howard Tatum's younger brother was then working at St. Mark's Mission in Nenana. The twenty-fifth anniversary of the Episcopal Church in Alaska, in 1912, had brought several young volunteers to Alaska. Robert G. Tatum, twenty-one, of Knoxville, was one of them. Although inexperienced, the younger Tatum possessed strength, enthusiasm, and commitment to the church. During the winter of 1912, his first in Alaska, he had assisted in a relief effort for the mission at Tanana Crossing; the following summer he joined a survey crew.

Stuck had initially selected an Athabascan youth, Arthur Wright, as a member of the team, but when Wright went Outside for medical treatment and high school, Stuck selected Robert Tatum to replace Wright as camp cook. Tatum committed to the expedition in August. As part of his duties, Tatum organized and catalogued the climbing supplies shipped to St. Mark's. When Karstens stopped in Nenana en route to the Kantishna, Tatum helped load extra freight, transfer fuel, and dog food. Stuck declared Tatum another "fine young fellow," but as he discovered on the mountain, a complex and brittle one.

Just prior to his departure for the mountain, Stuck chose two other students at St. Mark's Mission, John Fredson and Esaias George. Molded by the strong cold and their Athabascan heritage, these Native boys were skilled dog drivers and winter travelers. Very little is known of Esaias "Essie" George. He was born on January 20, 1896, and grew up in Stevens Village, a small Athabascan village on the Yukon Flats. John Fredson was the ninth child of "Louise" and "Fred," nomadic Natsit Gwich'in Athabascans. He was born about 1895 near the Sheenjek River in northeastern Alaska. As a child he acquired the name *Zhoh Gwatsan*, "Wolf Smeller," but to whites was known as John Fred. When his mother died giving birth to her tenth child, his father took his youngest children to Circle City and turned them over to the Episcopal Church, unable to support them all on a subsistence lifestyle.

Hudson Stuck first met John Fredson in Circle in 1905. When Fredson turned fourteen, he was sent to St. Mark's in Nenana, a step toward advanced education. One teacher described John as "the most capable and reliable of all the boys," and a "prize student." "We hope to make him a clergyman," Stuck said. "He is a very intelligent boy. But better than that, he is a true-hearted loyal youth. His word I would take absolutely, about anything." The archdeacon's high opinion was well placed. Later in his life, Fredson would wage a successful battle to preserve and protect his traditional lands, becoming a leader hailed as the "George Washington" of his people.

From solely a mountain climber's perspective, Hudson Stuck's team was completely untrained and unlikely to succeed. None were experienced alpinists, just another bunch of Alaskan rookies. Two were seventeen-year-olds; one a raw cheechako; the leader a skinny, aging preacher. Only Walter Harper and the sinew-tough Harry Karstens appeared to have the physical strength necessary to make the summit. Like the Glen Creek boys, however, this expedition held trump cards. All members, save Tatum, were absolutely at home in the wilderness and accustomed to the rigors of winter travel. They might have ice in their blood, but not in their souls. Karstens viewed climbing the mountain as just another trip, a new challenge to defeat with hard work, perseverance, and courage. They had done their homework and knew where they were going. The route, explained by people who had pioneered it, was seared into their brains. "We conquered Mount McKinley," Belmore Browne had said that fall, "and when some day a party stands on the highest snow they will have followed our trail to the last dome." Stuck pictured the route as vividly as his study allowed; Karstens could see it as clearly as the day Sheldon had pointed it out.

In the days leading up to departure, Harry Karstens had considered every detail of the expedition with a focused seriousness rooted in his profound respect for the sub-arctic environment. In the days ahead, on the towering slopes of Mount McKinley, all four climbers would enter the wholly unknown territory of high altitude, but also a familiar landscape of snow and ice. Only time would tell if their cumulative experience would prevail where others had failed.

Hudson Stuck (left) and Harry Karstens at camp on
Clearwater Creek stand facing Mount McKinley.

17. The Coldest Mountain on Earth

DAWN STEALS ONTO THE SUMMIT of Mount McKinley with a faint blush of pink. With each passing second, the color strengthens and a line of crimson creeps down the sheer North Face. The shafts of amber, magenta, and claret light reveal the mountain's rugged, hewn surfaces. Icefalls, fissures, outcrops, and ridges, backed by blue shadow, jump to life in sharp relief. When fully engulfed in glowing red, the mountain seems almost alive, the warm beating heart of Alaska. Sunlight bathes most of the mountain well before the nearby peaks even capture a hint of light. The pastel alpenglow fades rapidly as the sun pulses above the horizon, illuminating the entire range in gleaming sunlight.

Anyone who has ever gazed on the mountain at dawn or dusk has wondered about the view from the top. How would it feel to stand on the summit, looking out over the vast sprawling wilderness below? Would that sprawling vista change one's life? Could the key to heaven be buried there? For a climber, a mountain man, the lure would be overpowering. *The lure of a first ascent!* Irresistible.

Judge Wickersham loved mountains but desired fame as well. Frederick Cook sought prestige, McKinley a mere stepping-stone on the road to glory. Tom Lloyd wanted bragging rights. Herschel Parker and Belmore Browne were true mountain men, enthralled and exhilarated by the high and wild. One long look was enough to capture Hudson

Stuck, a Victorian romantic. Harry Karstens reveled in challenges and knew none bigger than capturing the summit. What all of these pioneer climbers had yet to understand, though, was the very *nature* of the mountain itself—the challenges, and risks, posed by altitude and latitude.

Mount McKinley rises near the geographic center of Alaska, a scant two hundred miles south of the Arctic Circle. It is the coldest mountain in the world, and stormy two out of three days a year. Summer temperatures sometimes plunge as low as −40°F. Winter blizzards combined with −70°F temperatures can flash-freeze exposed skin. Conditions change violently and dramatically. But cold weather is only part of the story. Eight groups had attempted the mountain prior to 1913, yet because of its sheer enormity, it remained largely unexplored.

Although the mountain is the highest point in North America, it does not rank among the world's one hundred tallest mountains. Dozens of higher peaks reside in the Andes or Himalayas, but none are so far north. In a list of the world's "peaks of prominence," however, McKinley ranks third, only behind Everest and Aconcagua. (In topographic terms, the prominence of a peak is the height of the peak's summit above the lowest contour line encircling it. Topographers also apply the phrase "peaks of autonomous height" to describe peaks of prominence.)

Since the Earth's other tall mountains rise nearer the equator, most high-altitude ascents are made in temperate climates. It is possible, for example, to climb South America's tallest peak, Aconcagua, 22,841 feet, without crossing snow or ice of any kind, perhaps riding close to the summit on muleback. Some of the highest peaks in the Himalayas can be approached and provisioned with pack animals. Climbers attempting Everest can access the Tibetan base camp, at 18,192 feet, without encountering snow. Because of its sub-arctic climate, Mount McKinley requires almost 15,000 feet of snow and ice travel compared to a maximum of 5,000 feet on other mountains.

North America's tallest peak is a granite giant sheathed in ice. Five large glaciers flow off the summit slopes. The Ruth Glacier streams to the southeast and the Kahiltna Glacier to the southwest. The Peters

Glacier flows from the northwest side of the mountain. The Traleika Glacier flows to the east and merges with the Muldrow Glacier wending northeast from the basin between the mountain's north and south summits. The thirty-four-mile-long Muldrow is the longest glacier on the north side of the Alaska Range.

Towering ridges flank both sides of the upper Muldrow Glacier. To a climber's right, the sheer rock walls of Pioneer Ridge soar toward the north summit. A break in that ridge—McGonagall Pass—opens onto the Muldrow Glacier and cuts off sixteen miles of travel from the basal moraine. The climbing distance from the pass to the summit is eighteen miles, with a vertical rise of 14,600 feet, all of it over ice and snow.

The ridge on the left, which Browne and Parker called the northeastern ridge, separates the Muldrow from the Traleika. At the head of the Muldrow, at about 11,500 feet, a nearly vertical icefall blocks further advance up the glacier. Near the base of the icefall, the northeastern ridge provides a way around the icefall and a practical route of ascent. Both the 1910 and 1912 expeditions climbed this ridge en route to the summit.

For every climber, each step at high altitude becomes a test of will, the physiology of heart and lungs holding him or her back. While climbers then knew that "thin air" at high altitude affected performance, the full impact on human physiology was not understood. The amount of available oxygen to sustain mental and physical alertness decreases markedly above 10,000 feet, with roughly one-half less oxygen at 18,000 feet than at sea level. It is the reduction in air pressure at altitude that causes hypoxia, or altitude sickness.

Hypoxia causes a host of complaints: headaches, breathlessness, cough, diarrhea, nausea, lack of appetite, and mental confusion. Nonspecific symptoms acquired at high altitude resemble a case of flu, carbon monoxide poisoning, or a hangover. In most cases, the symptoms are temporary and usually abate with acclimatization to altitude. In severe cases of altitude sickness, the lungs and brain fill with fluid, and without immediate rapid descent and treatment, the results are almost always lethal.

We now know that there are no specific factors that correlate with a person's susceptibility to altitude sickness; it is difficult to determine before an ascent who will be affected and how badly. Even extremely fit people may sicken worse than anticipated. The speed of ascent, the altitude attained, and the amount of physical activity at high altitude, as well as individual susceptibility, are contributing factors to the onset and severity of high-altitude illness. Given the rapidity of Frederick Cook's alleged ascent, the mere fact that he made no substantive mention of the effects of altitude, other than shortness of breath, casts serious doubt on his story. To one degree or another, it appears that all of the 1910 and 1912 climbers displayed some symptoms of altitude sickness.

Extreme cold and altitude tests both body and brain. Impaired judgment results in bad, perhaps fatal, choices. When Belmore Browne made the crucial decision to descend from near the summit in 1912, his thinking was clear and rational. He was able to make the right choice. In that storm, a decision to go on, made with clouded judgment, would have killed all three climbers.

Modern climbers on Mount McKinley do not use supplemental oxygen but acclimate to altitude for two to three weeks prior to a summit attempt. While route-finding or relaying loads up a mountain, a cardinal rule of modern climbers is to climb high but sleep low. Today's climbers also try to eat twice as much food as normal to keep up their energy. Proper hydration is also a concern. Drinking copious amounts of water allows the body to retain more heat than it loses. Frostbite is more likely to occur as a body cools and body heat is channeled to the core, the extremities going cold. Proper hydration and nutrition are essential to peak performance at high altitude.

McKinley's pioneer climbers unwittingly acclimated themselves to altitude while relaying supplies or waiting out storms. Most of the Alaskans were expert winter travelers, inured to and undaunted by extreme conditions. Nonetheless, the threat posed by the mix of sub-zero cold and high altitude would be the greatest danger the 1913 climbers would face.

Without all the hoopla and chest-thumping that had attended Tom Lloyd's 1910 departure from Fairbanks, Harry Karstens, Walter

Harper, Karstens, and Stuck (from left to right) prepare to leave Fairbanks on March 13, 1913. Judge Cecil Clegg and Reverend Charles Betticher, both at far right, stand witness in this never-before-published photo.

Harper, and Hudson Stuck left town on March 13. Only a few friends were on hand when the trio mushed away from Saint Matthew's Church on the south bank of the Chena River. Until the day before, Stuck had succeeded in keeping the climb secret from what he called the "hungry stupid little Fairbanks papers." When the story broke, Stuck lamented that "I could keep it from them no longer." The story left the impression that Karstens was Stuck's hired guide.

The three principles had only recently come together. Stuck and Harper had just returned from a 450-mile-long round-trip to Tanana Crossing to deliver much-needed supplies to the mission. They lay over in Fairbanks just three days before starting for the mountain. Karstens had been cutting and hauling cordwood for resale, and attending to last minute climb preparations. (He had also been courting a beautiful young nurse named Frieda Louise Gaerisch.) The scheduled morning departure had been delayed until early afternoon when the tent-maker finally delivered the mountain tents.

Stuck originally had planned to set out on March 1, but the re-supply effort to Tanana Crossing dashed that date. He wanted to have the cached supplies relayed to the mountain by mid-month. Instead, they pulled out from Fairbanks two weeks behind schedule. March and April are prime travel months, the weather often clear and settled; lost days are irreplaceable.

Karstens and Stuck broke trail with a sense of relief to be finally under way. Harper and the dog team followed them down the Chena and out onto the Tanana River. That night they stopped at Twelve-Mile Roadhouse. The next day, in cold, clear weather, they made slow progress over the Wood River cutoff to Fisher's Roadhouse on the Nenana River. "A fine first glimpse of Denali at sunset," Stuck exulted in his journal.

Early the following morning they mushed into the village of Nenana and were met at St. Mark's Mission by the three other members of their party, Robert Tatum, John Fredson, and Esaias George. After Palm Sunday services, the company returned to Fisher's Roadhouse, crossing paths with the mail carrier who had a package for Stuck—the amber snow glasses he'd ordered months before from Abercrombie & Fitch.

Harry Karstens and Walter Harper left the roadhouse early on March 17, breaking trail ahead of the two seven-dog teams, driven by Fredson and George. Robert Tatum and Hudson Stuck trailed well behind. "The Archdeacon is very nervous," remarked Tatum.

Karstens knew the Kantishna Trail intimately; he'd been over it dozens of times since 1905. Without major incident, they covered the fifty-five miles to Knight's Roadhouse in two days.

High pressure had settled over Interior Alaska, bringing the finest weather of the year, subzero mornings warming to near zero in late afternoon. The new trails froze hard overnight; the clear, calm, sun-splashed days were perfect for the dogs, and men toiling on snowshoes. They could not have hoped for better conditions.

At the roadhouse, an important waypoint on the trail, Karstens greeted the proprietor and his wife, old friends who shared the local news. February had been relatively warm, with few subzero days, the unseasonable weather persisting into early March. Travelers from the Kantishna had reported poor trail conditions, soft snow, open water, and abundant overflows. Only recently had temperatures dropped, with trail conditions dramatically improved.

From Knight's Roadhouse the trail turned up the Toklat River and led into the foothills, providing hazy glimpses of Mount McKinley growing ever closer. Sometime during that day's trek, the anxiety that had been dogging Hudson Stuck drained away. "This has been one of the most enjoyable days of travel that ever I remember," he wrote.

Another two days took them fifty miles up the Toklat to its Clearwater Fork, up its tributary, Myrtle Creek, to the divide, and down the other side to Moose Creek, the heart of the Kantishna Mining District. On the high divide, they paused to study the mountain rising into the clear, azure sky. While Karstens and Harper went on ahead to break trail, Stuck made numerous photographs of what he called an "incomparable view" of his magic mountain.

On Good Friday the expedition continued down Moose Creek to Eureka Creek, where they encamped at Jack Hamilton's cabin, their headquarters while relaying supplies from Diamond City, a little over twenty-five miles away. "We had trails and weather far beyond our expectations and made splendid time here," Tatum explained.

The next day they mushed with empty sleds to Glacier City, another of the relic boom camps left over from the 1905 stampede. They set up camp in a cabin owned by Billy Taylor, one of the 1910 climbers. Their dogsleds had taken a terrible beating on the river ice and on the high, bare ground above Moose Creek. With tools and a forge at hand, Karstens began repairing the sleds and runners. "Karstens is an ingenious mechanic," Stuck exclaimed after watching his partner replace broken stanchions and runners.

Easter Sunday dawned bright and clear. Four miners joined expedition members for morning services, the archdeacon delivering a sermon about flowers and their meaning to humanity. After lunch Karstens went back to work on the sleds.

Late the next day, the sleds rebuilt and strengthened, the whole party broke trail ten miles to Diamond City, where the previous autumn Karstens had cached the bulk of their freight. They found everything intact except for the "depredations of mice," which had eaten or destroyed fifty pounds of cornmeal and oats.

Harper, Fredson, and George went right to work relaying their outfit to Hamilton's cabin, via an intermediary stop at Glacier City. Stuck and Tatum meanwhile began preparing food for the climb, boiling a pot of ham and beans, and baking a large batch of doughnuts. From the outset, Karstens had been unhappy with the ice creepers, or climbing crampons, that had been made in Fairbanks. Now he took the time to work on them, especially the heelpieces, which he knew would not work well with moccasins. The creepers would vex Karstens throughout the climb.

One afternoon, Pete Anderson stopped by the cabin to see Karstens, and the two engaged in a long, serious talk. "Anderson maintains that he and Taylor actually got to the top," Stuck noted in his journal, "and

Hudson Stuck and lead dog Muk

set-up a fourteen-foot flagstaff there. Which they maintain is there yet. Karstens believes him and I do too, though the task of carrying a fourteen-foot pole up that mountain must have been enormous and the feat sounds incredible."

On March 30, with the last load of freight relayed from Diamond to Eureka, Karstens broke trail on snowshoes nine miles to a cabin near the McKinley River. While he was gone, Stuck and Tatum baked 250 biscuits and 50 more doughnuts, and mixed up a gallon of syrup. (Instead of doing their own baking, Browne and Parker had freighted in 96 *pounds* of canned hardtack.) Charley McGonagall dropped in for a visit.

After talking with Anderson and McGonagall, Hudson Stuck felt certain of Karstens's chosen route to the mountain. "There has been no need [for us] to make reconnaissance for routes," Stuck explained, "since these pioneers blazed the way; there is no other practicable route."

From the very outset of the trip, Stuck had worried about footwear. The climbing boots he'd ordered from New York were too small and had been left behind. Perhaps due to an old frostbite injury, cold feet were a perpetual problem for him. McGonagall and Anderson both swore that moccasins were the only footgear to use high on the mountain. They recommended canvas or moose-hide moccasins worn over *five* pairs of socks. "McGonagall's experience shows that moccasins with the great creepers under them are the only footwear for the mountain," Stuck later recalled. Miners collected dozens of moccasins for the climbers, a typical example of what Stuck described as their "most kindly and generous . . . assistance."

April Fools' Day dawned bright and clear, the last day of preparation for the final move to the base of the mountain. Using some of McGonagall's sourdough starter, Tatum baked six loaves of bread and added them to their larder. Laundry was hand-washed and dried by the woodstove. Fredson and George relayed the first loads of freight to the McKinley River cabin. By nightfall, the remaining food, clothes, and extra footwear were packed and stowed, ready for an early morning departure.

The expedition set out the next morning with two heavily loaded sleds. En route to Wonder Lake, Karstens stopped at a friend's cabin to borrow a rifle, a tent, and a gallon of alcohol left by Browne and Parker. By lunchtime they had their entire ton and a half outfit cached at the McKinley River cabin.

After lunch, while the rest of the party took the teams downriver to Clearwater Creek, Karstens snowshoed across the river to Tom Lloyd's old tent camp, searching for ice creepers that had been left there the year before.

Late that day, Karstens rejoined his companions a mile up Clearwater Creek, where they were setting up camp for the night. After dinner he and Stuck broke trail upstream. "It turned cold immediately," Stuck complained, "and my feet were nearly frozen before we returned to the tent." Soon after dark, the temperature plunged to thirty below. Karstens that day had snowshoed a total of sixteen miles, much of it through deep, soft snow. At one point, he lost patience with Stuck, unleashing an angry tirade. The cause of the outburst was not recorded, but it was a harbinger of future conflict.

The date was April 3, three years to the day from when McGonagall, Anderson, and Taylor had made the first ascent of McKinley's North Peak in 1910.

The next two days were spent putting in a trail upstream through deep snow, skirting open water and overflows. "A very bad trail full of potholes," Tatum described it. "Got through the canyon and the drifted, dangerous places." Seven miles above the mouth of the creek, the expedition pitched camp in the last stand of timber, their tent facing the mountain looming in the near distance. The woods camp would be an important stop. Here they would gather firewood for use in their stoves, cut poles for bridging crevasses, and gather willow wands for marking their high trail.

Nearly two weeks of brilliant weather settled in, the nights cold, down to forty below, with the afternoons warm enough for shirtsleeves. Harper, Fredson, and George spent the next days relaying their supplies from the McKinley River cabin to the new camp.

While the young men were engaged in freighting, Karstens scouted the way ahead, breaking trail to Lloyd's old Willows Camp on Cache Creek. He then launched a list of chores, cutting firewood and repairing sleds and gear. Stuck and Tatum sewed canvas rucksacks and prepared food for the mountain. One afternoon while making sourdough bread, Tatum dropped the starter, spilling the contents over everything, thus earning his nickname, "The Sourdough Kid."

Despite an endless list of chores, Hudson Stuck seemed quite detached. While everyone else worked, he neglected his tasks and spent what he described as "a lazy day" reading the book *An Economic Interpretation of History*.

While Karstens prospected a trail up Cache Creek to the glacier, Fredson and George hauled equipment, firewood, and poles to the cache at Willows Camp. Stuck stayed in camp, reading, writing, or taking short jaunts to photograph the mountain. One evening he led a sing-along, afterward commenting, "so far it has been a very pleasant party and I think it will so continue."

On April 9, the expedition began the move forward, establishing the climb's base camp at the forks of Cache Creek, just two and a half miles from the Muldrow Glacier. It had taken them less than a month to reach this point from Fairbanks. In contrast, it had taken Belmore Browne and Herschel Parker nearly eleven weeks to reach the same general location, their strength and supplies perilously diminished on the journey up from the coast. Only one other group, that led by Tom Lloyd, had reached this location so easily.

News of the expedition's trek to the mountain spread throughout the region, even to a Native village near Lake Minchumina. One day an Athabascan couple arrived at base camp in order to have their baby baptized. The archdeacon christened the baby and then officially married the couple.

Two days later, Karstens and Stuck broke trail to McGonagall Pass, 5,720 feet, affording Stuck his first look at the "splendid curve of the glacier [descending] from the west and south, with the peak of Denali closing the view." While eating lunch in the warm sun, Stuck spotted the tracks of a snowshoe hare. "What on earth can Brer Rabbit find to interest him on the Glacier?" Stuck mused. "Perhaps he was trying to make the first rabbit ascent of Denali." After recovering a Yukon sled cached by Tom Lloyd, the two returned to camp.

One last important task remained before the assault on the mountain could begin: pemmican making. Browne and Parker had blamed their failure to reach the summit on their choice of canned pemmican. By the time they started for the summit, Browne said, "we were worn down to bone and sinew." He explained in his book that "pemmican was our staff of life; on it we depended for strength and heat to carry us through the toil and cold of our high climb." Other than pemmican, they had packed no other staple to their high camp. At their moment of greatest need, their principal food was inedible.

Learning from others was second nature to Karstens and Stuck. The blueprint for their climb was drawn on the successes and failures of previous expeditions. "The immediate cause of their failure was the mistake of relying upon canned pemmican, hauled with infinite labor from the coast," Stuck said. In what Karstens knew to be "the finest game country in the world," freighting in pemmican of any kind, especially a variety not blended for high-altitude consumption, was inexplicable folly.

Everyone but Tatum and Stuck went hunting. Karstens shot a caribou; Harper killed á sheep. George shot three more caribou. The animals were butchered, the meat and fat boiled in a makeshift cauldron. The boiled meat was finely chopped and diced. Stuck and Tatum mixed the minced meat with rendered fat, marrow, butter, salt, and pepper into two hundred baseball-size orbs, and left them out to freeze. "We made our own pemmican of the choice parts of this tender, juicy meat and we never lost appetite for it or failed to enjoy and assimilate it," Stuck later reported. During the climb, their main food would be a stew of pemmican, rice, and *erbswurst* (a thick German pea soup) served with biscuits.

On April 15, with the spring thaw at hand, Esaias George reluctantly said good-bye to his companions and started with seven dogs on the 125-mile return trip to Nenana. All were sorry to see their "loyal, faithful assistant" leave, but two dog teams were unnecessary now, so George's work was over. He would have to travel at night to make it make back to the mission before breakup rendered the trails impassable.

Karstens continued to prepare for the climb. The heavy basket sleds that the dogs had been pulling would be a burden on the glacier, so he refurbished both Lloyd's toboggan sled and another that Browne and

Parker had left behind. The ice creepers continued to worry him and he made further alterations for use with moccasins. Stuck described the final design as "terribly heavy, clumsy rat-trap affairs" but they later proved indispensable on the iron-hard ice below the summit.

Karstens next fashioned "rough locks" for the snowshoes by lashing a wedge-shaped bar of hardwood underneath each shoe, just above the tread, and screwing calks along the sides. Rough locks prevented the shoes from sliding backward on steep slopes. Finally, Karstens peeled and fire-hardened an eight-foot-long piece of spruce to use as a sounding pole.

On April 16, Karstens and Tatum crossed over McGonagall Pass and down on to the Muldrow. They broke trail four miles up the glacier to where it curved south and the first crevasses fractured the ice. Harper and Fredson relayed the first loads of wood and gear to the summit of the pass, establishing a cache overlooking the glacier. The attack on the mountain had begun.

Karstens breaking trail on the Muldrow Glacier just below the
Lower Icefall, an area largely devoid of dangerous crevasses

18. The Highway of Desire

TOM LLOYD NAMED IT THE "WALL STREET GLACIER" for the slab-sided ridges that line it. Belmore Browne and Herschel Parker simply called it the "McKinley Glacier." Harry Karstens and Hudson Stuck knew it by its official name, the Muldrow. Back in 1898, the topographer Robert Muldrow calculated Mount McKinley's towering height using the rudimentary tools of his time, missing by only 144 feet. This river of ice, named for the topographer, is the most natural, perhaps easiest, route to the summit. Archdeacon Stuck described it as "the highway of desire."

The glacier over the first four miles above McGonagall Pass is relatively smooth with a gentle incline. Where the glacier sweeps south, the way grows steep. Numerous crevasses cleave the surface, with enormous blocks of ice and avalanche rubble impeding movement. Overall, the glacier rises in steps, with fairly level stretches broken by sharp upthrusts. The first serac, now called the Lower Icefall, rises about a thousand feet. Above it, the slope moderates until reaching the second serac, or Great Icefall, which rears 4,000 feet. From there the glacier inclines steeply to its head, a vast basin dominated by a tremendous icefall.

On April 16, Harry Karstens broke trail up the glacier five miles until checked by the yawning crevasses near the base of the Lower

Icefall. Near this point two days later, the expedition established its first camp, elevation roughly 8,000 feet.

After lunch on April 19, Tatum, Karstens, and Stuck roped up with Karstens leading the way. Just above camp they encountered a maze of crevasses—some of them enormous, yawning breaks in the ice, others hidden by drifted, crusted snow. Before each step, Karstens gingerly probed ahead with his sounding pole. As the climbers trudged upward, winding around crevasses and house-size chunks of ice, they marked their trail with willow sticks.

In midafternoon Stuck switched places with Karstens. "I had led for about an hour," he recalled, "while prodding . . . the pole slipped out of my hand and went hurtling down into unknown depths."

Karstens and Tatum stared in dismay. Without the sounding pole, there was no alternative but to turn back. That night Tatum recorded a telling observation in his journal: "Archdeacon Stuck through his desire to display his knowledge and authority, which he did not happen to have, twice took Mr. Karstens place and lost our only good pole." Back in camp, Karstens fashioned a poor substitute out of a tent support.

After losing the sounding pole, Hudson Stuck never again led any significant portion of the climb, his lack of experience obvious even to his loyal cheechako assistant, Tatum.

The next day, while Walter Harper and John Fredson relayed from Cache Creek to the glacier camp, their partners extended the trail upward. Above the Lower Icefall, the three roped climbers found easier going, yet Karstens probed every forward step. They advanced almost three miles, gaining 1,400 feet, to a point near the Great Icefall.

On the way down, Karstens broke through a snow bridge into a crevasse, but was saved by the rope. Many of the snow bridges that they had crossed earlier were thin and unlikely to support dogs and loaded sleds. Some of the crevasses could be stepped over, others were wide and deep; all of them would have to be bridged and reinforced.

All that day Harper and Fredson used the dogs to relay the expedition's gear, food, and firewood. The six dogs had been divided into two teams of three, each team pulling one of the refurbished Yukon toboggan sleds. For these young men, the move from Cache

After climbing to well over 11,000 feet, John Fredson, seventeen, kept the camp at Cache Creek, saving sugar, tea, chocolate, and milk for the returning climbers.

Creek to the glacier camp was little more than typical winter freighting, entailing hard work and patience, but relatively unchallenging. Karstens approved of both boys' dog-handling abilities. They seemed born on dogsleds.

Snow the next day prevented further trailbreaking. While Harper returned to base camp for more firewood, the others stayed in camp.

Stuck continued to fuss with his footgear, cutting caribou skin liners for his felt boots. "The footwear question still bothers me," he wrote. "I do not see how we will keep our feet dry in moccasins or felt shoes, for surely the sun will melt the snow at noon even on the high levels."

After lunch, Karstens's eyes began to pain him, which Stuck believed was due to negligence with his snow glasses the day before. Liberal applications of boracic acid failed to relieve the symptoms. In-grown whiskers also pained Karstens. Old-timers shaved in winter, reducing the risk of frostbite from ice buildup, and grew beards in summer, as a hedge against mosquitoes. For some reason Karstens had decided to sport whiskers, and he was paying a terrible price. Tatum, at Karstens's urging, used a magnifying glass and tweezers to pluck the offending hairs. After yanking just a few, Tatum bolted out of the tent to vomit his breakfast onto the ice.

Snow again the following day slowed the search for a good trail. Walter Harper roped up for the first time ever, all four climbers trudg-ing up the glacier in search of a better route for the dog teams. A snow bridge gave way under Karstens, but again his fall was arrested by the rope. It seemed unimaginable that the novice climbers of 1910 had traversed this glacier unroped without a serious fall.

Prior to the climb, Stuck had described his companions as volun-teers, skilled in snow and ice travel but without climbing experience. "But the nature of snow and ice is not radically changed by lifting them ten or fifteen or even twenty thousand feet up in the air," he explained. The collective experience was now paying off.

Expert winter travelers like Karstens knew how to read snow, judge the lay of a frozen river, and watch for subtle warnings of dan-ger. Karstens looked for undulations or depressions in the snow, the hint of a shadow that might indicate a hazard. Even smooth, invit-ing surfaces could disguise treachery. Picking a route up a glacier was not much different from mushing over suspect lowland trails. For Karstens, falling into a crevasse, protected by a safety line, may have seemed less hazardous than breaking through river ice, with its risk of frozen limbs and gruesome death.

Sobered by his second fall, Karstens carefully assessed his position. Clearly Hudson Stuck was ill-prepared and inexperienced to be the climb leader. "I had to solve the problem of glacier travel," Karstens said later. "None of the others seemed to know a thing about it and the Deacon worst of all. I had to figure out bridging crevasses, good snow, from bad snow. Ice bridges natural and homemade, it surely was some interesting."

Glacier travel, as Karstens found out, is a game of roulette. The location of hidden crevasses can never be gauged precisely. The strength and durability of snow bridges may vary with time of day and temperature. The climbers could never let down their guard against sudden falls. They had to believe that their precautions were equal to the hazards.

None of the climbers, with the exception of Stuck, had previously tied into a climbing rope. Although they relied on their ropes for protection, their skills were rudimentary at best. Ropes, however, do not guarantee safety. The proper use of them—knots, spacing, and technique—is paramount. Most falls stop in split seconds, but it takes a team effort to react and arrest a fall.

A sudden fall can result in serious injury, even death. Broken limbs and concussions are common injuries. A rescue might take hours to effect. Crevasses tend to gradually narrow as they deepen, and a climber can wedge in so tightly as to be almost inextricable. The upper portion of a crevasse can be lined with soft snow and be unclimbable. Getting a victim past an overhanging eave can pose a major challenge.

There is no indication that Karstens and Stuck practiced, or even discussed, rescue or extraction techniques. In some expedition photos, their ropes and knots appear to be used correctly, in others, incorrectly. The sudden shock of a fall was taken up en masse, their combined strength and body weights stopping the plunge. Team effort yanked the fallen up and out of the crevasse.

Their simple technique carried substantial risk. Pulling can saw the rope deeply into the lip of the hole and bind it, compounding the difficulty of extraction. A climber pulled against an overhang needs help to get out. Many modern climbers prefer mechanical ascenders and devices, rather than hauling, to extract themselves from a crevasse.

In light of their inexperience, it is remarkable that the Stuck-Karstens climbers had so few falls, and none that resulted injury. The previous year, Browne and LaVoy had multiple close calls, but were saved each time by their rope, Herschel Parker providing the expertise missing in 1913.

It took several days for Karstens to unravel and mark a route suitable for the dogs. Stuck and Tatum marked his winding trail with willow sticks. Hours were spent building bridges stout enough for the dog teams. Spruce poles were laid across the chasms and covered with layers of snow.

Near what is now called the Great Icefall, the glacier pinches down between the slab-sided ridges to about a half-mile wide. On the right, or north side, of the glacier, a long section of heavily crevassed ice passes below the sheer slopes of Pioneer Ridge. On the left, or south side, two peaks draped with ice, now named Carpe and Koven, loom over the glacier. The slopes between the two peaks are a dangerous avalanche zone. Karstens, like the men in the previous two expeditions, chose the left side of the glacier for the ascent, as the ice seemed smoother and less riven by crevasses.

In quick succession, Karstens broke two sounding poles, the untempered, dry spruce unable to withstand the constant prodding and bending. Moving past the Great Icefall, Karstens switched the lead with Harper, a quick learner open to direction. It "was very interesting and exciting for a while," Harper said, "but after standing around and getting one's feet cold, one gets very weary." They spent an inordinate amount of time building a long snow bridge. "My feet grew miserably cold waiting," said Stuck, echoing Harper. Later, back in camp, while Tatum heated the daily stew, Harper made dumplings and baked a pie. No canned pemmican or hardtack for these Alaskans.

In late evening the next day, the team reached the head of the glacier, which they estimated to be 11,500 feet (actually 10, 800 feet). After returning to camp from the twelve-hour trek, the indefatigable Harper decided to walk another eight miles to Cache Creek to spend the night with Fredson in preparation for another round of freighting.

Early on April 25, the climbers again left camp for the head of the glacier. A brisk subzero headwind cut like a knife. Karstens, Harper, and Tatum took turns leading. Even on the marked trail, they used

Karstens, left, and Harper, on the belay, wait for Tatum to pass up a block of snow for the snow bridge they are constructing over a crevasse.

their sounding pole before moving forward. Use of the pole was physically too much for Stuck, "with Walter kind enough to take my turn," he wrote.

The glacier above the Great Icefall rises steeply for some three miles before ending at a stupendous 4,000-foot icefall that rises to the basin above. The icefall, now named the Harper Icefall, is unclimbable except by technical experts. In midday the team reached the base of the northeast ridge, which circumvents the Harper Icefall. Both the Lloyd party and Browne and Parker had camped nearby for the attack on the ridge. "[The head of the Muldrow] is a great basin with hanging glaciers all around and the Great Icefall coming from between the North and South Peaks," Karstens explained later to Charles Sheldon. "Our ascent was a continual round of sounding for crevasses, some being covered by a light coating of snow which falls in as soon as one touches it. Some you can distinguish from surrounding snow by darker shadows and others can only be told by feeling for them. They range in width from a foot to fifty feet and hundreds of feet in depth."

A search for Lloyd's Tunnel Camp and a cache left by Browne and Parker turned up nothing, not surprising in a zone that gets fifty feet of snow per year. Before turning back, Karstens and Stuck agreed on a site for their high camp, well outside the limit of avalanche danger. They'd already seen thundering slides and they were taking no chances now. During the ascent, Karstens had crossed snowshoe hare tracks at 8,000 feet and again at 9,000 feet, miles from any browse. He failed to say if the hare was still on the ascent, or returning from the summit.

At the foot of the icefall, the sky was clear but the wind fierce. When the climbers started down at five o'clock, the glacier below was shrouded in dense clouds. As soon as they entered the mists, they were engulfed in heavy snow. Much of the trail was already obliterated, visibility nil. They safely followed their willow markers back to camp.

At dinner that evening, Hudson Stuck, done in by thirteen hours of hard slogging, was uncharacteristically quiet. "I realized already that the climbing of this mountain is going to tax my strength to the uttermost," he wrote, "and that I am fortunate in having those with me who will save me all they can."

Tatum also recorded a hint of his own malaise: homesickness. His emotional upset would worsen with each passing day, especially when storms or terrain stymied activity. Karstens, too, had physical complaints. He had hurt his wrist while breaking trail with Tatum, but did not speak of his injury. Although he had gingerly shaved, his face was still a mess. Dating back to before Charles Sheldon's time, Karstens also suffered from a chronic digestive disorder that not only was painful but ruined his sleep and disposition. Intestinal parasites, a typical malady of professional dog drivers, may have been the problem. Neither man was helped by the elixirs or powders doled out by Stuck.

Hudson Stuck's weakness was so apparent the next day that his partners left him behind when they led the dogs beyond the icefall for the first time. Uncertain of the trail, the climbers took only firewood to cache at the head of the glacier. Karstens and Fredson escorted one team, Harper and Tatum the other. One roped climber led the dogs while another followed just behind them. Progress over the buried trail was agonizingly slow, with both men and dogs pulling for all their worth. The advance was measured by yards instead of miles.

Some of the snow bridges proved inadequate for the dog teams and had to be strengthened or relocated. A bridge gave way and the lead dog, Snowball, fell into a relatively shallow crevasse. Harper was lowered into it and he and Snowball were pulled to safety. A snow bridge also broke under the dog Tace, suspending him in harness above the chasm. He too was yanked to safety, but the trail had to be rerouted to firm snow. By late afternoon, the teams had only reached the halfway point. The firewood was cached and the climbers headed back to camp, stopping along the way to reinforce some of the bridges.

Early that morning, Karstens had lashed out at Harper. "There was an unpleasant incident between K. and Walter," Stuck recorded. "The latter, in his careless way, leaving things just where he had used them and K. very roughly reprimanded him with threats. I am sorry the boy's feelings were hurt but he needed the calling down." If Harper bore resentment, he never showed it, doing more than his share of the day's work.

Two more loads of firewood were hauled to the makeshift cache the next day, the trail having hardened during the subzero night. Sunday afternoon was spent in religious observance and camp chores.

Through alternating days of snow and subzero cold, blistering sun and wind, the relay of firewood and gear continued. "I think I have never seen any other region where the weather changes with such frequency," Stuck said. "The Muldrow Glacier seems to have a climate of its own." Only with the sled dogs could the expedition's entire outfit and firewood be transported so effectively between storms.

On the morning of April 28, Karstens again exploded, this time at Stuck, berating the archdeacon for what he saw as laziness and his sometimes imperious behavior. By Karstens's estimation, everyone but Stuck had been "drilling" hard to forge a trail up the glacier. Whenever Stuck stayed behind to "lay in the tent," Karstens regarded it as a breach in Stuck's promise to "get in and drill" like everyone else. By now Karstens had had enough, and he hotly "shamed [Stuck] as [he] never wish to shame another man and he got out that morning and worked like a good one." Later Karstens would write Charles Sheldon that "what I wanted was him to live up to his agreement."

For his part, the archdeacon blamed Karstens's outburst on "his bad stomach" and resentment over a firewood contract with Saint Matthew's Church that had gone bad, something Stuck had no control over. Stuck seemed unable to grasp the simple truth: the climb agreement called for equal effort, and by delegating so many simple tasks to others, and sending the camp cook, Tatum, out in his place, Stuck was breaking his word, which to Karstens was a solemn trust. "I am so dependent upon him in this expedition that I have to put up with any bad temper he may show," Stuck wrote that night. "I like him and have always liked him and he must be taken with his limitations."

Everyone but Fredson then made two trips to the halfway cache, stashing more firewood and gear. With a rope over his shoulder, Stuck pulled as hard as anyone, teaming with Harper on both trips to the cache. After the first relay, Karstens said he took Stuck aside and explained exactly how he felt and "to quit his whining and get in and help himself. We were out roughing it not at a first class hotel. He promised to do better but forgot all about it the next day." At day's end, Karstens made a note in his own journal: "Deacon on rope, relieved my depression."

On the last day of April, the five men and dogs pushed five miles through heavy snow to the head of the glacier and cached 250 pounds of gear at the site chosen for their next camp.

Now their entire outfit, except minimal camp equipment, was either at the halfway cache or at the head of the glacier. The next morning, weather permitting, they planned to move camp to the high cache.

A storm moved in overnight, dumping several inches of snow. Yet again, the trail had to be broken and packed down. After striking camp, the climbers pushed slowly upward, trudging from one willow marker to the next. By midafternoon, men and dogs were spent. "I think I never worked harder in my life," Stuck exclaimed. Heavy snow forced a stop at the halfway cache, where they pitched their tent in the shelter of a slab of ice. Tatum assisted with dinner and other chores but seemed unable to shake his growing malaise.

Dawn broke clear, calm, and cold, −13°F, ideal conditions for breaking trail and freighting. The first relay, two sledloads of firewood, took most of the morning, with one man breaking trail ahead of the dogs, the others pulling. All morning the climbers labored upward, reaching their high cache by midday. There they took a much-needed break, drinking hot cocoa from their thermos bottles and snacking on doughnuts. Karstens and Stuck smoked their pipes.

Several hours later as they neared the cache with a second load of freight, they saw smoke. Stuck stared in disbelief. "Had some mysterious climber come over from the other side of the mountain? Had he discovered our wood and our grub, and perhaps starving, kindled a fire . . . smoke must mean man." The climbers pressed forward over an intervening rise. "When we came in sight of the cache," Karstens recalled, "we could see it on fire. We left the loads and made the quickest time we could and found nearly everything that we had cached there, except the wood, burned up.

The cause of the fire slowly dawned on them. "It is probable that as we sat smoking at noon a match was dropped on one of the silk tents and it smoldered unnoticed and was put back in the cache and covered with the canvas still smoldering," Stuck said, adding that he was not "downcast. . . . It will delay us, and that is unfortunate." But by Karstens's account, Stuck despaired. "The Deacon started yelling we were ruined until I told him to keep still till we found out how badly we were set back."

A quick inventory revealed the loss of the lightweight climbing tents, socks, spare clothes, an ax, and Karstens's camera and film, as well as most of the film for Stuck's camera, and staples like flour, biscuits, and doughnuts. A huge blow, but with ingenuity, not the disaster first feared.

"All the sugar was gone, all our powdered milk and our baking powder; a case of pilot bread, our dried apples, our dried fruit and all sorts of other supplies were burned," Stuck recounted. "[Afterward] we were without sugar for a month and without bread for a couple of weeks." By pure chance, the pemmican, sausage, milk chocolate, and other essentials reserved for the higher elevations were still below.

Also safe were the expedition's instruments—thermometer, mercurial barometer, boiling-point hypsometer, and prismatic compass—with which Stuck determined the height of the camps and would hopefully use on the summit.

A somber party returned to the midway camp that afternoon. "Who would think of a fire on a glacier at 11,500 feet in the air?" Karstens wrote that night. "Think of the months of labor getting those things up there. Even with the loss we are going on."

On May 3, the expedition broke camp and pushed ahead, and in early afternoon established their camp at the head of the glacier. With only one more load of gear to ferry up from the midway camp, they now could take stock of their loss and refit for the attack on the northeast ridge. It had taken eighteen days of struggle to reach the head of the glacier. By comparison, Browne and Parker, using just one dog team, had freighted six hundred pounds of food and gear to this same location in just ten days.

Much has been written about the impacts of the 1912 earthquake on the upper portion of the mountain, but it is likely that it also affected the glacier. Browne and Parker had witnessed monumental avalanches sweeping the range, without question dumping tons of snow and ice rubble onto the Muldrow. Natural snow bridges must have collapsed in the cataclysmic shake-up. The glacial surface in 1913 was likely very different from that encountered the previous year.

The temperature had been −13°F at the outset of the day's march, but quickly the heat became intolerable. At altitude, the sun blasting off the snow and ice can blister skin and cause severe overheating. "It was a terribly tough grind, coming up the glacier," Stuck wrote, "but before we were halfway up the sun's heat was intense and we all suffered from it." Karstens could not agree more, his face scorched and "in awful condition."

The exhausted, dehydrated climbers spent the afternoon setting up camp; building an igloo to store their supplies; and walling their tent with blocks of hard snow. They broke up wooden and cardboard boxes for tent flooring, crisscrossing the pieces over the packed snow.

Although Hudson Stuck lamented the time it had taken to ascend the glacier, he had realized one part of his cherished dream. Despite the fire, he had one month's worth of food and firewood marshaled at the base of the ridge, the route to the summit now at hand. Writing in his journal that night, he noted that no dogs on earth had ever been taken so high. He seemed unaware that both previous Muldrow expeditions had also mushed dogs to this point.

The day quickly cooled. "Just as soon as the sun went behind the north ridge of the north peak," Harper wrote, "the thermometer went to 26 below zero." The firewood, freighted twenty miles from the Clearwater camp, was, according to Stuck, "worth its weight in gold."

The next morning Stuck insisted that Karstens stay in the tent to protect his face from the glare. Everyone else descended to the midway cache to retrieve the remaining supplies. The day was a repeat of the last—subzero cold followed by desertlike heat. "It scarcely seemed possible that surrounded by nothing but ice and snow it could be so hot," Stuck exclaimed. "Anyone who thinks that the climbing of Denali is a picnic is badly mistaken."

The final relay took just four hours, and when the party returned with the heavily laden sleds, they found that Karstens had "an excellent dinner ready." While Karstens spent the afternoon out of the sun, again tinkering with the ice creepers, Stuck investigated and salvaged what he could from the ruins of the fire. Later, Harper and Fredson set out on the long trail back to base camp for dog food, canvas to sew into tents, a reserve of sugar and food, and "what socks can be found for *all* our socks are burned."

Hudson Stuck estimated that the fire would delay their ascent by two days. Although the setback seemed onerous, they all knew that from this location Anderson and Taylor had climbed to the summit of the North Peak in a single day and that Browne and Parker had conquered the northeast ridge in under a week. Despite the fire, both Stuck and Karstens expected a similar rapid ascent. They were dreadfully mistaken.

Karstens leading Tatum on the final descent
of the northeast ridge

19. The Shattered Ridge

"THE GREAT PEAKS WERE BRILLIANT in the morning light," Hudson Stuck wrote. "Far away to the north the whole wide prospect of tangled mountain ranges was illuminated and even in the distance where the great flats of the Tanana valley spread out, the sun was lighting up the scene." Inspired by his reading of a psalm, he saw a divine touch in his camp at the head of the Muldrow.

For days the weather had been "glorious", the new camp at the base of the ridge "comfortable" and pleasant. Despite the surrounding grandeur, however, a sense of unease gnawed away at both Stuck and Karstens. The northeast ridge looked nothing like "the steep but practicable snow slope" described by Belmore Browne. Instead of elation at achieving a major goal, they felt uneasy and doubtful.

On May 5, while Karstens stayed in camp to salvage gear and again repair ice creepers, Stuck and Tatum roped up to make the first attempt to gain the summit of the ridge. Instead of the "easy scramble up a snowbank" as Browne had described it, their way was blocked by ice-encrusted rock and iron-hard snow. Stymied, they traversed beneath the ridge before finally gaining the top. From the summit, they gaped at the Traleika Glacier far below and the jumble of ridges and peaks to the south.

A view of the route above was daunting. "Difficulties appeared that were not so apparent below," Stuck noted. "There is a bad break in the ridge that may not have existed when Parker climbed a year ago, but may have been caused by the great earthquake. . . . We must try to strike the ridge above that break; yet that will be difficult." Herschel Parker had told Stuck that the ridge's 30- to 40-degree slope was without major technical challenges. Although the view up the ridge was limited, the archdeacon saw enough to know that their work was only just beginning.

Late that evening Walter Harper and John Fredson returned from Cache Creek with supplies and material necessary to replicate some of the items lost in the fire. This last relay, in good weather and with a marked, solid trail, took just nine hours, ending the freighting phase of the expedition.

The next day Harper and Fredson, with Stuck's permission, climbed to the ridge for a view of the world below. While they were gone, Karstens cut a sled cover into sections for a six-by-seven-foot tent, Stuck scissored a sleeping bag liner into socks, and Tatum baked biscuits to replace what had been burned. They still needed to make a climbing tent, a shelter tent for reading instruments, more socks, and other items. The repairs and jury-rigging would take days. Only a few rolls of film were spared by the fire. The lost film and cameras were irreplaceable.

Two days after their first foray to the ridge top, Stuck and Tatum tried to find another route to the top but without success. As they were descending in late afternoon, a tremendous avalanche roared down from the icefall, "500 feet of ice carved from the great hanging glacier [that] threw dense clouds of snow 1000 or more feet into the air."

The next day Tatum and Stuck both complained that the altitude had affected their sleep, although they should have been acclimated by now. Karstens and Harper seemed unaffected. Was it really the altitude? Throughout his adult life, Stuck had been plagued by insomnia, his friends relating his occasional irascibility to sleep deprivation. Tatum's homesickness had been growing more intense, his depression deepening.

On May 8, Karstens, Fredson, and Harper set out for the ridge. Karstens ignored the route taken by Stuck and forged straight up a gully to the top, cutting steps the entire way. Once on top, the climbers proceeded slowly along the crest to a jumble of ice shattered by the 1912 earthquake. Cautiously Karstens flanked the break, his team chopping steps in the hard snow beneath it.

"There is no doubt in my mind that the shake up of last year has broken up the snow and left the ridge in the condition it is in," Karstens explained. "Great blocks of ice stand on top of the ridge . . . blocks stand over one another which look as though they would tumble over by whispering at them." By Harper's reckoning, they had climbed halfway up the ridge before turning back, declaring in his journal that "cutting steps is a long, tiresome business."

Tatum and Stuck had stayed in camp to finish sewing the tents but kept a worried eye on the climbers. "My occupation all day long was chiefly watching them," Stuck said. "I grew very anxious." Stuck's anxiety was not misplaced. Karstens had never tackled anything like this before, and his climbing partners were two young Athabascans, born and raised on the Yukon *flats*. There's no indication, however, that either young man faltered in the slightest way on their foray into unknown high-elevation terrain.

By day's end, Fredson had reached his high point on the mountain, perhaps 12,500 feet or better. The next day he had to take the team down to base camp, their dog food in high camp all but exhausted. On May 9, Tatum and Stuck accompanied Fredson and the dogs to a point below the Great Icefall and beyond the most dangerous section of crevasses. When Stuck bade Fredson good-bye, he told him to look for their return in two weeks. "Johnny has been a good, faithful boy to me and his fidelity shall not be forgotten," Stuck wrote. "We would all have liked to keep him with us."

On the ridge, Karstens and Harper found it "ruined" for good climbing, with "very slow work cutting steps at difficult angles." Karstens located a flat spot at 12,100 feet to use as a cache or possible campsite. Progress up the ridge was hard-won. Tremendous cornices of snow, which he said were "liable to break off at any time," awed Karstens. Undaunted, Karstens and Harper worked ever higher. That evening in camp Harper told Stuck that the way ahead looked even worse.

A "high boisterous wind" the following day pinned the climbers in camp, an advance on the knife-edged ridge impossible. The archdeacon declared it "Whit Sunday" and began the morning with psalms.

Karstens leads Tatum on the perilous ascent of the northeast ridge;
parts of the overhanging ice and snow were hacked away to allow for
the passage of climbers burdened with heavy packs.

After services, Karstens fashioned an alcohol stove out of a piece of can and some scrap metal salvaged from the fire. By afternoon he was boiling tea. Stuck spent the afternoon working on his book, reading the Bible, and dictating passages to Harper. Tatum read the Bard, for his ongoing study of *Henry IV*. Evening prayers were augmented with lessons for Whit Sunday, Harper and Tatum reading the passages.

Throughout the climb, the daily routine included morning and evening prayers and religious instruction for Harper and Tatum. Although Karstens was an Episcopalian, he found confinement with what he called "the three sky pilots" somewhat draining.

The next morning, despite snow and low clouds, the four climbers started out with heavy packs to establish a cache on the ridge. Stuck's first foray up Karstens's route revealed the difficulties already conquered. On the ridge "we began an intricate twisting in and out amongst the huge blocks of ice of its crest; there is no longer a snow slope on the ridge; it is a jumbled mass of rocks and ice with snow lying at an unstable angle on either side. We passed the gap by steps cut almost perpendicularly in the great ice gable."

The climbers inched along, visibility seldom more than a few yards. Even the powerful Harper found the climbing difficult. "We had heavy packs on our backs," he wrote, "and we toiled up the ridge gasping for breath."

After depositing their thirty-pound packs at the cache site, the team continued upward into the snow and roiling mist. Karstens and Harper led the way, taking turns cutting steps with their axes and shovels. Stuck found the process "slow and toilsome."

A short distance above the cache, a house-size chunk of ice blocked further advance. The block, "as big as a two-story house and weighing hundreds of tons," perched precariously on the ridge, leaning toward the abyss. A few well-placed blows from Karstens's ice ax sent the monster "tumbling thousands of feet below," where it exploded unseen with the roar of a cannon.

Now the ascent became very steep and movement slowed to a crawl. Dense, driving snow turned the climbers back, Harper "skillfully and carefully" leading the way down.

On May 12, the climbers again ascended to the cache in falling snow and visibility of less than fifty feet. Just as they started, Karstens erupted at Tatum for his dawdling and fussing with inconsequentials. The team made it as far as the cache, deposited their loads, and then retreated, further advance impossible. On the way down, the beating snow made it difficult to even see their feet, the descent more perilous than the morning climb. "We found our trail entirely wiped out," Stuck recalled, "and we were sometimes at a loss for the direction of camp."

It was treacherous going, with sheer slopes dropping away on either side. Each person had to move carefully and precisely. If one man fell, all four might be yanked down. Again, Harper, under Karstens's direction, led most of the way. "I thanked God heartily that we got safely down from the ridge for snow had already begun to slide down its steep slopes," Stuck wrote that night.

Now at least the expedition had all its mountain food, the mercurial barometer, and fuel for two weeks, stowed at the high cache. To advance further they needed an extended break in the weather, but they didn't get it. More snow that night and again the next day kept them in camp. Stormbound, Karstens worked on plans for a boat he wanted to build, Stuck drilled Harper with diction from Shakespeare, and Tatum again studied *Henry IV.* To pass the time, Stuck outlined his book about the first ascent, listing chapters, title, and publishing details. He was not unaware of the absurdity of planning a book on an outcome yet to be determined.

Stuck was worried that enforced confinement would exacerbate Karstens's already bad temper. Karstens liked to read—just not the books on economics, religion, philosophy, and the classics that his companions carried. In Fairbanks, rather than a saloon, his main hangout was Hall's bookstore. It was absolutely true that Karstens was a man of action who did not fare well when confined indoors. He would rather work than read, no matter how strenuous the task.

Another day of storms kept the party tentbound, the temperature dropping to twenty below. Tatum, already suffering from homesickness, now complained of tonsillitis and neuralgia. Nothing in the medical kit seemed to help. "Oh, for good weather," pleaded Karstens.

The morning of May 15 dawned clear, calm, and cold, the camp buried in eight inches of new snow. The ailing Tatum stayed behind while his companions tackled the ridge. On the crest, Harper took the lead, forging ahead one shoveled step at a time.

By midday the climbers had exceeded their previous high point and proceeded through a scatter of pinnacles and ice blocks. At day's end, they stopped and tried to visually parse out the route ahead. Stuck pointed to a rock pinnacle at the head of the ridge, an outcrop he named Browne's Tower, and described the route from there into the basin between the north and south summits.

"It is quite impossible to identify any of the places mentioned by Belmore Browne on this ridge," Stuck wrote. "The only 'col' is the prominent rock at least 2500' above the glacier. This we have called the 'Parker Col', or 'Parker Pass.' The rest of the ridge is simply a jumble of rocks and ice with precipitous slopes on either hand." (A *col* is a gap or

Karstens belays while watching Harper cut steps around an obstacle, on the ascent of the earthquake-fractured northeast ridge.

pass in a ridge. The reference here is somewhat inaccurate, because it was neither a gap nor a pass but something more akin to a shoulder or flat spot in the ridge below the tower of rock.)

That evening Stuck and Karstens sketched out a plan for the next day. Karstens and Harper would push ahead to Parker Pass while Stuck, and Tatum, if recovered from his illness, would relay loads to the cache.

"Dirty weather" the next morning dashed their high expectations, wind and snow ushering in five days of frustration. Trail was broken and rebroken, steps chopped and rechopped, new snow shoveled from "staircases" and then reshoveled. An ascent that one day took two hours, took six the next. Karstens and Harper took turns leading and hacking at the ice and snow, while Tatum and Stuck remained in camp.

"Tatum's tonsillitis kept him awake all night and we left him in the tent again today," Stuck recorded. "I grow a little uneasy about him: what shall we do with him if he does not quickly recover, I do not know."

Breaks in the weather would lure the climbers out and onto the ridge, and then quickly close in again, imperiling them in exposed positions. "The Ridge looks easy from a distance," Karstens wrote, "but *Oh! my.*"

By fits and starts, the high-altitude gear and rations were relayed to the high cache. Karstens was positive that given a break in the weather, he and Harper could reach Parker Pass in one day. Good weather was not in the offing. "Shoveling out steps is becoming monotonous," Karstens said.

The "comfortable camp" became unpleasant in the continuing cold and storm. The tent, despite the surrounding ice walls, shook in the wind, and the dwindling supply of firewood meant a cold camp, everyone taking to their sleeping bags and robes to stay warm. During dinner one night, the Primus stove, which would be the sole and critical cooking appliance for the summit attempt, overheated, melting some of the solder holding it together. "Karstens with his usual ingenuity has repaired the primus stove," Stuck noted.

Instead of getting better, Tatum's condition worsened, a gnawing headache and rheumatism in his shoulder adding to his woes.

High wind and blowing snow prevented movement on Trinity Sunday, May 18. The day dragged by. Stuck again dictated passages from the Bible for Harper to memorize; Tatum slept or read from his prayer book; and Karstens snored through the long, slow hours. The lack of exercise affected everyone, Tatum more so than the others. Stuck tried to bolster Tatum's sagging spirits and promised help with his future studies. The archdeacon's patience and somewhat forced good humor, however, began to falter as "time passes unbearably tedious to me."

While the huddled climbers listened to avalanches thundering into the basin, they were acutely aware of the season. By the third week in May, the ice had gone out on the Yukon and Tanana Rivers, the luxury stern-wheelers again plying the waters loaded with freight and miners returning from Outside. Waterfowl and songbirds winged in by the thousands to nest, and the first moose and caribou calves were gingerly testing their wobbly legs. Bear cubs trailed their mothers; wolf pups whined for food. Spring flowers sprouted on the greening tundra below.

"It has its ridiculous side," Stuck wrote, "this enforced detention of ours. . . . Think of four men deliberately pitching a camp on the ice of a glacier . . . and then sitting down in it day after day, killing time as best they can. . . . And Heaven only knows how much longer we must remain where we are."

The dawn of May 21 brought a break in the weather. Karstens and Harper awoke at four o'clock in the morning and after breakfast, headed for the ridge. Again digging out the drifted snow from every step, they labored for six hours to reach the cache. The effects of the previous days of confinement, coupled with the altitude, shortness of breath, and fatigue, hampered their advance. By day's end, they'd reached a point 300 feet beyond their previous high point. By the time they turned back that day, Karstens was certain that they could reach the pass in less than a day given a break in the weather. "But oh! How hard the work was of clearing the steps," Harper wrote. "It took us six solid hours to make one mile."

Back in camp, Tatum and Stuck dragged all the bedding into the sun to dry. Stuck then spent the morning exercising, "marching up and down a promenade of 35 paces or so."

Clouds, wind, and snow the following morning again dashed expectations. The previous day's work would have to be done over again. "If only we could get the steps finished up to the unbroken part of the ridge," Stuck said, "we could probably progress. But the step cutting ends with some of the steepest and most broken parts of the ridge left to pass."

Tatum seemed better one day, then worse the next. One night he woke everyone with a fit of vomiting. Karstens and Stuck confronted him the next morning and offered to take him down to base camp. Tatum said that altitude was not the issue, just an illness he believed would soon clear up. He apparently made no mention of the depression, or "blues," dogging him. Karstens thought Tatum's malaise was simply due to confinement and lack of activity. Stuck was not so sure: "He wants to go up [but] it will be a dreadful business if he gets sick there and may knock the expedition out."

Now indigestion began to bother them all—altitude, or poorly cooked beans, wreaking havoc. Night cramps and diarrhea ruined everyone's sleep.

More snow on May 23 again altered plans. With growing frustration, Stuck suggested moving camp to the ridge cache and obviating the need for repeated step clearing. Karstens jumped at the idea, and everyone hurriedly packed their rucksacks. Born of frustration, their joint decision was hasty and ill-advised.

At 11:30 AM, the climbers left camp. A half hour later, they were back again. Even before reaching the base of the ridge, Stuck "realized that we were attempting altogether too much. . . . I told Karstens that I did not believe I could get my pack up to that ridge and after a little consultation it was decided to go back."

The next day, under light snow, the four climbers again started for the ridge, but this time carrying half the weight as the day before. In four and one-half hours, digging out every step, they reached the 12,100-foot cache site and wearily dropped their packs.

They dug down into the loose snow and pitched their handmade six-by-seven-foot tent, building a wall around the perimeter with blocks of snow that Harper and Karstens had cut from the drifts. In the afternoon, they made a second relay, bringing everything but their bedding and Primus. "Tomorrow we will come up . . . rain or shine," Harper wrote.

After Sunday morning prayers on May 25, the four left their glacier camp for the ridge, fervently hoping that they would not return until their final descent. Without steps to cut, the pace was brisk, so much so that Stuck called for frequent halts. They reached their new ridge camp by noon and settled in, the thermometer in the bright sun reading slightly above freezing, the warmest day in months. "It is certainly the hardest work I ever did in my life," Stuck wrote in his pocket diary, "and my breath up here, under any exertion whatever, is terribly short." He also noted feeling light-headed, or "giddy," a symptom of the altitude.

That afternoon, Karstens and Harper prospected the way ahead, cutting steps as they went. By four o'clock they were 500 feet above the new camp but only 100 feet beyond the previous high point. The work of cutting steps was slow, difficult, and dangerous. They had hoped to reach the unbroken snow at the head of the ridge, but after seven rigorous hours, returned to camp, fully confident of reaching the pass the next day. "Some very bad places," Karstens wrote, "chopping steps in ice today. The col a little nearer tonight."

For his part, Walter Harper was very happy to have moved camp to the ridge, remarking that it was "with a great deal of pleasure and satisfaction that we won't have to come down the old ridge that we were all tired of, and I specially for I am at the head always cleaning steps. I think I know every step of the way nearly."

Despite being warmer on the ridge, no one slept much that night due to indigestion. In that "abominably overcrowded" tent, if one man thrashed about or had to get up, it disturbed them all. The tent reeked of unwashed bodies, wet wool, damp animal skins, and scorched food.

Karstens's sudden illness the next morning again crushed hopes of reaching the pass. Stuck allowed Harper and Tatum to go on ahead while he and Karstens stayed in camp. The fine, calm weather was too much to pass up, yet sending Tatum was a calculated risk, since he had had the least experience on the ridge. Stuck kept an anxious eye on the two young men as they crept slowly higher. By midday, drifting clouds and intervening shoulders of ice hid much of their progress.

By late evening, Harper and Tatum had advanced some distance but were still shy of the final earthquake cleavage and the smooth slope beyond. "I wanted to go on," Harper reported, "no matter how late it was but Mr. Tatum got cold so we returned."

The following day, Karstens led Harper in the continuing attack on the ridge. Moments after leaving the tent, they disappeared in dense cloud, leaving Stuck and Tatum literally in the dark.

Neither Stuck nor Karstens had slept much the previous night. The inside of the tent was covered in frost and the slightest movement triggered an icy shower. Tatum had experienced a vivid dream of a girl back home and his father's death, causing him to cry in his sleep, even rousing Harper, who almost always slept soundly. The next morning, Tatum was despondent, "blue and ill at ease." In his journal, he recorded the source of his melancholia: "I rather fear climbing the ridge with Archdeacon but I will as it is my duty."

As worried as Hudson Stuck was about Tatum, he had no fears about Harper. "I envy that boy his splendid rugged strength and adaptability." He also fretted about Karstens: "His indisposition yesterday was mental rather than physical: the tedium of the undertaking is wearing on him and I seem to get on his nerves particularly." Stuck was entirely correct. Harry Karstens fared poorly when confined or constrained. Yet Stuck seemed unaware of the strain Karstens was under. As climbing leader, Karstens daily made countless decisions under extreme conditions and high risk. He knew by now he had not one, but two, weak, inexperienced companions to shepherd up a dangerous and lethal mountain, with only one person, Walter Harper, to count on. "Walter was a good one, 21 years old, strong and fearless and as fine and loveable disposition as I ever saw in a man," he would later tell Charles Sheldon. "He was my main standby. . . . I only saw him falter one time."

From Karstens's point of view, Stuck was too weak to lead, or cut steps, and Tatum "too green" for anything but packing. He had expected more from his partner. "I took it for granted that [Stuck] was a good man as he surely had traveled enough," he reflected later. He had not signed on as a *guide* but as an *equal partner*, the discrepancy glaring on the struggle up the ridge.

Despite Stuck's disquiet, he fully recognized Karstens's determination: "He will never give up so long as the slightest chance of success exists. He has that sort of dogged determination."

That day, Karstens and Harper tackled the most dangerous segment of the ascent. During the 1912 earthquake, an immense chunk of ice had sheared away from the ridge, creating an uncrossable cleavage. A huge slab of ice blocked the downhill side of the cleavage. On either side of the base of the slab, loose snow dropped sharply away. The blocking ice was nearly vertical, with a right-hand turn midway to the gap itself. At that point, the ice bulged out into an overhang.

To circumvent the block of ice, a long traverse had to be made around it. Karstens lead the way, hacking steps into the block of ice itself. One misstep would result in a fall, his life dependent on Harper's quick reactions.

"I took the lead myself always keeping Walter or myself on safe footing," Karstens explained later to Charles Sheldon. "I [usually] kept Walter in the lead while I studied out the route ahead but at times he would not understand what I wanted so it was easier to go ahead myself than try and explain, not casting any reflections on Walter as he would have gone anywhere I told him."

The steps had to be oversize, the wall itself hewn away at shoulder height to accommodate climbers with packs. The exposure for the full team, burdened by packs, would be severe.

Late that afternoon, after hours of stress and toil, Harper and Karstens finally reached the smooth snow above the cleavage. The way was now open to the pass. Just as the two reached the unbroken slope, they heard a great shout from below and saw Stuck waving at them from camp. They responded with a cheer of their own. "This is the best thing I have been able to record for three weeks," Stuck wrote. "It means that we can now advance to the basin, and gives renewed and invigorated hope of reaching the summit."

At the foot of the snow slope, Karstens found remnants of Browne and Parker's camp from the previous year. "It looked as though it had been left yesterday," Harper said. "There were empty cracker boxes and raisin boxes."

The climbers briefly celebrated on their return to camp. Karstens told of some "hair-raising passages," but the route to the top of the ridge was open. Everyone except Tatum slept peacefully that night. "The feeling of uncertainty of what lies ahead," Belmore Browne said the year before, "is what makes an attempt on Mount McKinley as exciting as the heart could desire." And, until today, neither Karstens nor Stuck knew if the *ridge* was even surmountable.

Early on May 28, despite a keen, slicing wind, Harper and Karstens set out for Parker Pass. Stuck and Tatum packed their rucksacks for a relay up the ridge. "I feel very blue and ill at ease," Tatum wrote, "and nervous." Nevertheless, Tatum and Stuck safely relayed their packs to a point below the cleavage, caching them near what Stuck called "a sensational traverse around ice cliffs that leads to the bold cleft face of the ridge."

Back in camp, Tatum tried to start the Primus stove to make tea. In the process, he broke off the wire pick used to clean the fuel orifice.

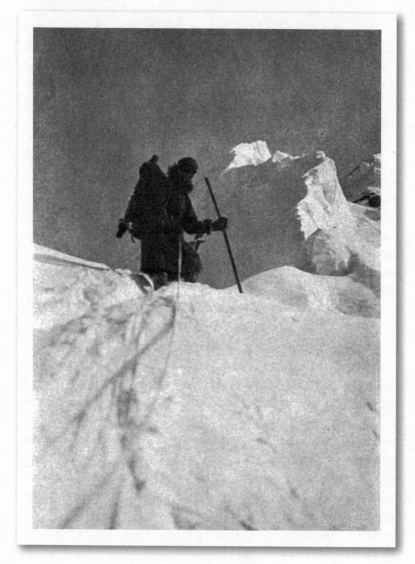

Karstens on the ridge

Stuck exploded, haranguing Tatum. How many times had he warned him to be careful? On the verge of success, they now faced ignominious defeat. "This is the worst accident that can befall the primus," Stuck complained. If irreparable, "it might easily knock our expedition on the head for we could not proceed without some means of cooking our food and drying out clothes."

A sudden storm drove Karstens and Harper back from a point shy of the pass. Limited visibility slowed their descent, but they returned safely. Karstens immediately went to work on the stove. After much tinkering, he succeeded in repairing it ("with his usual ingenuity," remarked Stuck). After that episode, Stuck forbade Tatum from ever touching the Primus again.

After another uncomfortable, restless night, Karstens and Harper got under way early, determined to reach the pass. According to Tatum, "Mr. Karstens was dreadfully displeased about something" when he left, but did not say what or why. With the advance party far ahead, Stuck and Tatum relayed two more loads to the cache below the cleavage.

Late on the afternoon of May 29, Karstens's "dogged determination," combined with Harper's "splendid rugged strength," finally won out when the two reached Browne and Parker's old camp at the summit of the northeast ridge. Finally, after "hewing a three-mile-long staircase of ice," the campsite at Parker Pass below Browne's Tower, 14,600 feet, was theirs.

The next day, after twenty-three days of toil and hardship, the expedition pitched their tent at the pass, a spot that had taken Browne and Parker just five days to reach. The place they called Parker Pass was the open door to the summit.

Stuck later acknowledged Karstens's accomplishment: "Those who think that a long apprenticeship must be served under skilled instructors before command of the technique of snow mountaineering can be obtained would have been astonished at Karstens's work on the Northeast Ridge." And to this day, the name, Karstens Ridge, honors his brilliant piece of mountaineering.

Karstens at 18,500 feet on the approach to McKinley's summit,
on a slope covered in rubble from the 1912 earthquake

20. The South Summit

NO ONE SLEPT WELL THE FIRST NIGHT at Parker Pass. Harry Karstens tossed and turned under his heavy wolf sleeping robe. Hudson Stuck slept not at all. Even Walter Harper, who could sleep through a caribou stampede, tossed and turned. Neither the altitude nor the subzero cold was to blame. There, on the shoulder of North America's highest mountain, pushing the envelope of exploration, those four tired climbers spent a miserable night for want of warm caribou skins.

They had made their ascent the day before burdened under heavy packs. The bulky caribou skins, used to insulate their sleeping bags and robes, had been left below at the cache. Their bedding directly atop the snow did not keep them warm. Every movement in that cramped tent affected everyone. If one person turned, they all turned, making undisturbed sleep nearly impossible.

Dawn broke, calm and brittle, the sun shining at three o'clock in the morning. After breakfast, Tatum and Harper started down the ridge to retrieve supplies, including the precious caribou skins.

For the first and only time on the expedition, Karstens and Stuck roped together to prospect the route ahead. Karstens, cutting steps where needed, led across the slope below the cliffs, finding the traverse uncomplicated. Stuck trailed at the end of the rope, his "feet and toes numb the whole way." As feared, his moccasins were inadequate for the cold.

Where the slope flattened out, Stuck switched places with Karstens, the sun and added toil warming him. To his great relief, the traverse into the lower plateau was as easy as Browne had described.

The altitude and lack of sleep wore on them both, notably a pronounced shortness of breath. By early afternoon, the two men had climbed to 15,000 feet, where they picked out a spot for their next camp. "The prize of this first ascent seems now within our grasp," Stuck wrote that night. "Two more camp removes, and then a good day for the final dash are all that lie between us and our heart's desire."

That night, with the warm, insulating caribou skins under them, the climbers slept well, including Stuck, who "slept better than I have for a long time." June 1 was spent relaying supplies. After Sunday prayers, Harper and Tatum again descended to the cache; Karstens and Stuck relayed loads to the edge of the Grand Basin.

Burdened as they were with "comforts," food, and instruments, Karstens knew his party was less mobile than Browne and Parker. It takes "us three loads each to move our outfit complete," he lamented in his journal. In Stuck's mind, however, the 1912 expedition was "too mobile," without enough food to wait out the weather.

A building wind raked Harper and Tatum on their last relay from the cache. To their left, a wall of rock and ice dove 5,000 feet to the Traleika Glacier; to their right, a sheer slope plunged to the Muldrow 2,000 feet below. "The wind was so strong that in several places on the narrow ridge I nearly lost my balance with the heavy pack on my back," Harper remembered. If he had fallen, Tatum would have been pulled off the ridge as well, the fall killing them both. (Just such an accident occurred at this place years later, when a sudden fall pulled four experienced climbers off the ridge. One died, one sustained serious injury, and all of them would have perished had not a tiny shelf of snow arrested their plunge toward the Muldrow.)

That afternoon, after bowls of *erbswurst*—which Harper dismissed as "pea soup again"—Karstens, Tatum, and Harper relayed a second load to the high cache. Stuck remained in camp to read the mercurial barometer.

As soon as the sun dropped below the North Peak, the temperature immediately dropped to −9°F, then colder. "While we were having our evening service it was so cold that we had to wear our parkas," Harper commented. The good weather held, and the next morning the expedition packed for the move to the plateau camp, which they reached at noon. The uphill grind sorely taxed Hudson Stuck. "I had a great fight for breath," he explained, "and had to call innumerable halts." Yet despite his fatigue and the subzero cold, Stuck called it "the finest day in three weeks . . . the high South Peak is entirely visible and free of cloud." They pitched the tent and spread their belongings to dry in the sun.

After lunch, Harper and Karstens prospected the way ahead, searching for an advance campsite. While toiling upward, Karstens and Harper crossed Browne and Parker's trail, their crampon marks still visible in the ice a year after their climb. Late that afternoon, they located a place for their next move, not far from Browne and Parker's highest camp, at 16,400 feet. The North Peak towered above them, the sun blasting off the rock and ice.

Hudson Stuck's patience was wearing thin. "I am much overstayed on this enterprise already," he told Tatum. So, too, was everyone else. Yet the discord that had marred the ascent to the ridge top had completely disappeared. "The last week has grown a much better feeling amongst all the members of the party," Stuck noted. "There is no more of that irritability of temper which marked the tedium and suspense of the glacier camp. Thank God for that."

Nonetheless, both Stuck and Tatum fretted that the cold would worsen as they climbed higher, the wind sweeping down from the summit already bitter. Stuck complained about cold feet, "no matter how many socks I wear." Tatum's rheumatism flared up again.

In the Grand Basin, which Stuck later named the Harper Glacier in honor of Walter and his father, Arthur Harper, the doubt that had dogged Stuck momentarily evaporated. "With the exception of the ridge, Denali is not a mountain that presents special mountaineering difficulties of a technical kind," he said. "Its difficulties lie in its remoteness, its size, the great distances of snow and ice . . . the burdens that must be carried over those distances. We estimated that it was twenty miles of actual linear distance from [McGonagall] pass . . . to the summit. . . . But the Northeast Ridge, in its present condition, adds all the spice of sensation and danger that any man could desire."

On June 3, the expedition struck camp for the move higher. They advanced at a snail's pace, slowed by the struggling archdeacon. The altitude affected them all, but especially Stuck, who paused every six steps to gasp for breath. He carried only his instruments, but even his lightweight pack he found "a terrible burden." Karstens declared flatly that Stuck would from then on pack nothing more. "When it was evident that the progress of the party was hindered by the constant stops on my account," Stuck wrote, "the contents of my pack were distributed amongst the others and my load reduced."

At one rest break, Walter Harper let out a cry and pointed to a rocky outcrop on the ridge below the North Peak. "The flagstaff! The flagstaff! I see it." Then Karstens spotted it too. Through binoculars, they all saw the spruce pole, proof positive of the 1910 ascent, and full vindication for Anderson, Taylor, and McGonagall.

When the expedition returned to Kantishna and reported seeing the flagpole, some of the miners believed that Browne and Parker must have seen it the previous summer but had kept it secret. Mountain experts claim that no one else but the 1913 expedition saw the flagpole. Woodbury Abbey, who surveyed the park boundaries in 1921, said he spotted it several times through his transit from various prominences in the Kantishna, and using his transit, showed it to his family as well. Critics charge that a transit is not powerful enough to spot a tiny pole at such distances. However, thermal inversions are common in Alaska, and an inversion can create a superior mirage that causes an object to appear higher and nearer than it is.

Harper's sighting of the flagpole altered the expedition's plans. After first climbing the South Peak, Stuck had proposed to climb the North Peak, settling once and for all the claims of Cook and Lloyd. "Now we will not have to climb the North Peak at all," explained Tatum.

That afternoon they pitched camp at 16,400 feet, amid blocks of ice and snow rubble from the great earthquake.

On June 4, Karstens and Harper again advanced in search of a higher campsite, hopefully their final one before the attack on the summit itself. The day was incredibly hot, the sun roaring off the snow and ice and cooking the men as they toiled under their heavy packs. By evening their faces were roasted a deep brown, their lips blistered and cracked. Luckily, the amber snow glasses that Stuck had purchased prevented the snow blindness that had plagued Browne and Parker.

While Karstens and Harper pushed ahead, Stuck and Tatum followed with a relay of gear. Partway up the new trail Stuck, who had insisted on carrying a pack, cut the relay short and returned to camp.

The archdeacon, so near his cherished goal, was failing. For days, he had been convulsed by choking and shortness of breath and near blackouts. In his preparations for the climb, he had cut his smoking down to two pipes a day and had given up smoking altogether once he had reached the ridge. None of it helped.

"The medicine chest held no remedy for blind staggers," he said. That he had gotten even this high was a powerful testament to both his extraordinary will and the excellence of his companions. "Deacon having hard time breathing but we will get him there somehow," Karstens wrote that evening. Stuck, realizing his situation, could only agree: "I have realized for the last two days that there is quite a chance that it may be physically impossible for me to reach the top of the mountain. Karstens says I shall get to the top even if he has to pack me."

In camp that night, Karstens reported that he had found a good campsite and had identified Browne and Parker's route to the top. He also said that he had located what looked like a better route to the top. "Their last camp may have looked good to them," he said, "but the next basin above looks better to me. One thousand feet less to climb at the final ascent means a great deal in this changeable climate. If they were camped where we will make our climb from they would have made it."

On June 5, the expedition again broke camp and began the move to 17,500 feet. Karstens and Harper went first; Tatum and Stuck followed an hour later, Stuck carrying only his barometer. "I dread the remove to the next camp with its steep serac climbing," Stuck admitted, "as much as the final ascent."

As the climbers ascended the next icefall (which Stuck had called a "serac"), clouds poured in over the ridges and the day rapidly cooled. Karstens and Harper stopped shy of their goal and hastily pitched the tent before the storm hit in earnest. After lunch—"more pea soup"—the four climbers dozed off to a hard wind rattling the canvas. They stirred some time later to bright sun and clear sky. The feared storm had petered out.

That afternoon, while his companions went back to relay supplies, Stuck stayed in camp to cook a supper of bacon and beans. The bacon stubbornly refused to cook even after boiling for three hours. Alone he mused at the changes in his companions. "Karstens has become very considerate of me," he wrote that afternoon, "as he recognizes that it is a simple physical impossibility for me to pack anything further, and that there is some question whether I may be able to get myself to the top of the mountain. It will have to be slow, patient work, a few steps at a time."

Snow that evening dampened everyone's spirits; they had had enough of foul weather and delay. June 6, however, dawned clear but windy, the world below smothered in clouds. When the wind died down, the sun again "scorching," according to Stuck, the climbers broke camp for the next, and hopefully final, move. Karstens and Harper went first, Tatum and Stuck fifteen minutes behind. As before, Stuck carried only his barometer, everyone else heavy packs.

The trail wound upward, broken by frequent stops. In two hours, the climbers reached the plateau Karstens had chosen for the final camp. "I congratulated Karstens on pitching the highest camp ever pitched on the North American continent," Stuck said.

That afternoon, while everyone else went back to retrieve the rest of the outfit, Stuck again stayed in camp, carving an inscription on a tent pole he hoped to erect on the summit as part of a cross.

By early afternoon, the packers were back and camp organized for an extended stay. Stuck inventoried enough pemmican, erbswurst, and rice to last ten to twelve days or longer with rationing. Extras like chocolate, tea, sugared almonds, figs, and raisins were in short supply, but "our worst lack is the lack of any kind of bread," Stuck said.

Determined not to be caught by bad weather and low supplies, the expedition had relayed enough food and fuel to last through a series of storms, creating five camps as they leapfrogged ahead. By comparison, Browne and Parker had made just three camps in the Grand Basin.

If the weather held, however, their stay at 17,500 feet would be brief, with the final ascent coming the next day. "We expect to make the final dash by leaving tonight about midnight," Tatum explained.

That night Walter Harper took his turn as camp cook, boiling the usual stew and adding a lot of "flour paste," which they called "noo-dles." Already they had found the noodles to be what Stuck called "a heavy and I fear indigestible compound."

Should the summit bid fail, Karstens had a fallback plan. "Harry says if we cannot reach the summit easily from this camp," Stuck wrote, "he will put another on the ridge itself. But all we need is one fine day now." After all the toil, suffering, and time spent by the party to achieve this height, the ascent by Anderson, Taylor, and McGonagall, fueled by doughnuts and hot chocolate, must have seemed incredible, if not impossible.

Within hours of dinner, everyone except Harper was sick. Instead of sleeping, the climbers huddled around the Primus with blankets

Camp Two in the Grand Basin, the Muldrow Glacier far below. The little hand-sewn tent, protected from wind by snow blocks, was a tight fit for four.

and robes wrapped around them, their stomachs churning. "No one slept though we tried," Karstens remembered. "My stomach was bad and I had one of the most severe headaches." According to Harper, "The Archdeacon could not move without losing his breath and our spirits were all pretty low."

By four in the morning, the sun already blasting off the North Peak, the climbers were up, packed, and under way. "If it were not for the final climb I should have stayed in camp," Karstens admitted, "but being the final climb and such a promising day I managed to pull through." *Those damn noodles!*

Since Harper was least affected, Karstens put him in the lead and "took second place on the rope so I could direct [him] and he worked all day without a murmur," chopping steps wherever needed. Hudson Stuck was third on the rope, followed by Tatum.

The morning temperatures dropped to –17°F, a sharp north wind biting at exposed flesh. The climbers wore multiple layers, enough to sustain them on the trail at –50°F, yet they were still cold. At every break, each man took time to pound some warmth into his hands and feet. Karstens stomped his feet so often and so hard that later he lost two toenails. "It was bitterly cold," Stuck said. "There is no question that cold is felt more keenly in the thin air of nineteen thousand feet than it is below."

Karstens's chosen route led straight up a steep snow-covered ridge south of camp and then around the peak itself to a gentle incline to the summit. Even near there, earthquake damage forced the climbers off a direct line to their destination.

The altitude pummeled them all. With pounding headaches, roiling guts, and shortness of breath, they measured their progress at two steps forward, a pause for rest, a few more paces, stop again. "Altogether we were a somewhat feeble folk," Stuck acknowledged. Every four or five steps, Stuck called a halt, his lungs seemingly incapable of expanding. He thought of failure and death but prayed for triumph and life.

When Harper topped an incline thought to be the summit but pointed ahead to yet another rise, Stuck almost quit. "I confess my heart sank, for I had realized all day that I was very near my altitude limit," he confessed, "and had been apprehensive that I might be

Hudson Stuck on Athabascan-style snowshoes ascending
the Muldrow Glacier, on Ascension Day 1913

physically unable to get to the top." Harper doubled back to where
Stuck knelt in the snow and took the mercurial barometer, the last
item in the archdeacon's pack. All Stuck had to do now was keep moving. Avoiding fissures wrought by the earthquake, the climbers slowly
rounded the north end of the peak and gained the horseshoe-shaped
ridge that culminates at the true summit.

Just past midday, Walter Harper stopped. After weeks of toil, he
had reached the summit of North America's tallest mountain. Karstens

was right behind him, followed by Tatum, with Stuck last on the rope. "I had to be hauled, puffing and panting into the hitherto secret place of the greatest mountain of the continent," Stuck remembered. Reaching the summit, he collapsed "in enthusiasm and excitement somewhat over passing [my] narrow wind margin." Later he would muse, "Have I climbed a mountain? I climbed it largely by [Harper's] legs. Have I made memorable journeys? I made them largely by his powers."

Despite the piercing cold and pounding fatigue, the climbers exulted in the panorama. "To the south and east . . . the near-by peaks and ridges stood out with dazzling distinction," Stuck wrote, "and the beautiful crescent curve of the Alaskan range exhibited itself from Denali to the sea." On one side of the range, the great drainages rolled south to Cook Inlet and the North Pacific; on the other, the rivers pulsed to the Yukon and on to the Bering Sea. Wildfire haze obscured the lowlands to the north. Nothing that Frederick Cook had described matched what they were seeing from the summit, nor did his description and photographs look like the summit itself.

No other humans had ever seen these stupendous sights and, not surprisingly, the Archdeacon of the Yukon beheld the power of God. "Yet the chief impression was not of our connection with the earth so far below, its rivers and its seas," he remembered, "but rather of detachment from it. . . . Above us the sky took a blue so deep that none of us had ever gazed upon a midday sky like it before . . . it seemed like special news of God.'"

Before beginning his scientific measurements, Stuck gathered his companions for prayers of thanksgiving. They then pitched the tiny instrument tent with Tatum's hand-sewn American flag streaming from the top. Inside, Stuck read the boiling-point thermometer and the mercurial barometer. Outside, Tatum took readings with the prismatic compass.

Once the tent was struck, Harper fashioned a cross from the tent pole, and he and Karstens planted it at the highest point. Then everyone gathered around for the *Te Deum*, a Christian hymn of praise. A number of photographs were taken, but at −4°F, with a hard wind blowing, numb fingers fumbled the controls and almost all of the summit pictures were double and triple exposed. "There

A rare photo of Hudson Stuck using the boiling-point thermometer
on the summit of Mount McKinley

was much photography that I should have liked to have done," Stuck explained, "that was impossible to do." It was just too cold to change film. Karstens, himself a keen photographer, lamented the loss of his camera in the cache fire.

"The miserable limitations of the flesh gave us continual warning to depart," Stuck recalled. "We grew . . . still more wretchedly cold." In all, they spent an hour and a half on the summit before starting down.

The descent was a "long weary grind" made longer by a search for the thermometer that Herschel Parker had cached "in a crack of the western side of the last granite boulder of the summit ridge." The search took them a mile out of their way and provoked some grumbling about "a needle in a haystack." Stuck attributed the failure to recover the thermometer to the changes wrought by the great earthquake. During the search, they collected pieces of granite from the highest exposed rock. Thirteen hours after leaving camp, the climbers returned "tired but happy."

"Only those who have for long years cherished a great and almost inordinate desire," Stuck explained, "and have had that desire gratified to the limit of their expectation, can enter into the deep thankfulness and content that filled the heart upon the descent of this mountain." Stuck wrote, "I remember no day in my life so full of toil, distress, and exhaustion, and yet so full of happiness and keen gratification."

Harper exulted in his accomplishments. Tatum called it "a red letter day." Karstens, never one to brag or posture, expressed his satisfaction in his journal: "Hurrah. The south summit of Mount McKinley has been conquered."

In the tent that evening, Hudson Stuck considered his ailments. "If someone would discover a remedy for shortness of breath . . . climbing Denali would lose its terror for me. My throat is hard and dry and my whole abdomen is sore from my continual panting and I twice lost consciousness for a moment. How much further I could have gone I do not know." He fully recognized that he never would have achieved the summit without Karstens and Harper. "There seemed no reason why Karstens and Walter . . . should not go another ten thousand feet, were there mountains in the world ten thousand feet higher than Denali," he acknowledged.

One modern climbing analyst has concluded that the climbers, especially Stuck, were suffering from "acute altitude sickness." But were they really? That night, all of them slept peacefully and soundly, their minds finally at peace. They rose late the next day without mention of any indisposition of any kind. It was *those damn noodles!*

The next morning, the temperature –21°F, the climbers broke camp, taking advantage of the settled weather to head down. At Parker Pass, the site of their ridge-top camp, they took a long rest break, boiling a huge pot of tea and refilling the thermoses. Stuck placed a thermometer in the rocks nearby and carefully described its location. (When found two decades later, the instrument had recorded an uncalibrated minimum of –90°F, with an estimated minimum of –106°F.)

In the Grand Basin, Harry Karstens adjusts the much-maligned handmade ice creepers.

Finally, the maligned and much-repaired creepers came in for praise. "The creepers have proved themselves invaluable," Stuck wrote. "We could never have ascended or descended the slopes without them."

At 3:15 PM, they started down, roped in pairs. Karstens, followed by Tatum, took the lead on the first rope; Stuck, followed by Harper, on the next—the two strongest climbers shepherding the weakest. In addition to his own gear, Harper carried most of the archdeacon's. "I am grateful to the boy for his thoughtfulness," Stuck remembered.

The slope below the pass was exceedingly steep and buried in almost two feet of new snow that obliterated their hewn steps. The day was hot and conditions ripe for avalanche. The descent was perhaps the most perilous part of the climb.

Ever so cautiously, Karstens descended the slope, shoveling out new steps as needed. With only Tatum to belay him, Karstens must have felt quite exposed. Stuck said he felt safe with the powerful Harper behind him.

It took an hour and a half to negotiate the slope and reach the treacherous and difficult cleavage. Soft, loose snow spilled away on either side of the jutting wall of ice. One step could trigger a lethal fall or avalanche. Gingerly, Karstens cleared the new snow, cutting and shoveling the critical steps around the rupture.

Pinnacle by pinnacle, challenge by challenge, the climbers descended the ridge and at six o'clock reached their first ridge camp, the worst now behind them. "One feels upon reflection that we took more risk in descending that ridge than we took at any time in the ascent," Stuck recalled.

After a brief rest, Karstens forged on. Six hours after leaving the pass, the climbers trudged into their glacier camp, now all but buried in snow and ice.

That night after dinner—with sourdough bread—the climbers rolled into their bedding for a hard-won rest. "Karstens led most carefully and skillfully," Hudson Stuck wrote before turning in. "He has become already an accomplished mountaineer. Tatum and Walter both did their full duty and did it handsomely."

Stuck then wrote out the text for a 160-word telegram to be sent as soon as they reached civilization. The message covered the high points of the climb, including sightings of the 1910 flagpole, and concluded: "Chief credit our success due to Karstens's good judgment, resourcefulness, caution. No mishap whatever."

On June 9, after another fine sleep, the party broke camp on the mountain for the final time. They loaded essential gear onto their Yukon sled and discarded or cached the rest. Downhill progress was slow. They trudged in deep snow from one willow marker to the next. Time and again during the descent, they detoured around collapsed bridges and yawning crevasses. Many of the bridges they'd built during the ascent failed as they tried to cross.

Below the Lower Icefall, and on safe, flat ice, the climbers finally relaxed. The last hazards were behind them. The lower glacier was covered in standing water, and they plodded on in soaking-wet moccasins. At the base of McGonagall Pass, they cached their Yukon sled and on the summit reveled in the sight of purple flowers, "thus jumping from winter to summer in one day," Harper recalled. Countless mosquitoes swarmed them.

Late that day, as the haggard and battered climbers approached base camp, "we began to be very anxious about Johnny," remembered Stuck. "What had happened to the boy? Had he grown alarmed at our prolonged absence, and sought to make his way to the nearest men, fifty miles away?" Instead of two weeks, Fredson had been alone for thirty-one days.

"It was a joy and an enormous relief to find the boy well and happy," Stuck exulted, "both the dogs and Johnny were fat and well-favored. I shall never forget the great load that was lifted from my heart as we approached the base camp. . . . He gave a great shout . . . and came running, and never stopped until he had reached us and taken the pack from my back and put it on his own."

John Fredson's fidelity awed them all. In camp, the men dined on a feast of fresh sheep steak, biscuits, and coffee laced with sugar and milk. The selfless boy, Stuck wrote, "had not touched a spoonful of either [milk or sugar] that on our return we might enjoy what we had been so long deprived of!" Near the summit, Stuck had collected a small piece of granite, which he planned to have made into four scarf pins, one for each climber. Months later, the grateful archdeacon gave his to Fredson. "I am very happy and contented tonight and full of gratitude to Almighty God for the successful issue of our enterprise," he wrote.

In contrast to the world of ice and snow, the piedmont blazed with flowers and green grass. The next day, the climbers rested, making packs for the dogs and preparing for the cross-country trek. To stroll on moss and tundra, to pet the dogs, to drink hot coffee and eat fresh biscuits baked nonstop by Fredson—sheer delight! The mosquitoes were the only downside to the day.

Stuck said he burned to write the tale of the climb, his mind whirling with phrases and descriptions. "For the first time in my life," he noted in his journal, "I have something entirely adequate to write about."

If the summit was "like looking out the windows of Heaven," as Tatum said, then the two-day cross-country trek to the Kantishna was, for him, *Hell.* Cold rain and hail drenched them; clouds of mosquitoes tormented the dogs and men without relief. While crossing the McKinley River, Tatum tangled with a dog and tripped headlong into the icy rushing water. Karstens, already across, rushed back and grabbed Tatum, pulling his head clear of the water. Harper, who was carrying Stuck across the river so that he wouldn't get wet, deposited his patron on the bank and hurried to aid in the rescue. Stuck was appalled. "Tatum lay [on the bank] and bellowed like a baby," he reported. "He is a strange mix of pluck and effeminacy; of cowardice and courage . . . it was a scare pure and simple." Stuck clearly did not realize that Tatum's fear was based on his distrust of his mentor's climbing ability and frailty.

Tatum, however, was convinced that Karstens had saved his life, openly weeping in gratitude for his rescue from drowning. Sadly, the young man lost his ice ax in the river, the one souvenir he most cherished. For his part, Karstens never spoke poorly of Tatum, describing him as a "good worker but slow and green at trail work." If someone pitched in and tried their best, that mattered a lot to Harry Karstens.

The expedition stopped briefly in Eureka, where Jack Hamilton fed them a lavish meal. Moving on to Glacier Creek, they stayed at Quigley's cabin where Fannie McKenzie "filled us full—too full—of good things." McGonagall came for a visit, and Karstens delivered the news of his friend's vindication.

Late on June 17, the expedition loaded its dogs and supplies in the poling boat that Karstens had stashed at Diamond and began the three-hundred-mile river float to the village of Tanana. Before setting out, according to Tatum, the climbers agreed "to say nothing to the outsiders about our little differences."

Early on June 20, three months and six days after they left Nenana, the party reached Tanana. Stuck telegraphed the triumphant news to Seattle and Fairbanks newspapers. Quickly the story spread around the world. In Alaska, the news sparked celebrations. "There was unanimous rejoicing but no trace of surprise," a newspaper exulted. "It has remained for true Alaskans to clinch and to win." Harry Karstens also sent a telegram, but to a pretty young nurse in Fairbanks: "Reached top am going on to Ruby return Fairbanks direct."

That afternoon, Karstens caught a riverboat for the downriver trip to the mining town of Ruby. After retrieving the gas launch *Snoqualmie* from winter storage, he returned to Fairbanks. Passing through Nenana on July 2, he spent the night at Hudson Stuck's cabin. It was the last time the two ever spoke.

The Tiffany's pin, made from granite collected near
the summit, which Stuck presented to each of the four
climbers, displayed on the head of Karstens's ice ax

21. Aftermath

HARRY KARSTENS WAS BOILING MAD. By the time he returned to Fairbanks from Ruby, he'd seen headlines blaring *"STUCK CLIMB-ERS REACH SUMMIT OF SOUTH PEAK"* and *"STUCK'S ASCENT OF MOUNT MCKINLEY."* The barrage of references to the "Stuck Expedition," "The Archdeacon's companions," or "Stuck's associates" inflamed Karstens's sense of fair play and honesty. Other than a brief statement from Hudson Stuck that gave Karstens credit for the expedition's success, the press, especially the Outside papers, referred to Karstens merely a *member* of the "Hudson Stuck Mount McKinley expedition."

The exception to the one-sided reporting ran in the tiny *Ruby Record-Citizen* on July 5. Based on an interview with Karstens, who was in Ruby to retrieve his launch, *Snoqualmie*, the article gave a succinct but factual account of the summit climb, without hyperbole or exaggeration. No mention was made of Stuck's physical shortcomings or conflict of any kind. The headline—"Stuck-Karstens Expedition"—gave equal credit to both men.

In fairness, Hudson Stuck was not responsible for the headlines used or the content of news stories, yet, right or wrong, Harry Karstens blamed Stuck for the inaccuracies that downplayed Karstens's leadership and the efforts of Walter Harper.

In Fairbanks, Karstens made several brief statements, largely controlling his pique. "The successful explorer is very modest about the marvelous feat performed by the party," wrote one reporter, "yet he felt a little aggrieved at the local papers for characterizing the party as the 'Stuck' expedition as he was equally interested with the archdeacon, each of them having a separate part to look after." Karstens told the *Fairbanks Daily Times* he preferred the title "Stuck-Karstens Expedition," asking only for equal credit.

If mountain climbing tests endurance, strength, and ability, it also teaches lessons of ego, ambition, loss, and loneliness. On the slopes and glaciers, and in the storms and high camps, the very fiber of a person's being is laid bare for his companions' examination. No fault goes unexposed or unexplored. During the climb, both Stuck and Karstens had revealed their individual strengths and weaknesses. In the aftermath, instead of glory, Karstens felt betrayal. He and Walter Harper had done the work, carried Stuck to the top, and now were overlooked.

For Harry Karstens, the rift that had opened on the mountain now yawned wider than any crevasse that he'd seen. In truth, Hudson Stuck and Harry Karstens never would have been close friends, their divergent temperaments and outlooks irreconcilable. If indeed, Karstens had been a hired guide rather than an equal partner, Stuck's failings, and apparent exaggerations, would not have been so damaging and inflammatory. Guides are accustomed to clients lacking experience and physical ability, and then later embellishing their contributions to the enterprise.

Hudson Stuck did not learn the extent of his partner's displeasure until late July. He had been engrossed in church business and in writing a magazine story about the climb. On board the steamer *St. Michael*, on the first leg of his journey Outside, Stuck saw a letter to the editor from Karstens, correcting a story in the *Fairbanks Daily Times*.

Stuck immediately wrote the editor:

> "In your issue of 10th July is a communication from Mr. Harry Karstens in which he takes a very natural exception to the continual reference to our expedition as the 'Stuck' expedition. I desire to join my protest to his. Before leaving on that enterprise

*I explained to your reporter that Mr. Karstens and I were part-
ners in the affair. The telegram sent to you from Tanana (and
a copy thereof) sent to the Seattle Times is the only statement
made by me about the ascent. I am not in any way responsible
for the headlines . . . . I feel perfectly free to say that without Mr.
Karstens we should have never reached the top of the mountain.
. . . Karstens was always the real leader."*

Prior to the climb, Stuck had characterized Karstens to the *Times*
as a *guide*, a misstatement he now was finding difficult to correct.

A few days later, in response to yet another story, Stuck again
reiterated his position: "Mr. Karstens, who was my partner in this
enterprise, organized the whole expedition of six men and boys and
fourteen dogs so that every person in the party had his own special
duties to perform, without Harry Karstens's leadership and ability we
would not have succeeded."

The successful ascent had altered Stuck's plans. He cut short his
planned summer ministry and headed Outside on a fund-raising trip.
Even before leaving Alaska he said that he had not climbed the mountain for financial gain but did it merely "for the sake of climbing the
mountain." He claimed that Karstens also had no expectation of profit.
"I have already declined a lecturing tour that would have tied me up all
the winter, for I am a missionary first and a mountain climber afterwards," Stuck told the *Fairbanks Daily Times*, "and my visit Outside is
primarily in the interests of missionary work in Alaska."

Stuck's comments appear disingenuous. Perhaps the statement is
accurate if he meant *personal* reward, but from the very beginning, he
had calculated the financial gain for the church.

Karstens was infuriated by what he was hearing. He was seriously
short of money. By the time the party had reached Tanana on June 20,
Karstens had missed the lucrative spring freighting season. It appears
that Stuck grasped neither Karstens's financial sacrifice in undertaking
the trip nor his expectations in the wake of its success. "Before I promised to go [on the climb]," Karstens wrote Charles Sheldon, "I had a nice
little sum of money now I am broke and in debt working my head off to
get even so I can go on the new stampede at the head of the Tanana."

Karstens had obviously believed that a successful climb would result in handsome remuneration. On more than one occasion, he had listened to Stuck criticize Cook's financial windfall. He also knew that Tom Lloyd had been paid well for the full story of his fanciful climb. Stuck had made statements that encouraged Karstens's expectations of monetary gain. "The expedition will not be without the likelihood of financial value, and that these will be returned to you for the time and the labor," Stuck assured Karstens prior to the trip, "It will be satisfaction enough to me to have made the ascent." Stuck also added a subsequent caveat: "But it will not be my fault if there is not compensation to you."

Shortly after the climb, Stuck signed a contract to write a book and magazine article detailing the first ascent. Even before leaving Alaska, Stuck had written and sent out his eight-thousand-word article for *Scribner's Magazine*. Although Stuck received double the usual advance for the book, the publisher seemed more excited about the sales potential for Stuck's first book, *Ten Thousand Miles with a Dog Sled*, which he finished during the climb.

In mid-August, in response to enquiries from Charles Sheldon, Karstens wrote a long letter describing the climb and bluntly stating his true feelings about Hudson Stuck.

> *"Sheldon 'O' Sheldon why didn't you come in and make the trip as you suggested doing . . . why shouldn't I have a man with me one worthy of the ascent and not an absolute parasite and liar. I told you about the Deacon trying for years to get me to go on this trip, and how fine he was to me now I understand to my sorrow.*
> *"We were equal partners. He was to finance the expedition and it was not to cost me a cent. I was to furnish the experience."*

He saw the archdeacon's public accounts of his exploits as gross exaggerations. Hudson Stuck "would talk of his hardships and long trips to show what a good man he was . . . (I woke up after the first day)."

Karstens felt that Stuck had failed to uphold his end of their bargain. Because Stuck misrepresented his climbing skills and accounts of the climb, Karstens considered him a liar. He called Stuck a parasite for the manner in which he shifted most of his chores to his assistants, allowing everyone else to do the work. He also believed the "Preacher" to be shamelessly self-aggrandizing, a damning flaw. Now it looked to Karstens as if the archdeacon did not care if he raised money to compensate Karstens for his time, effort, and lost income.

Upon his arrival in Seattle in early August, after the steamship voyage down the Alaska coast, Stuck received the galley proofs for his *Scribner's* article on the climb. In response to Karstens's criticism, he inserted in the draft a paragraph giving Karstens equal credit.

In New York in early September, Hudson Stuck once again tried to redress the original oversight. "I have noticed that many newspapers have referred to the expedition as the 'Stuck expedition,'" he told the *New York Sun*. "It could be more properly called the Stuck-Karstens expedition. . . . Karstens was my colleague to the very top. . . . Some of the papers referred to Mr. Karstens as my guide, which wasn't fair to him. He is entitled to just as much credit as I am." Despite his comments, the *Sun* called Stuck the "Conqueror of the Peak" and hailed him as the "first man to reach the summit of Mount McKinley."

The archdeacon spent the winter writing, lecturing, and lobbying for Alaska missions. His appearances drew large and enthusiastic crowds. He was feted as guest of honor at the annual dinner of the American Alpine Club in Boston. He spoke at the Explorers Club and the American Geographical Society, the recipient of his climbing records. He also met with Charles Sheldon in Woodstock. His fame spread around the world, and he was named a Fellow of the Royal Geographical Society.

Stuck spoke to the crowds about his work with Alaska Natives, the need for enhanced funding, and his hardships on the trail while spreading the Gospel. His comments about the Cook controversy were politic. The story of the first ascent drew the loudest applause and he responded with a plea for the restoration of the mountain's Native name, *Denali*. Cook had argued that the mountain should retain President McKinley's name, as befitting a patriotic icon of US identity. Stuck's advocacy for Denali, like Sheldon's, offered a fundamental shift in the importance of naming the mountain—a way to remind the nation that whites were not its "discoverers." The return of McKinley to its Native name,

Stuck told his audiences, will "show that there once dwelt in the land a simple, hardy race who braved successfully the rigors of its climate and the inhospitality of their environment and flourished."

The press continued to laud Stuck as "the first who reached the highest point on the American continent." The *Pittsburgh Dispatch* reported that Stuck described the climb as "a vacation stunt more than anything else." According to the article, Stuck had addressed a large crowd saying that the mountain called for "none but the bravest" to attempt. He described his companions thusly: "I started with a party of two white men and an Indian boy . . . my men all trained to hardships of the northland." It was naive of Stuck to believe such elitist and demeaning comments would not filter back to Alaska, exacerbating already raw feelings.

The honors bestowed on the archdeacon, and on Frederick Cook before him, would have never been given to Anderson, Taylor, Harper, or Karstens, even had their true accomplishments been recognized. Adventure and sporting clubs of the era were solely the province of the upper class, and America back then was as class-conscious as imperial England. Cook, by training, and Stuck, by calling, easily mingled with the "better classes" that excluded and disdained people of the "working class."

Despite Stuck's expressed "uneasiness" in the "sensationalism" of finding himself famous as the conqueror of Mount McKinley, he exploited it to wring money from his large audiences for his missionary work. He easily met his primary goal and came home with $50,000 for hospitals at Tanana and Fort Yukon. Stuck told Karstens he rebuffed a climbing lecture tour because it conflicted with his established church fund-raising schedule. Without it, personal financial reward for the climb would be nil. "I think I should not bother with [profiting from the climb] were it not for you, but I have made up my mind to try to make at least $1,000 for you," Stuck wrote Karstens. In the end, Stuck paid Karstens half of the $2,300 he eventually earned in engagement fees and royalties, a far cry from the tens of thousands Cook had received.

The inaccurate stories and headlines trailed Stuck's lecture tour, each new one rekindling Karstens's ire. Charles Sheldon also took umbrage at the spate of inaccuracies, and fired off letters to the editor to correct them. After reading the galley proofs of Stuck's *Scribner's* article, Sheldon appealed to the editor for fairness. The editor responded:

> "We shall certainly do everything in our power to give credit to Mr. Karstens which we know from his repeated statements that Archdeacon Stuck desires him to have, and I think it possible you do not know—owing to the fact that it was done after he had returned the proofs you may have seen—that the Archdeacon sent to us for insertion near the beginning of the article a paragraph very emphatically stating the substance of what your note tells me. I feel sure that it will be impossible for anyone to read the article without doing the fullest justice to Mr. Karstens's part in the expedition."

In September, Hudson Stuck visited Sheldon at Woodstock. Among several topics, the two men talked about Harry Karstens and the upcoming article and book. "In the original article [Stuck] did not clearly credit Karstens with his full share in the expedition," Sheldon later explained. "Stuck has left the record in such a way that he can point to it as indicating that he mentioned Karstens as member of the expedition. But he never emphasized it and permitted the public to retain the impression, which is strong today, that he was the leader and Karstens was a mere assistant acting as one of his helpers."

During Stuck's visit, Sheldon also extended an invitation to Walter Harper, then attending Mount Hermon Academy in Massachusetts, a college preparatory school. Sheldon wanted to meet the stalwart that both Stuck and Karstens admired and who had rescued Stuck several times during their epic dog trips, twice on a single trek down the Yukon.

"My stay at your house was very enjoyable and I look back at it and at the discussion we indulged in with much pleasure." Stuck wrote Sheldon afterwards. He also included a revealing note about Harper:

> "I am very fond of the boy and ambitious for him. I think you will like him because everybody likes him and therein lies my chief anxiety for him. I am afraid that his amiability may reveal

itself as weakness of character when the real test comes. It seems to me a very difficult thing to inculcate strength of purpose and independent conscientiousness of attitude with a boy of equivocal racial status. I am profoundly convinced that it could not be done at all by any system that ignored the divine sanctions of conduct. The boy is sensitive to praise and blame: could easily be spoiled by excess of one or the other and, in a word is the subject of a good deal of anxious thought to me just now."

Hudson Stuck's *The Ascent of Denali* was published in early 1914. Stuck's narrative, like those of Cook and Browne, follows the literary and cultural traditions of the era's adventure stories. Critics hailed the book as a "full, clear, and interesting" record of the climb. Geographers hailed it for fairness, candor, and sparkling style. One reviewer used the following quote to highlight Stuck's "humility": "There is no pride of conquest, no trace of that exultation of victory that some enjoy upon the first ascent of a lofty peak, no gloating over good fortune that had hoisted us a few hundred feet higher than others who had struggled and been discomfited."

Most expedition memoirs of the era rarely mentioned the conflicts and personality clashes that are an inescapable part of human nature in times of challenge and stress. Robert Dunn's book, *The Shameless Diary of an Explorer*, in which he exposes the conflicts and mistakes of the Cook expedition, was the notable exception. This was not Stuck's style. In fact, he once described Dunn's book as "a vivid but unpleasant production, for which every squabble and jealousy of the party furnishes literary material. The book has a curious, undeniable power, despite its brutal frankness. . . . One is thankful, however, that it is unique in the literary world." Not surprisingly, when it came to writing his own book, Stuck clung to tradition and left out all mention of acrimony, glossing over every conflict and shortcoming.

The Ascent of Denali inflamed Harry Karstens, if for no other reason than the liberal use of the word "we." Many events that Stuck described with the editorial "we" occurred while the author was in camp, with everyone else hard at work. Several passages gave a distorted impression of reality, such as this blatant example: "We took more risk in descending that ridge than we took at any time in the ascent. But Karstens was most careful, and in the *long and intensive apprenticeship of this expedition* [italics added] had become most expert." Apprenticeship? To whom? The reader gets the unmistakable message that the author was the master, Karstens the apprentice.

When Stuck's book came out, the *Fairbanks Daily News-Miner* termed it a "Novel" and renamed it *Stuck's Ascent of "Damlie,"* referring to the author as "ArchStuckon."

It would be unjust, however, to claim that Stuck deliberately tried to slight the man to whom he owed so much. He clearly was not solely responsible for newspaper shorthand that simply left out mention of Karstens and Harper. Rather, his words and actions may have been the result of his inherent egocentrism, his inability to see things from another person's point of view. Despite the archdeacon's genuine piety, he nonetheless was prey to the same dangerous dreams and impulses that drive all explorers to risk their lives in wild places. At times, his ego did get the best of him.

This was not the first or last time that one climber received more credit than his companions for a first ascent. On May 29, 1953, New Zealand explorer Edmund Hillary and Nepalese Sherpa mountaineer Tenzing Norgay became the first climbers to reach the summit of Mount Everest. Afterward Hillary was knighted and hailed as an international hero. He was eventually named one of the one hundred most influential people of the twentieth century. Although Hillary had cited his companion's support, Norgay felt slighted.

In his own book, *Tiger of the Snows*, Tenzing Norgay wrote:

> "[Hillary] is a fine climber and a fine man, and I am proud to have gone with him to the top of Everest. But I do feel that in his story of our final climb he is not quite fair to me; that all the way through he indicates that when things went well it was his doing and when things went badly it was mine. For this is simply not true. . . . All the way up and down we helped, and were helped, by each other—and that was the way it should be. But we were not leader and led. We were partners."

And what about Walter Harper? What did he make of the Stuck-Karstens contretemps? Did he feel slighted or angered by the lack of recognition for his grand achievement? Was he so beholden to his mentor that honors and recognition meant nothing? Stuck regularly mentioned his protégé's fidelity and kindness, but in the press Harper was almost totally overlooked. Harper undeniably had done as much, or more, work than Karstens, his efforts and thoughtfulness enabling Stuck to reach the top. As the first person to stand on the summit of the mountain, Harper stood out as an important symbol of Alaska Native legitimacy. If Harper felt any disquiet, however, he forever kept it to himself.

Stuck seemed genuinely baffled by Karstens's displeasure and could not understand why he did not respond to his conciliatory letters. "I am altogether at a loss to understand why you should cherish any but the kindest feeling to me. I have given you . . . the fullest credit for your great part in our *joint enterprise*," Stuck wrote Karstens. He tried to explain about the money. "I could have made much more if I had been content to give up everything else and devote myself exclusively to lecturing; but I am a missionary first and mountain climber afterwards."

He followed that statement with a particularly patronizing and insulting one: "I saw you hailed in the local paper the other day as 'the world-famous explorer.' I have no quarrel with the description whatever, but I would point out that if you are 'world-famous' it is I who have made you so. . . . I have sung your praises . . . whoever heard of you before? Sheldon has written nothing of you. You must remember that in this matter of fame it is not enough to be able to do things, it is also necessary to be able to tell about them."

Despite Stuck's repeated attempts at reconciliation, Karstens never forgave him. "I have never written to him at any time since we were on the mountain, as he had entirely disgusted me with his untruthfulness from the time I first joined in the enterprise with him."

For all his days, Karstens regretted not making the climb with Charles Sheldon. "'O' Why, 'O' Why . . . didn't you take a chance at that hill," he wrote Sheldon. "We would have had one of the grandest trips ever made on a hill for you know me and my failings and I know *you*. [W]e could have taken Mrs. Sheldon and made it easy."

In spite of their feud, both men deserve due credit; their inability to reconcile did a disservice to their grand success. As Charles Sheldon put it, "Stuck has credit for his part in starting the expedition. Without his interest, it never would have been thus attempted. But Karstens was the man who put it through and who really by his ability and leadership made the climb possible—he should receive in the annals of Mountaineering full credit for this fact."

To Robert Tatum belongs the credit of hard work and accomplishment far beyond his experience. And to Walter Harper goes the credit for being the first person to reach the top of North America's highest peak. He *earned* that honor.

Harry Karstens,
first superintendent, Mount McKinley National Park

22. Alaska's First Ranger

BELMORE BROWNE FELL IN LOVE with the wilderness on the north side of Mount McKinley. The country and wildlife so enthralled him he called it "God's Country." Soon after returning home from the 1912 expedition, he visited a family friend, the secretary of the interior, and proposed establishment of a Mount McKinley National Park. In subsequent public lectures devoted to the expedition, he took time to promote his park concept.

Browne was unaware that Charles Sheldon harbored similar sentiments and that he had been laying the groundwork since 1908. After Sheldon made his first public pronouncements in mid-1915, the two men met and forged a powerful partnership. Their vision and dedication is a vital reminder of the key element of conservation so often neglected: love of place inspires protection.

Sheldon enlisted influential backing within the Department of the Interior and approached his friend James A. Wickersham, now Alaska's delegate to Congress, for help. Wickersham, however, was then publicly opposed to the park's creation. He recognized the park's tourism potential but resisted any attempt to inhibit mining. Sheldon argued, perhaps halfheartedly, that the two were not exclusive. They struck a compromise: miners could continue to locate claims within the new park.

On April 16, 1916, Delegate Wickersham introduced his park bill. "It is particularly fitting that Mr. Wickersham, who was the first man to attempt to climb Mount McKinley in 1903, should have introduced the bill . . . and it is fitting also that the bill should bear his name," read a statement of support from the influential Boone and Crockett Club.

If all the Mount McKinley controversies and heroics accomplished anything, they brought notice of this great mountain to the public. Instead of a far, distant place, Mount McKinley had become a household name. Park advocates traded on the notoriety to gain congressional and public support.

On February 24, 1917, after years of political struggle and turmoil, President Woodrow Wilson signed into law the act establishing Mount McKinley National Park "for the benefit and enjoyment of the people." The pen he used to sign the act was later presented to Charles Sheldon in recognition of his work and seminal idea.

In its first years, the park was a park in name only. Illegal hunting and trapping continued unabated. An initial appropriation to protect park wildlife was rejected by Congress. Attempts to secure park funding evaporated in the heated days of World War I. Without funding, there would be no rangers, and without rangers, there would be no end to the wildlife slaughter.

From the outset, Charles Sheldon had lobbied for Harry Karstens to be the park's first ranger. "I want Harry Karstens appointed the warden if he'll take it. He was there with me in 1906 and 1907–08 and later pulled Hudson Stuck to the top of McKinley. He is honest and will take pride in the work and knows the country better than others," Sheldon avowed. Karstens responded favorably to Sheldon's entreaty to take the position, but as the years rolled by with no official job offer, his initial interest drained away as each false start and promise of funding failed to materialize.

In the summer following the climb, Karstens had kept busy with river freighting and guiding. He hauled supplies and miners to the diggings and brought the gold back to town. In September, he guided Dr. Joseph Holmes, first director of the US Bureau of Mines, on an inspection trip to the remote Nenana coalfields. An early, severe blizzard in the mountains dumped eighteen inches of snow on them. A horse stepped on Holmes's ankle, but the "prince . . . never murmured during the whole trip," Karstens said. Karstens's reputation soared in the wake of Holmes trip. "Among the youngest of the old pioneers, Karstens has won an enviable reputation for himself as a trailblazer and true Alaskan," a reporter intoned.

That winter Karstens led Deming Wheeler on an epic fifteen-hundred-mile dog team circuit of the upper Kuskokwim River near the base of Mount McKinley. Despite fearsome cold, "the long trip was without incident of particular note or hardship," Karstens said. Judging by his comments concerning Holmes and Wheeler, it is obvious that Karstens was more than willing to assume most of the work if his companions didn't complain and pitched in as best they could.

A series of events brought changes in Karstens's personal life. That winter he received word from Chicago that his father had died. As per custom, the eldest son, John Henry, inherited the entire estate. Then, on July 31, 1914, Karstens married Frieda Louise Gaerisch in a small

Karstens, left; Deming Wheeler "The Mystery Man of the North," and Scotty Dalton, on their 1,500-mile dog sled trip to Mount McKinley and the upper Kuskokwim River in 1915

ceremony in the Fairbanks home of an old friend. Louise, as she was known, was born in Benton, Minnesota, and came to Alaska in 1905, from Portland, Oregon. She was a nurse, and her skills were in high demand in the Alaska Territory.

If Louise expected Harry to settle into the role of a stay-at-home businessman, she was mistaken. Karstens would later tell Sheldon, "[My] wife is trying to civilize me but it is a hard job. Every once in a while I take a trip for a month or so and when I get back she is glad to see me. When she remembers she has a job on hand I'm off on another trip but she says she hasn't lost hope yet."

The hunting season opened the day after the wedding. For weeks Karstens had been preparing for a four- to five-month hunting trip to the Toklat River. On August 9, Karstens and his clients left Fairbanks bound for Diamond City. "Say Sheldon, this is tough luck," he wrote his friend. "Married 10 days and off up here [on the Toklat] for four or five months."

His three hunters, who were friends of Sheldon, were scions of some of America's wealthiest families. The trio came north prepared to shoot "everything from mice to moose," both for themselves and for Cambridge's Museum of Comparative Zoology. The hunters settled in to Sheldon's old cabin on the Toklat, and "showed no inclination to return for several months."

An unseasonably warm winter, with the Toklat and Nenana Rivers running almost ice-free, delayed the party's planned return to Fairbanks by two and one-half weeks. With each passing day, Louise grew increasingly worried. Her husband's prolonged absences were something she'd never get used to.

On January 7, 1915, Karstens, accompanied by one of his hunters, mushed into Fairbanks with a giant load of furs, hides, horns, and antlers. After a brief reunion with Louise, Karstens returned to the Toklat to bring back his other two hunters and the remaining trophies. In town, the hunters bragged that the hunt had been the best-equipped and guided ever afield in Interior Alaska and credited Karstens for their success and safe return after months in the wilderness.

The year 1915 was a watershed for Interior Alaska, with change literally in the air. The first airplane to fly in Alaska took off from

Fairbanks on the Fourth of July 1914. Harry and Louise Karstens joined the excited crowd as the plane circled the ballpark, which doubled as an airstrip. The implications of the flight were not lost on Karstens. In minutes, an airplane could transport passengers and freight to destinations that would take days by dog team. Although the aviation age was a few years off, the door had creaked open.

That same year Delegate Wickersham wrote an act authorizing construction of a railroad to span the wilderness from Seward to Fairbanks. Already motor vehicles had transformed the Richardson Trail into a highway. Clearly the age of the pioneer, and dog-team freighting, was drawing to a close.

Quick to embrace practical change, Karstens bought a "Tin Lizzy," a Ford Model T, and inaugurated a highway transportation business. In 1916, with construction of the Alaska Railroad booming, Karstens announced an express passenger service between Fairbanks and Nenana, the northern division headquarters for the project. Over the next five years, dozens of dog drivers and horse wranglers hauled freight for the railroad, the first massive public works project in Interior Alaska. Perhaps only a few of those pioneers realized that the railroad would end their careers.

Harry and Louise lived in a small, well-kept home in Fairbanks that also doubled as headquarters for Karstens's transportation service. The couple associated with old-timers and cheechakos, Natives and miners, frontiersmen and merchants. A few minutes after midnight on May 1, 1917, just weeks after President Wilson signed the bill establishing Mount McKinley National Park, Eugene Henry Karstens, the couple's only child, was born in the government hospital in Nenana. The proud father was soon back on the road.

Karstens's travels, combined with the "small town" aspect of Alaska, brought him frequent word of his fellow climbers. He heard that after the climb, with Walter Harper away at school, John Fredson took Harper's place as the archdeacon's field assistant. In winter, Fredson mushed dogs with Stuck, and in summer, piloted the *Pelican*. He "was proud he'd been chosen to do the job Walter Harper had done so well for nearly ten years," Fredson's biographer wrote. Fredson was the first of his family to graduate from eighth grade. In 1916 he left Alaska to attend school at Mount Hermon. Later, Karstens helped Fredson attain summer employment to help pay for school.

In Nenana, Karstens crossed paths with Robert Tatum, working at the mission there and at Tanana. Tatum eventually earned his degree from the University of the South. He returned to Alaska, where Bishop Rowe ordained him a priest. For three years, the Reverend Tatum served as superintendent of Tanana Valley Missions, the start of a forty-three-year career as an Episcopal minister.

Alaska congressional delegate James Wickersham, left, a Fairbanks gold assayer, and writer/lecturer Frank G. Carpenter stand with gold ingots, circa 1916.

Walter Harper returned to Alaska in 1917 to assist Hudson Stuck on one last epic journey. Back home, however, Harper was felled by typhoid, a multiday fever that soared to 105°F and tested his powerful constitution. The long-planned Arctic trek seemed dashed, but to Stuck's "great joy," Harper made a rapid recovery. Only nine days after Harper first sat up in bed, the two men left Fort Yukon, the temperature, −38°F. The ensuing six-month, 2,500-mile trip by dog team took them from Fort Yukon west to Kotzebue Sound, then north along the coast to Point Barrow, and east to Herschel Island, before circling back to Fort Yukon.

On September 4, 1918, in Fort Yukon, with Archdeacon Stuck presiding, Walter Harper married Frances Wells, who had nursed him during his illness. After returning from their honeymoon, a hunting trip up the Porcupine River, the couple packed for a trip Outside to join the war effort, she in the Red Cross, he in the army. In late October, the newlyweds caught the steamer to Dawson, and then the train to Skagway. Just before their departure from Skagway, they learned of Germany's military collapse. Now Harper could go directly to college with a bright, limitless future ahead of him.

What happened next shocked Harry Karstens and devastated Hudson Stuck. On October 23, 1918, the SS *Princess Sophia* left Skagway loaded with passengers, freight, and gold. In a heavy south wind and blowing snow, she ran aground at 2:00 AM on Vanderbilt Reef, about thirty miles northwest of Juneau. Rescue attempts failed. Two days later, she slipped off the reef in a storm and sank, drowning all 350 people on board. The territorial governor personally notified Hudson Stuck that Harper's body had been recovered. "The most terrible thing that has happened in my experience," Stuck mourned.

Two years later, on October 10, 1920, Archdeacon Hudson Stuck died of bronchial pneumonia, one month shy of his fifty-eighth birthday, in the hospital in Fort Yukon that he had helped build. According to his wishes, villagers buried him in the Alaska Native graveyard there. Fort Yukon's aging Chief Jonas addressed the memorial gathering: "My relatives; with weeping and great sorrow I speak to you again of the Big Preacher; for we loved him. What great work he did so that our future might be good! . . . My relatives, a man who loved us greatly has labored among us; so let us truly seek to live as he did." In New York City, at Saint John the Divine, a huge crowd turned out for a memorial service for Hudson Stuck.

On April 12, 1921, four long years after the establishment of Mount McKinley National Park, Harry Karstens was appointed ranger-at-large, with an annual token salary of ten dollars. His responsibilities included Glacier Bay and Katmai National Monuments, neither of them funded or staffed. Charles Sheldon's friends donated money to get Karstens into the field ahead of the start of the fiscal year, when his promotion to park superintendent and funding began.

Karstens brought all of his courage, tenacity, and capacity for hard work to the new post. The man who had spent most of his adult life in view of the mountain, and knew it more intimately than all but a handful of others, now was charged with protecting the mountain's treasures, the wilderness and wildlife at its base. Charles Sheldon's dream, hatched a dozen years back in a tiny cabin on the Toklat River, had become a reality with Karstens's appointment as park protector.

Local opposition to the park was strong, Alaskans viewing its regulations as hindering mining and hunting "rights." Poachers and market hunters pushed back, threat and conflict part of the strain of opening the new park. In his seven years as superintendent, Karstens constructed headquarters facilities still in use today, established the rule of law that protected park wildlife, and developed a ranger corps that patrolled the park by dog team and snowshoes, covering thousands of miles each winter in any and all weather.

Twice during Karstens's tenure, the National Park Service announced that Karstens would again climb Mount McKinley "in the interest of science." The second climb had a stated goal of retrieving the recording thermometer that he and Hudson Stuck had left on the mountain in 1913. Both times, the plans for a second ascent were scratched due to Karstens's heavy workload.

In early 1924, Harry Karstens learned that he'd been nominated as one of two Americans to accompany the British expedition to climb Mount Everest. With the North and South Poles conquered, Everest, the highest peak in the world, ranked as the earth's last great challenge. Adventurers of all stripes clamored for the chance to join the expedition. William Colby, former president of the Sierra Mountain-eering Club, recommended Karstens.

Ascending to Everest's north col then required a minimum of two full days of step cutting. The "staircase" Karstens and Harper had hewn in the ridge above the Muldrow Glacier was widely admired by climbers around the world. Karstens, then forty-five years old, was not sure that he still possessed the stamina for high-altitude work. The Everest base camp on the Rongbuk Glacier was just 3,000 feet lower than the summit of Mount McKinley. For several reasons, Karstens stayed home. On June 8, 1924, the British expedition's climbing leader, George Mallory, and his partner, Andrew "Sandy" Irvine, disappeared near Everest's summit. Mallory's frozen body was found seventy-five years later at the 27,000-foot level on Everest's North Face.

Karstens seldom spoke of his role in Mount McKinley's first ascent. Interviews were few and far between and were often brief and trun-cated. As time passed, he allowed the conflict with Hudson Stuck to fade. He rarely mentioned the archdeacon's name and when he did, it was seldom, if ever, with acrimony. An old-style Alaskan, he was unconcerned with what cheechakos made of him or his part in the climb, but cared a great deal about what his friends and peers thought. The "gentry of the trail" knew what had happened, knew what he had done, and that was good enough for Karstens. The surviving members of the Yukon Order of Pioneers and the Pioneers of Alaska knew what the old days, the pioneer days, had been like, and they honored their brethren such as Karstens, the Seventymile Kid. They had all faced the savage cold, the wilderness, and isolation, and almost daily per-formed great deeds without fanfare. They had no need to brag to those who could never know the tribulations of breaking trail.

There was one exception to Karstens's silence. On certain summer nights, in the years before he resigned as park superintendent in the autumn of 1928, he would visit Savage Camp, the tent lodge inside the park, and speak to the visitors crowded around the evening campfire. According to his son, it was always an extraordinary moment.

With minimal introduction, Karstens would step into the firelight, and with the ice mountain glowing on the far horizon, begin to weave a tale of his ascent of those perilous slopes. This angular, weather-beaten man described fissures big enough to swallow a team of horses, avalanches that could carve stone, and told of a jumbled, ice-encrusted ridge that barred the way to the summit. He told of hacking a path around house-size pinnacles of ice, crossing dangerous slopes, and the constant threat posed by storm and altitude. He spoke of Walter Harper, the first to the summit, and of young John Fredson who kept the base camp. With a physical presence both confident and inspiring, he wove a story that totally beguiled his listeners. His was the way of the northern storyteller, the keeper of traditions and histories that all but vanish and are lost if not passed on or written down. His version of what really happened on the mountain disappeared in the smoke of those fires and with the people who knew him best.

Nearing the end of his life, when young climbers like Brad Washburn and Francis Farquhar visited him and Charley McGonagall, he seemed to sense that these interlocutors did not quite believe their versions of the pioneer ascents. Desiccated, ailing, and nearing the end of the trail, these self-educated frontiersmen were less impressive physically and

Old partners and lifelong friends, Charles "Mac" McGonagall (left), eighty-one, and Harry Karstens, seventy-three, in Fairbanks in 1951

verbally than the more refined and affluent climbers. They clearly were not of the same class of Browne, Parker, and the new generation of privileged and educated climbers. Their reticence to promote themselves or their adventures was easily misconstrued. Some forty years after the first ascent, Karstens, uncaring what others thought of him, told his son, Eugene, "Don't let anyone make a fuss over me."

Harry Karstens's pioneer contributions to Interior Alaska have been largely forgotten, especially his role in the first ascent of Mount McKinley. Karstens once made a telling comment about Anderson and Taylor's climb to the North Peak. "The old timers are not mentioned," he said. "Such is life for those who accomplish things but have no influence."

Henry P. "Harry" Karstens died of congestive heart failure on November 28, 1955, in Fairbanks. The following spring, when the ground thawed, a small group of mourners gathered in the rain for the burial at Birch Hill Cemetery. On the hillside overlooking Fairbanks, family and friends gathered below the gravesite to hear the pastor's eulogy and finally lay to rest a man whose life had been one of constant motion, constant action.

The pastor spoke well, but plainly, pausing often to judge the effect of his words and gauge the patience of his audience. When the light rain let up, a chill wind rose and swirled through the birch and aspens covering the upper hillside, the forest seeming to sigh with impatience, or sadness.

An unusual pause late in the service drew the mourners' eyes upward to the pastor, who stood rigidly staring off into the distance. One by one each person turned and looked south to where the clouds had parted, revealing the Alaska Range and the brilliant dome of Mount McKinley at its heart. Somewhere in the near distance, a dog yard of tethered huskies yapped into the sky. Forty-two years had passed since the Seventymile Kid had stood on the summit of that far pavilion and now it had appeared as if to say a final good-bye to the man who had spent most of his life in its shadow. With nothing more to be said, the pastor, uttering a soft amen, closed his book.

Sources

Research for this book began in the late 1980s in the holdings of Denali National Park and Preserve. The first words were written in 1991, but after two conversations with Harry Karstens's son, Eugene, the idea for a biography of the Seventymile Kid was shelved while the author pursued research for and the writing of a two-volume history of the pioneer era of Mount McKinley National Park. Some of the material in this book was also discussed in those two volumes. After completion of that project, the author once again approached the Karstens family about writing the biography of a remarkable pioneer Alaskan.

This book would not have been possible without the assistance of Gene Karstens, Harry Karstens's grandson, and Ken Karstens, Harry's great-grandson. They generously opened their research collection to me and assisted in every way by answering endless questions and providing rare photographs. Together the three of us painstakingly ferreted out details of Harry Karstens's early years in Chicago and his eventual migration north to Alaska.

Harry Karstens began and left unfinished five attempts at an autobiography, most covering the same events but each providing additional details. Long letters to Charles Sheldon, preserved at the University of Alaska Fairbanks, the Smithsonian Institution, and in the Karstens family collections, provided invaluable quotations and source material. His journals, some of his correspondence, and his memorabilia have been preserved by the family and provide a wealth of insight. In addition, Karstens wrote two long letters, the most important to Charles Sheldon, describing the first ascent and the conflict with Hudson Stuck.

David Dean's detailed biography of Hudson Stuck, *Breaking Trail: Hudson Stuck of Texas and Alaska*, along with editions of the Episcopal Church's publication *The Spirit of Missions*, are the source for background on Hudson Stuck. James A. Wickersham's diary of his 1903 expedition contains rich details, especially those of personal conflict, published in his collection of memoirs, *Old Yukon: Tales, Trails, and Trials*. Books by Belmore Browne, Frederick Cook, and Robert Dunn, mixed with newspaper articles and unpublished letters from various archives, have provided details of the expeditions of 1903–1912. Some early Chicago background and information were gleaned from Erik Larson's book *The Devil in the White City*.

In addition to Susan Peschel at the University of Wisconsin and Peter Lewis of the American Geographical Society Library, the staff of the Alaska and Polar Regions Collection at Rasmuson Library, University of Alaska Fairbanks, and staff of the Special Collections at Consortium Library, University of Alaska Anchorage, provided able and valuable assistance. Over the years, Jane Bryant, cultural resources specialist at Denali National Park and Preserve, added support and help whenever called upon. Park scientists Rob Burrows and Denny Capps commented on geology and glaciology passages. I am indebted to everyone for their help, but any errors are mine. For clarity, some journal and correspondence quotations have been edited for proper grammar and spelling.

Other key sources, as well as general reference materials that were helpful in my research and writing, include the following:

PERIODICALS
Alaska
Alaska Gazetteer and Directory (1915–16)
Alaska Journal
Alaska Sportsman Magazine
Alaska-Yukon Magazine
American Alpine Journal
National Geographic Magazine
Outing
Pacific Monthly Magazine
Pathfinder
Mentor Magazine
Spirit of Missions

NEWSPAPERS
Alaska Citizen
Alaska Weekly
Dawson Daily News
Dawson Record
Fairbanks Daily News-Miner
Fairbanks Daily Times
Fairbanks Evening News
Fairbanks Miner
Fairbanks Weekly News
Iditarod Pioneer
Jessen's Weekly
Klondike Nugget
Knoxville News-Sentinel
Nenana News

Sources

New York Sun
New York Times
Nome Nugget
Pittsburgh Dispatch
Ruby Record-Citizen
Skagway Alaskan
Tanana Miners' Record
Tanana Semi-Weekly Miner
Tanana Weekly Miner
Valdez News
Washington Post
Yukon World

1913 CLIMBING JOURNALS

Walter Harper Journals. (Various published versions; see especially Terris Moore's *Mount McKinley: The Pioneer Climbs*.)

Henry P. Karstens Journals. American Alpine Club, Golden, CO.

Robert G. Tatum Papers. Special Collections, University of Tennessee Library, Knoxville.

Hudson Stuck Journal. American Geographical Society, Brooklyn.

ARCHIVAL SOURCES

Alaska State Library, Juneau.

Alaska State Probate Records. Alaska State Archives, Juneau.

Archives, Alaska and Polar Regions Department. Rasmuson Library. University of Alaska Fairbanks.

Archives of the Episcopal Church, Austin, TX.

Charles Sheldon Papers. Edward W. Nelson Collection. Smithsonian Institution.

Eagle Historical Society, Eagle, AK.

Grace and John Vincent Hoeman Papers. Consortium Library. University of Alaska Anchorage.

Museum Archives , Denali National Park and Preserve.

National Archives and Records Administration, Washington, DC.

Nenana Recording District Mining Records, Fairbanks, AK.

Rauner Special Collections, Dartmouth College.

BOOKS/REPORTS

Adney, Tappan. *The Klondike Stampede*. Harper & Brothers, New York, 1899.

Baker, Marcus. *Geographic Dictionary of Alaska*. G.P.O. Washington, DC, 1906.

Sources

Balch, Edwin Swift. *Mount McKinley and Mountain Climbers' Proofs.* Campion and Company, Philadelphia, 1914.

Bates, Robert H. *Mountain Man: The Story of Belmore Browne—Hunter, Explorer, Artist, Naturalist.* The Amwell Press, Clinton, NJ, 1988.

Bayers, Peter L. *Imperial Ascent: Mountaineering, Masculinity, and Empire.* University Press of Colorado, Boulder, 2003.

Beeman, Marydith. *Lost and Found in Alaska and the Klondike,* Volume 1 and 2. Private Printing, Eagle River, AK, 1995.

Berton, Pierre. *The Klondike Fever: The Life and Death of the Last Great Gold Rush.* Alfred A. Knopf, Inc., New York, 1958.

Bolotin, Norman. *A Klondike Scrapbook: Ordinary People, Extraordinary Times.* Chronicle Books, San Francisco, 1987.

Brooks, Alfred H. *Blazing Alaska's Trails.* University of Alaska Press, Fairbanks, 1953.

------. *An Exploration to Mount McKinley America's Highest Mountain.* Journal of Geography, Washington, 1903.

------. *The Mount McKinley Region, with Description of the Igneous Rocks of the Bonnifield and Kantishna Districts.* G.P.O. Washington, 1911.

Browne, Belmore. *The Conquest of Mount McKinley.* G.P. Putnam's Sons, New York, 1913.

Bryce, Robert M. *Cook and Peary, The Polar Controversy, Resolved.* Stackpole Books, Mechanicsburg, PA, 1997.

Buzzell, Rolfe G. *Drainage Histories of the Kantishna Mining District, 1903–1968.* National Park Service, Alaska Region, Anchorage, 1989.

Coates, Ken, and Bill Morrison. *The Sinking of the Princess Sophia: Taking the North Down with Her.* University of Alaska Press, Fairbanks, 1991.

Cohen, Stan. *A Klondike Centennial Scrapbook: The Great Klondike Gold Rush.* Pictorial Histories Publishing Company, Missoula, 1997.

------. *The Streets Were Paved with Gold: A Pictorial History of the Klondike Gold Rush, 1896–1899.* Pictorial Histories Publishing Company, Missoula, 1977.

Cole, Terrence. *The Sourdough Expedition.* Alaska Northwest Publishing Company, Anchorage, 1985.

------. *Crooked Past: The History of a Frontier Mining Camp: Fairbanks, Alaska.* University of Alaska Press, Fairbanks, 1991.

Cook, Frederick. *To the Top of the Continent: Discovery, Exploration and Adventure in Sub-Arctic Alaska. The First Ascent of Mt McKinley, 1903–1906.* Doubleday, Page, and Co., New York, 1908.

Dean, David M. *Breaking Trail: Hudson Stuck of Texas and Alaska.* Ohio University Press, Athens, 1988.

Sources

Dodson, Peggy Rouch. *Girl in the Gold Camp: A True Account of an Alaska Adventure 1909–10.* Epicenter Press, Seattle, 1996.

Dunn, Robert. *The Shameless Diary of an Explorer.* Modern Library, New York, 2001.

Farrell, Ed. *Biographies of Alaska-Yukon Pioneers 1850–1959,* Vol. 3. Heritage Books, Inc., Juneau.

Gates, Michael. *Gold at Fortymile Creek: Early Days in the Yukon.* University of British Columbia Press, Vancouver, 1994.

Haigh, Jane G., and Claire Rudolf Murphy. *Gold Rush Women.* Alaska Northwest Books, Portland, OR, 1999.

Hales, David A. *An Index to the Early History of Alaska as Reported in the 1903–07 Fairbanks Newspapers.* Rasmuson Library, Fairbanks.

Herron, Edward A. *Conqueror of Mount McKinley: Hudson Stuck.* Julian Messner Inc., New York, 1964.

Hunt, William. *Golden Places: The History of Alaska-Yukon Mining.* National Park Service, Anchorage, 1990.

------. *North of 53°: The Wild Days of the Alaska-Yukon Mining Frontier, 1870–1914.* McMillan Company, New York, 1974.

------. *Whiskey Peddler: Johnny Healy, North Frontier Trader.* Mountain Press Publishing Company, Missoula, 1993.

Johnson, James Albert. *Carmack of the Klondike.* Epicenter Press, and Horsdale & Schubert Publishers, Ganges, BC, 1990.

Larson, Erik. *The Devil in the White City: Murder, Magic, and Madness at the Fair That Changed America.* Vintage, New York, 2004.

Mackenzie, Clara Childs. *Wolf Smeller: A Biography of John Fredson, Native Alaskan.* Alaska Pacific University Press, Anchorage, 1985.

Mitchell, William L. *The Opening of Alaska.* Cook Inlet Historical Society, Anchorage, 1981.

Moore, Terris. *Mt. McKinley: The Pioneer Climbs.* University of Alaska Press, Fairbanks, 1962.

Mozee, Yvonne. *The Ascent of Denali: Containing the Original Diary of Walter Harper, First Man to Achieve Denali's True Summit.* The Mountaineers, Seattle, 1977.

Murie, Adolph. *The Wolves of Mount McKinley.* Fauna of the National Parks of the United States, Fauna Series #5, GPO Washington, 1944.

Norgay, Tenzing. *Tiger of the Snows: The Autobiography of Tenzing of Everest.* As told to James Ramsey Ullman. G.P. Putnam's Sons, New York, 1955.

Pearson, Grant, and Philip Newill. *My Life of High Adventure.* Ballantine Books, New York, 1962.

Potter, Jean. *The Flying North.* Curtis Publishing Company, New York, 1945.

Sources

Prindle, L. M. *Bonnifield and Kantishna Regions*. US Geological Survey Bulletin 314, Washington, 1907.

Rand McNally Guide to Alaska and Yukon for Tourists, Investors, Homeseekers and Sportsmen. Rand McNally and Company, New York, 1922.

Saleeby, Becky M. *The Quest for Gold*. C.R.I.M.M., National Park Service, Alaska Region, 2000.

Scull, E. Marshall. *Hunting in the Arctic and Alaska*. John C. Winston, Co., Philadelphia, 1914.

Service, Robert. *The Spell of the Yukon*. Dodd, Mead, & Company, New York, 1953.

Sheldon, Charles. *The Wilderness of Denali*. Charles Scribner's Sons, New York, 1930.

Slemmons, Mary Anne. *James Wickersham, US District Judge of Alaska: Transcripts of Diaries 1–13, January 1, 1900–February 13, 1908*. Alaska State Library, Juneau, 2000.

Stuck, Hudson. *The Ascent of Denali*. Charles Scribner's Sons, New York, 1913.

------. *Ten Thousand Miles with a Dog Sled*. Charles Scribner's Sons, New York, 1914.

Washburn, Bradford. *Mount McKinley: The Conquest of Denali*. Harry N. Abrams, Inc. New York, 1991.

Washburn, Bradford, and Peter Cherici. *The Dishonorable Dr. Cook: Debunking the Notorious Mount McKinley Hoax*. The Mountaineers Books, Seattle, 2001.

Waterman, Jonathan. *High Alaska: A Historical Guide to Denali, Mount Foraker, and Mount Hunter*. The American Alpine Club, Golden, CO, 1988.

Webb, Melody. *Yukon: The Last Frontier*. UBC Press, Vancouver, 1985.

Wickersham, James. *Old Yukon: Tales, Trails, and Trials*. Washington Law Book Co., Washington, 1938.

Photo Credits

Frontispiece, Harry Karstens in 1906, Karstens Library, #041.

Table of Contents, Ice ax, courtesy of shutterstock.com.

p. 10, Harry P. Karstens Diary, 1913, courtesy of the American Alpine Club.

p. 14, Harry Karstens, age twelve, Karstens Library, #599.

p. 19, John Henry Karstens, courtesy of Randall J Krueger.

p. 22, *Al-ki* steamer by E. A. Hegg, courtesy of the University of Washington Libraries, Special Collections Division, Eric A. Hegg Collection, PH 274, Album 16, Page 40, #864.

p. 31, Henderson Creek claim filing receipt, courtesy of Karstens Library, #1897108.

p. 36, Tanana Crossing, courtesy of the University of Nebraska Press.

p. 50, Harry Karstens and Frank Cotter, courtesy of Karstens Library, #0895.

p. 59, Harry Karstens by Leon Kellum, courtesy of Denali National Park and Preserve, Museum Collection, #28/0.3.

p. 61, Miners and dance-hall girls, courtesy of Karstens Library, #0028.

p. 66, Judge Wickersham, courtesy of the Alaska State Library #PCA #277-18-43.

p. 80, Frederick Cook, courtesy of Ken Karstens Collection.

p. 89, Peters Glacier, courtesy of the author.

p. 92, Fanny Hall, courtesy of Karstens Library, #0029.

p. 100, Karstens hauling mail, courtesy of Karstens Library, image #84.

p. 103, Karstens and Fannie McKenzie by Joe Quigley, courtesy of Karstens Library, #0470.

p. 108, Kantishna Mail and Express Route banner, courtesy of William Kotsenburg.

p. 112, Frederick Cook in New York, 1909 by George Grantham Bain, courtesy of the Library of Congress, Bain Collection, #LC-USZ62-119525.

p. 120, Karstens on Toklat River, courtesy of Denali National Park and Preserve, Cultural Resources Collection, Wilderness of Denali.

p. 134, McGonagall and Tom Lloyd, courtesy of Alaska State Library, #PCA277-4-89.

p. 147, Lloyd party, 1910, courtesy of Archives, Alaska and Polar Regions Collection, Rasmuson Library, University of Alaska Fairbanks, VF ADD. Expeditions, #80-84-113.

p. 150, Parker Expedition, courtesy of the Library of Congress, Frank and Frances Carpenter Collection #99614364.

p. 154, Herschel Parker and Belmore Browne in the Great Basin, courtesy of Ken Karstens Collection.

p. 156, Hudson Stuck, courtesy of the University of Nebraska Press.

p. 168, Karstens, courtesy of Karstens Library, #382.

p. 171, Karstens in front of the R.C. Wood Co., courtesy of Karstens Library, #596.

p. 176, Charles McGonagall, courtesy of Karstens Library, #0015.

p. 178, Parker-Browne Expedition, courtesy of the Library of Congress, Frank and Frances Carpenter Collection; #99614459.

p. 181, Martin Nash on Pioneer Ridge by expedition leader Ralph Cairns, courtesy of Archives, Alaska and Polar Regions Department, Rasmuson Library, University of Alaska Fairbanks, Charles Sheldon Collection, Box 2, Folder 2.

p. 182, *Fairbanks Times* Expedition, courtesy of Candy Waugaman.

p. 184, Parker-Browne Expedition camp by Merl LaVoy, courtesy of Ken Karstens Collection, #444.

p. 192, Frieda Louise Gaerisch Karstens, courtesy of Karstens Library, #3707.

p. 197, Freighters on the Richardson Trail, courtesy of Karstens Library, #66.

p. 202, Stuck and Karstens, courtesy of Project Gutenberg.org.

p. 207, Harper, Karstens, and Stuck, courtesy of Archives, Alaska and Polar Regions Department, Rasmuson Library, University of Alaska Fairbanks, H.H. Lumpkin Collection, #2010-0101-00026.

p. 210, Stuck and lead dog Muk, courtesy of University of Nebraska Press.

p. 216, Karstens on Muldrow Glacier, courtesy of Project Gutenberg.org.

p. 219, John Fredson, courtesy of Project Gutenberg.org.

p. 223, Karstens, Harper, and Tatum, courtesy of Project Gutenberg.org.

p. 230, Karstens leading Tatum, courtesy of Project Gutenberg.org.

p. 234, Karstens on northeast ridge, courtesy of Project Gutenberg.org.

p. 237, Karstens and Harper, courtesy of Project Gutenberg.org.

p. 244, Karstens on the ridge, courtesy of Project Gutenberg.org.

p. 246, Karstens on summit approach, courtesy of Project Gutenberg.org.

p. 253, Camp Two, courtesy of Project Gutenberg.org.

p. 255, Stuck on Ascension Day, courtesy of Project Gutenberg.org.

p. 257, Stuck using thermometer, courtesy of Ken Karstens Collection.

p. 259, Karstens adjusting creepers, courtesy of Project Gutenberg.org.

p. 264, Granite stick pin and ice ax, courtesy of the author.

p. 276, Ranger Karstens, courtesy of Karstens Library, #2301.

p. 279, Karstens, Wheeler, and Dalton, courtesy of Karstens Library, #0417.

p. 282, Wickersham with gold ingots, courtesy of the Library of Congress, Frank and Frances Carpenter Collection #96615009.

p. 286, McGonagall and Karstens, courtesy of Karstens Library, #0288.

Index

Index

Index

Index

Index

About the Author

A resident of Alaska for forty-seven years, **TOM WALKER** resides near Denali National Park. Like many Alaskans, he has a varied career background: conservation officer, wilderness guide, and log-home builder. A freelance nature photographer, writer, and lecturer, he has authored thirteen books of Alaska life and natural history, and published four compilations of his outdoor photography. He is the 2006 recipient of the Alaska Conservation Foundation's Daniel Housberg Award for Excellence in Still Photography. His illustrated book *Caribou: Wanderer of the Tundra* won the 2000 Benjamin Franklin Book Award in the category of Nature and Environment. His most recent books are *McKinley Station: The People of the Pioneer Park that Became Denali* and *Denali Journal: 20th Anniversary Edition*.

THE MOUNTAINEERS, founded in 1906, is a nonprofit outdoor activity and conservation organization whose mission is "to explore, study, preserve, and enjoy the natural beauty of the outdoors . . . " Based in Seattle, Washington, it is now one of the largest such organizations in the United States, with seven branches throughout Washington State.

The Mountaineers sponsors both classes and year-round outdoor activities in the Pacific Northwest, which include hiking, mountain climbing, ski-touring, snowshoeing, bicycling, camping, canoeing and kayaking, nature study, sailing, and adventure travel. The Mountaineers' conservation division supports environmental causes through educational activities, sponsoring legislation, and presenting informational programs.

All activities are led by skilled, experienced volunteers, who are dedicated to promoting safe and responsible enjoyment and preservation of the outdoors.

If you would like to participate in these organized outdoor activities or programs, consider a membership in The Mountaineers. For information and an application, write or call The Mountaineers Program Center, 7700 Sand Point Way NE, Seattle, WA 98115-3996; phone 206-521-6001; visit www.mountaineers.org; or email info@mountaineers.org.

The Mountaineers Books, an active, nonprofit publishing program of The Mountaineers, produces guidebooks, instructional texts, historical works, natural history guides, and works on environmental conservation. All books produced by The Mountaineers Books fulfill the mission of The Mountaineers. Visit www.mountaineersbooks.org to find details about all our titles and the latest author events, as well as videos, web clips, links, and more!

The Mountaineers Books
1001 SW Klickitat Way, Suite 201
Seattle, WA 98134
800-553-4453
mbooks@mountaineersbooks.org

OTHER TITLES YOU MIGHT ENJOY BY
THE MOUNTAINEERS BOOKS

Climbing the Seven Summits:
A Comprehensive Guide to the Continents' Highest Peaks
Mike Hamill

The first guidebook of climbing routes to the
highest peak on each of the world's seven continents

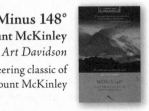

Minus 148°
First Winter Ascent of Mount McKinley
Art Davidson

A gripping, can't-put-down mountaineering classic of
the first winter ascent of Mount McKinley

The Mountain of My Fear and Deborah
Two Mountaineering Classics
David Roberts

The publication of *The Mountain of My Fear* in 1968 and *Deborah* in 1970
changed the face of the mountaineering narrative. Now these two classic
expedition narratives from acclaimed writer David Roberts are together
again in one volume.

Denali: A Literary Anthology
Bill Sherwonit

A literary collection about Denali and the broad shadow
it casts in history, culture, and nature

Alaska: A Climbing Guide
Colby Coombs and Michael Wood

The definitive climbing guidebook to Alaska's mountain peaks,
from the Southeast to the Brooks Range, including Denali

Steller's Island
Adventures of a Pioneer Naturalist in Alaska
Dean Littlepage

The fascinating account of eighteenth-century naturalist Georg Steller
and his discoveries along the north coast of North America

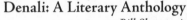

**The Mountaineers Books has more than
500 outdoor recreation titles in print.**
For details, visit
www.mountaineersbooks.org.